Abstracts from *The Clarksville Standard*
(Formerly *The Northern Standard*)

Volume 5
1856-1857

Richard B. Marrin and Lorna Geer Sheppard

HERITAGE BOOKS
2009

HERITAGE BOOKS
AN IMPRINT OF HERITAGE BOOKS, INC.

Books, CDs, and more—Worldwide

For our listing of thousands of titles see our website
at
www.HeritageBooks.com

Published 2009 by
HERITAGE BOOKS, INC.
Publishing Division
100 Railroad Ave. #104
Westminster, Maryland 21157

Copyright © 2009 Richard B. Marrin
and Lorna Geer Sheppard

All rights reserved. No part of this book may be reproduced or transmitted in any form or by any means, electronic or mechanical, including photocopying, recording or by any information storage and retrieval system without written permission from the author, except for the inclusion of brief quotations in a review.

International Standard Book Numbers
Paperbound: 978-0-7884-4912-3
Clothbound: 978-0-7884-8135-2

ABSTRACTS FROM *THE CLARKSVILLE STANDARD* [FORMERLY *THE NORTHERN STANDARD*] TEXAS, VOLUME 5, 1856 - 1857

Richard B. Marrin and Lorna Geer Sheppard

TABLE OF CONTENTS

Introduction. 1

Abstracts from 1856 5

Abstracts from 1857 133

Endnotes 211

Indices. 223

INTRODUCTION

Picture yourself, back in the mid 1850s, sitting on a bench in front of the Clarksville Hotel, right on the Public Square. A copy of the local paper, Charles De Morse's *Standard,* is on your lap. You are from Virginia and are in Texas for the first time. You had heard a lot about it, how thousands were moving there. You are yourself passing through town on your way farther west. It was too crowded back East. Lands were worn out. You are curious about this town. They tell you that Clarksville is now more than twenty years old, has a lot of schools, stores, churches and sturdy citizens, sort of like life back home. Things sure look to be thriving. You passed comfortable looking farms on your way in. A couple of wagons, full of merchandise for the stores around the Square, lumber by. Happy looking kids are passing by on their way to school. They looked and acted like the folks back home too. From where you sit, you can see a building that seems to be particularly busy. That, you are told, is the Courthouse and the Court is in session for the next two weeks. Lots of folks are in town; witnesses, parties, observers and the usual collection of attorneys who follow the Court from county seat to county seat throughout North Texas.

The period 1856/1857 was a seemingly peaceful one in the United States generally and in Texas in particular. In the mid 1850s, the population of the United States was about twenty-seven million, with Texas contributing some 400,000 of it. They were largely Protestant; ninety percent of the churches in the United States were Baptist, Methodist or Presbyterian. Like back home, more than half the population was engaged in agriculture. In Texas that meant mostly cotton but some wheat, corn and sugar as well. Times were good. People were at peace. Or so it seemed. But there were uneasy rumblings beneath the surface.

While largely Protestant and rural in the South, the cities back east were growing. Factories replaced farming. The Industrial Revolution had arrived as had immigration, especially

Catholics from Ireland and Germany. Friction was growing between the old timers and the newcomers. A new, secret version of bias appeared on the scene, called Know Nothingism. Cloaked in secrecy, it was anti-immigrant and anti-Catholic. Technology was arriving also and, with it, changes, both good and bad, to the old way of life. The telegraph and the railroads connected many of the States, although they had not yet come to Texas. Agriculture had its own leaps forward, which affected Texans more than those back East. Cyrus McCormick's wheat reaper could cut fifteen acres a day with three horses. Before, a farmer could not get enough help to cut that much wheat. Now he could do it with his sons. More wheat grown meant more to be threshed. Technology also assisted the small farmer with mechanical threshers worked by two horses and threshing 250 bushels a day. Business was booming too. There was a lot of money around, thanks to the gold from California and ready credit from East Coast banks. Cotton could be sent to the factories of New England in return for cash with which to buy the products of those and other factories. Times were good and people thought they would only get better. But, as we see periodically, economies can crash and peaceful times become more tense. That happened in the latter half of 1857; the New York banks closed and did not reopen for two months. Businesses shut down, unable to pay back their borrowings. Employees lost their jobs.

But the Panic of 1857 and the resentment against the immigrants were not the only storms brewing. Slavery was emerging as an issue of great magnitude. More demand for cotton resulted in even more slaves being needed in the South. By 1861, there were four million slaves. At the same time, slavery had been abolished in all the Northern States for decades and voices were demanding the South do so too. Slaves were lured by abolitionists to run away on the Underground Railroad to the North and slaves' insurrection conspiracies were uncovered. In 1857, the Supreme Court issued the Dred Scott decision. Slavery was legal in the new territories and Congress could not stop it. Southerners were delighted, but the decision caused a furor in the North.

All these stresses in society could be seen in the election of 1856. The Whigs were disappearing after years as a major party. The Democrats were split be between North and South, abolition and slavery. A new party, the Republican Party, was forming and rounding out the combatants were the nativist Know Nothings and their American Party. *The Standard's* Editor, Charles De Morse, was an avid Democrat and he followed – and reported – on it all.

Now, if you take that copy of *The Standard* off your lap and open it, you will see all those events which shaped our country, as they were happening. So too can be seen everyday life – the weather, what was on sale at the stores around the Square, how the crops were making out, the schools, the churches, marriages and deaths, etc. and other items of interest to the people who lived in Clarksville, Red River County and some two dozen surrounding counties in Northern Texas in the years 1856 and 1857.

1856

There was no issue of *The Standard* for January 5, 1856
****
From *The Standard*, January 12, 1856

new volume
This is the first number of a new volume – a good time to start a subscription.

the Templars
On the 8th, the votaries of cold water had a celebration made up of a march, a speech and a dinner, all of which were excellent in their way, as we are assured, the gastronomic portion of the performance, got up by the sisterhood, not being by any means the least. Indeed, it was, if we were to judge by the somewhat ecstatic eulogy of our Post Master who said in glowing language that he had never been so feted in his entire life. There were some bright eyes and laughing faces there, but [not this editor's] who stuck to his labors, although every member of the printing department left the office and gloated over the jollification until dark.
They marched up abreast our offices and, saying something about saluting the *Star Spangled Banner* (the whole of which we did not hear) they gave three jolly cheers to the flag that waved above our Sebastopol and then, turning off churchward, we heard the sounds of their music softening in the distance and heard no more, except as was relayed to us from the fervid lips of the Post Master aforesaid.

snow
The weather has maintained its severity and these last two weeks may be called "one of the severest spells of cold weather" that we remember to have felt in Texas. It has looked for most of the week that the clouds would like to let out a little of the superincumbent water, but it was so cold that it would not come. During Friday night a little bit of snow fell.
Last night it came - the long delayed snow - and this morning we have 8 inches of snow by measurement, covering the earth and

roof tops and adding bleak beauty to the town. Such a snow has never fallen in Clarksville before during the 13 winters we have passed in it previous to this.

snow ball fight
Apropos to the season, we have just received a challenge by a special messenger, from four ladies to meet them across the Delaware, in dangerous combat with snowballs. The missive is accompanied by our well made hard snow balls, carefully wrapped up in two newspapers. Our heart beats for the fray, but hard fate compels us to attend to *The Standard,* until late in the evening, when we shall storm the hill and expect to have a desperate encounter with a probability of being made to leave the ground to the enemy or to remain upon it only by courtesy.

protest
*(*from *The Louisville Journal)I*
The Editor of *The Boston Liberator* calls upon the ladies of the North to make use of nothing that is made of slave labor. He need no expect them not to use cotton. They will not expel so old a friend from their bosom.[1]

we call attention
to the professional card of Wilson Peacock, Esq. Paris, Lamar County;

to the new advertisement of Sims & Bloodworth, carriage repair, wagon making and black smithing;

to the advertisement of Shanahan and Brim's cabinet shop. Their chair manufactory is the first regular establishment of that sort that we have heard of in northern Texas.

to the advertisement of John Faulkner, saddler;

to the advertisement by L.G. Harman of Tarrant, Hopkins county that he has several years experience as a locator and survey and proposes to locate claims for one third of the land as compensation for locating surveying and procuring and free of expense to the claimant or for $.10 per acre for any claim of 1280 acres or more.

to the professional card of Mills & Mills. They will practice in all the courts of the Eight Judicial District and in Cass and Harris as well as in the District Court of the United States at Tyler and in the Supreme Court of the state. Address is Paris, Lamar County.

to the advertisement of L. H. King, watch repairer and jewelry maker, Mount Pleasant, Titus County. Mr. King will be supplied immediately with every requisite to a proper performance of his work.

McKenzie Institute
The Male department will have as its teachers J. W. P. McKenzie, Ragsdale Smith, B. F. Fuller, J. Kennedy; J. N. B. Henslee; the Female department teachers will be J. W. P. McKenzie, Ragsdale Smith and Martha Ragsdale; vocal and instrumental music to be taught by D. Danforth. The institution is located three miles west of Clarksville.

clothing store
J.P. Dale and Bros., merchant tailors in Clarksville, have just received from New York and Philadelphia, an assortment of ready made clothes.[2]

new stage line
Notice by Wm. Moss of Washington, Arkansas of a new stage line; the travel time to Shreveport and Little Rock is four days and the fare reduced to $18.

artesian wells
Thomas Long has settled in Clarksville and drills artesian wells.

drug firm dissolving
The Partnership of the Undersigned in the Drug business expired with the close of the year 1855. Mr. Williams retires and Dr. Wooten assumes the indebtedness of the firm and collects the

assets.
G. H. Wooten; J. D. Williams.

valuable town property for sale
Notice by John W. West of a business lot and house in Clarksville for sale; also one residence and three lots, consisting of a comfortable dwelling, kitchen, smoke house, a good cistern[3], good stable and cow lot; also one good black smith shop, wagon shop and cow house;
also for sale:
531 acre of land adjoining A. Morris stock farm in Titus County;
320 acres on Blundells Creek in Titus County, adjoining Mr. Jones;
700 acres in Grayson County on Choctaw Creek;
200 acres in Van Zandt County.
I also offer for sale one Negro woman, a field hand.
William B. Sims and S. H. Morgan are my agents in Clarksville
****

From *The Standard,* January 19, 1856

we are authorized
to announce John C. Easton as a candidate from McKinney, Collin County for District Attorney of the 16th Judicial District.

we are indebted to
John Henry Brown, Sherwood Pirkey, H. R. Runnels, Daugherty, Green and McKenney for late documents from Austin.

we call attention
to the card of the Clarksville Hotel under new proprietorship. Brahas Sims. The new Proprietor been here since boyhood and has grown up with the country. He will give close attention to his business and will doubtlessly make his house worthy of support from the labor given to its keeping as well as for patronizing in a small way an old acquaintance of most of the citizens and a correct man.

killing a panther
Early last Sunday morning, two panthers were discovered in the cotton field above Dr. Gordon's Red River plantation, below Rowland, in this County. They were immediately pursued by Mr. James Clark with dogs. One of them took a tree some 200 yards outside the fence when Mr. Clark shot him in the side by a discharge from one barrel of a shotgun and the panther dropped until finished by the dogs.

The other got out of sight and was seen no more. The animal killed was nearly 10 feet from the nose to the end of the tail, was enormously large and fat and very grey on head and neck, probably a veteran long accustomed to feed on pigs in the neighborhood. His tusks, 2 inches in length have been shown to us. The hogs belonging to the plantation had been turned into the field for protection and had been repeatedly missed of late sometimes, pigs, sometimes full-grown hogs. When the panthers were startled they had just killed and were eating a hog and pieces of the pork, as large as a man's hand, were found in the stomach of the animal killed. This is the second panther killed on this place in a year, although the place has been settled some 20 years and is immediately adjacent to the landing for this Town, known as Rowland[4], in a region one would suppose that these wild foragers of the woods would avoid. It may be that they come from the comparatively unsettled region on the Choctaw side opposite, the River having been so low for a long time as to interpose no obstacle of late being frozen over.

the weather and winter sport
Rare times the boys have had of it, since our last, including the old boys, for the venerable editor of this paper was nearly snowballed all day last Sunday by a fair array of females, who could not "pretermit' the unusual opportunity and pelted him occasionally, until after night fall. Commencing on Saturday, the boys took the town and filled the ears, and knocked the hats off, of nearly all the men who made themselves visible about the Square, and they had it all their own way, for the unlucky individual who showed signs of resistance or threatened vengeance had no chance against their numbers.

As to our case, we were formally challenged, as we reported last week, and had to go through a most desperate contest with numerous foes from which, however, we emerged satisfactorily, after a hard conflict in which the enemy, as may be presumed, displayed a great deal of tactical skill and perseverance. The snow is still lying upon th ground in patches and upon the shady sides of roofs, though the warm sun o the last two days, has removed nearly all of it.
During Saturday last, one to two jumpers or slides were hastily put up and put in requisition and, if good sleighs had been in command during Saturday and Sunday, the sleighing would have been as good as it is anywhere. Seven and a half to eight and a half inches was the general depth of snow on Saturday last. The weather has been cold ever since until yesterday.

the river
The river continues to rise slowly and as we hear of heavy rains above and a rise in the upper Red River, we are in hopes of having in a few days sufficient water to afford navigation for the largest class of boats. Since our last., the *Victoria, Marion* and *Hope* have arrived from New Orleans, the *Effort, Runaway, M. L. Daugherty* and *Lone Star* from the falls.[5]

strays
In Fannin County, a horse taken up by Cicero Brown, brought before J. C. Parish, Justice of the Peace; and appraised by Lewis Whitfield and E. J. Holland; notice given by S. Howell, County Clerk;

a mule taken up by Henry Smith and estrayed[6] before J. S. McKassan, Justice of the Peace and appraised by Benjamin Lankford and Miles Gore; at the same time a horse was taken up estrayed before J. S. McKassan, Justice of the Peace and appraised by M. Hart and J. P. Wilkinson; notice given by S. Howell, County Clerk.

administration of estates
Notice by Clarissa Fulton, *Executrix,* that she will sell cheap lands

in Cooke, Lamar or Fannin counties; belonging to Samuel M. Fulton ; inquire of her attorneys, Mills and Mills in Paris.

professions and place of origin of Texas legislators
Some of the occupation of the members of the Sixth Legislature of the State of Texas are lawyers (82); farmers (41); bear hunters (2); traders (8); stock raisers (1); mechanics (2); architects (1); printers (1); physicians (6), vacancy (1). They were from Tennessee (19); North Carolina (6) South Carolina (9); Virginia (11); New York (8); Canada (1); Alabama (9); Mississippi (8), Illinois (1); Pennsylvania (2); Connecticut (2) Georgia (10); Germany (1) Prussia (1); Missouri (1); Kentucky (4) and Texas (1).

****

From *The Gazette,* January 26, 1856

weather
The weather was cold and the sky clouded most of the week until Thursday afternoon when it rained gently until Friday morning at about five or six o'clock. Then commenced a very heavy rain which continued without intermission until four o'clock P. M. After that, the rain was light and the wind blew fitfully and strongly until late in the night.
This morning early, it commenced raining freely and continued for perhaps two hours. Then fell a little snow which melted on the wet ground. Since then, it has drizzled and still holds an appearance of dampness, with occasional snow.
The creeks are high and the river doubtless will be, if the rain has been general in the region bordering upper Red River, as we presume it has.
The stately Delaware which meanders through our Town is a sort of inland sea right now, sweeping around the bridge magnificently. Ordinarily its depth varies for 0 to 2 ½ inches, except in the holes which keeps itself for the domestic convenience of our citizens, from one to three feet in depth.

we are authorized
to announce that E. D. McKenney is a candidate for District

Attorney for the Eighth Judicial District;

to announce that John C. Easton is a candidate for District Attorney for the Sixteenth Judicial District.

we call attention
to the advertisement that the Bonham Hotel is for sale;

to valuable Red River land and Negroes for sale by Wm. C. Jones of Fannin County.

Probate Courts
The Legislature has before it a bill dividing the state into a convenient number of Probate Districts and for the election of Judges therein, with such salaries as will secure the series of men learned in the law. No courts has cognizance of matters of so much interest and consequences as the Probate Courts for the entire property of the country must at some time pass through them and it is a matter of the first importance that the vast and delicate interests committed to them, should be presided over by men of high legal and moral qualifications. It is notorious and lamentable that the Chief Justices of most of the Counties of the State are woefully deficient in the qualifications which the position demands.
The Bill proposes that the State be subdivided into a convenient number of inferior Judicial District, for each of which a Probate Judge is to be elected, to hold their place for a term of years at a salary of $1,200 a year, that the Clerk of the County Courts should be *ex officio* clerk of the Probate Court. Courts to be held four times a year.

new invention
The Terraqueous Transportation Company has put into use an invention by General T. J. Chambers, of a vehicle which, as he says, "by a natural combination of a few mathematical principle and mechanical powers, which has proven capable of traversing alike land and water with a convenience safety and velocity, surpassing any other mode of transportation heretofore used. It

will traverse our shallow bays and their Bars without difficulty and, upon a sloping coast like that of Texas, it will readily pass from the sea to the dry land and from the land to the sea."

telegraph
Telegraph lines in Northern Louisiana and Eastern Texas seemed to have proved an unprofitable investment. This is as we anticipated. We never saw anything in the commercial aspect of the county to warrant a supposition that they would even pay salaries for the operators and so it has been. The lines of wires through Eastern Texas are as we believe generally down and even to Shreveport the business has been entirely unremunerative.[7]

notice to settle accounts
All persons indebted to J. W. P. McKenzie, Smith Ragsdale and the McKenzie Institute are requested to make immediate settlement.

****

There are no copies available of *The Standards* of February 2 and February 9, 1956

****

From *The Standard*, February 16, 1856

we are authorized
to announce John A. Summers as a candidate for the District Attorney for the Eighth Judicial District.

we are indebted to
the Hon. W. H. Ochiltree of the Texas House of Representatives for a speech upon the Texas Debt Bill.[8]

election in the 16th Judicial District
Nat. M. Burford has been elected judge of the new District Court west of us, a position that he is both worthy and competent to fill. The contest between Col. J. C. Easton and J. C. McCoy, for District Attorney was undetermined at our last advices. In the election of either, the District has a competent prosecutor and a clever, gentlemanly representative.

Know Nothing intellectually
There is nothing more notable about the new party of the bigots and proscriptionists than their general want of brains. Not to say but that it does not have some intelligent men with it, but that it has fewer than any considerable body ever before organized in the United States, while of the mass is made up in a great degree of the most ultra ignorance which accounts for its bigotry and proscriptive notice.[9]

humor
A country girl, coming from the fields, was told by a cousin that she looked as fresh as a daisy kissed with dew. "Well, it wasn't any fellow by that name but Bill Jones that kissed me and confound him. I told him that everybody would find out."

shortage of beer back East
Lager beer has become so scarce in Newark, New Jersey that dealers of a refused to sell it to any but their regular customers.

notices of lost land certificates
by Geo. C. Dugan of a lost certificate, originally issued to William Tyler in Fannin County.[10];

by Joseph Baker of lost certificate originally issue to William H. Brown of Lamar County;

by Milton Grag of Titus Count for one third of a league of land in Red River County;

by Joslin Hopkins of Titus for a certificate originally issued to Henry Hopkins in Red River County.
****
From *The Standard,* February 23, 1856

the River
The River is said to be in boatable condition to a point above us. We understand that a fleet of boats is on the way up here. Cotton was taken from Moore's Landing our about the 20th by the *Hope.*

we call attention
to the advertisement of Bonham Masonic Female Institute;

to the advertisement of Bonham Hotel, under its new Proprietor, B.F. Christian; very favorably know to the citizens of Fannin County, who proposes to keep as a good house as can be kept in the country.

tidbit of wisdom
Fashion is the race of the rich to get away from the poor, who follow as fast as they can.

Christmas presents
A friend said he had two. A kiss from his wife and another from his daughter. The first he valued for its rarity and the second for its disinterestedness, being given for a bracelet.

****

From *The Standard*, March 1, 1856

we are authorized
to announce James J. Farrar as a candidate for Chief Justice of Lamar County.

Grayson County
Our correspondent in the county writes that the late immigration to this County is one too large to tell.

we call attention
to the advertisement of James G. Sutphin, general collecting agent for Dallas, Collin, Denton, Grayson, Cooke, Kaufman, Hopkins and Lamar counties;

to advertisement a very desirable Negro servants for sale by W. C. Jones; also valuable land;

to the advertisement of Wooley Daguerrean artist. His daguerreotypes are superior to most of those have been taken here;

to the card of J. J. Good of the law firm of Burford and Good. Dallas. Mr, Burford has been elected District Judge leaving the business of the firm to Gen. Good all alone. The General is a gentleman and a fine talent and correct business applications. Persons having legal business in Dallas could not put it in better hands;

to the advertisement be Paris Male Academy under the new organization. It opens, we are informed, under excellent auspices. Trustees are the gentlemen of high standing and the teachers are highly capable. The Trustees are John T. Mills, Isaiah W. Wells, Travis G. Wright; Geo W. Wright and P. W. Birmingham.

stray taken up
Notice by John P. Dale, taken up by James Parks and brought before him, a Justice of the Peace and appraised by James Caldwell and Samuel Smith. Notice given by George H. Bagby by deputy John M. Bivins .

stolen or strayed
Notice by Phandrum Brown of two missing mules.

****

From *The Standard*, March 8, 1856

we are authorized
to announce the honorable W. S. Todd as a candidate for Judge of the Eighth Judicial District;

to announce S. R. G. Mills of the Lamar County for District Attorney of the Eighth Judicial District;

to announce S. G. Bonners of Jefferson as a candidate for one of the District Attorney of the Eighth Judicial District;

to announce B. W. Musgrove of Hopkins County as a candidate for District Attorney of the Eighth Judicial District;

we call attention
to Judge Stout's advertisement of the fine, large engraving called *The Union,* embracing portraits of the most distinguished men of the country in 1850;

to the advertisement of Bryarly & Co who have received goods per late arrivals.

The Clarksville Messenger
This establishment, heretofore the *Weekly Messenger,* has become the property of Sutton and Darnell, the first the foreman of our office for the past two years and the last having learned the typographic art under our instruction. They are young men of integrity and good intent and will do their duty to the paper. The new Editor Mr. J. W. Thomas is well known Post Master of this village, a gentleman of good capacity, candor and integrity. Although it is not his intention to meddle extensively in politics, he takes occasion to say that "he is not only essentially Southern, but also essentially National in his views and decidedly anti democratic, so far as least as the principles of that party are in conflict with the great fundamental truths contained in the AMERICAN PLATFORM".

The 2nd of March
The Natal day of Texas Independence came on Sunday and the flag raised over our office was the only recognition here. On Monday, however, the Society of Odd Fellows made an imposing demonstration.
After a march around the Square, arrayed in really elegant attire, they filed in the Court House and were addressed by Judge Mills and Dr. J. A. Barry. We did not hear the speeches but were told they were both excellent. Following the speeches, came a very fine dinner at the Sims Clarksville Hotel, said to be the best dinner ever set in Town.
We hope to see the annual recurrences of this day observed hereafter. The several societies could not chose a better festival day and citizens en masse should honor the birth of Texas Independence.

fugitive slaves
The Syracuse Chronicle says that two hundred fugitive slaves have passed through that city in the past year and thirteen within the past twelve days.

the river
The river is in boatable condition. Since our last the *Fanny Fern*, the *Hope* and the *Runaway* have been at our landing. The two last arrived on Tuesday evening, passed up to Kiamitia and came down on Thursday. The *Hope* took away 20 bales of cotton at five dollars per bale. The *Fern* asked six dollars now but only got 40 bales at our landing. The *Runaway* would not take any cotton from our landing because the river was falling. He took some from above but we do not know how much. The arrival of the *Runaway* was most timely for us as she brought us a large supply of paper which had been on the way since July last and, but for which, we should have been out. The paper shipped in April is still in Jefferson in route to this place as the late difficulties of the highland navigation have detained it.

court
District court the court opened on Monday morning, the 26th, and has proceeded without delay unto the conclusion of the term on the eighth of this month.
The attorneys for other counties included John Mills, S. R. G. Mills, Williams and Milwee of Lamar; R. H. Lane, P. B. Smith, District Attorney and N. W. Townes of Grayson.
The *State vs William Powers,* his being charged with stealing money from James C. Duties, came up on Monday of this week. He was found guilty and sentenced to three years in the penitentiary. The case has been taken up but a new trial refused. The evidence was circumstantial. Mills, Summers and Murray for Powers. The district attorney, N. Sutton and Amos Morrill for the prosecution.
The *State vs. John Miflin Bates* for horse stealing resulted in the conviction of a sentence of penitentiary for five years. The District Attorney prosecuting, Mills and Mills for the defense.
The *Morrill vs DeMorse* case, after occupying all of Friday and

Saturday was finally given to the jury at about half past three o'clock on Sunday after the speech is by Messrs. Dickson, Murray and Morrill for the prosecution and the very able efforts of S. R. G. Mills, John Mills and Lane for the defendant. After brief retirement, the jury back part in a verdict for $8,000. Later, the trial judge and court informed that plaintiff had voluntarily remitted the damages and the court had adjourned.

lost certificate
Notice by George Dugan of lost land certificate in Fannin County, originally issued to William Tyler in Fannin County.

new stage route to Jefferson
We are indebted to R. W. Nesmith for the late New Orleans papers and for a letter from Judge Evans relative to a stage route between Clarksville and Jefferson. The Judge desires that his application to the Post Office department for the establishment of such route shall be strengthened by numerously signed petitions. Such a route is important to all this region of country and should be allowed, and probably will be, if urgent representations are made. All those interested can take notice.

****

From *The Standard*, March 15, 1856

thanks
We are indebted to James Gilliam for New Orleans papers and also to George H. Bagby.

We are indebted to Hon. T. J. Rusk for a some parcel of Spanish Spring Wheat. This wheat is purported to ripen within a hundred days of sowing.

weather
Today, Friday the 14th of March, presents the appearance of the very dead of winter. Today we had some sleet. The roads are impassible.

rain
Since our last, we have some moisture, but not enough rain to

have an influence upon the river. The ground is so saturated with water that every shower produces some effect at getting the river from its stage of low water. The first good rain of two or threes days duration would in all probability give us navigation for several weeks.

farming
Owing to the long spell of frosty weather and the subsequent rains, but little has been done in this region in the preparing for spring crops. When the weather does finally settle, our farmers will have busy times if they succeed in getting their crops in any reasonable period. Our wheat crop, which is unusually large, has said to suffer considerably from the recent frost.

****

From *The Standard,* March 22, 1856

we call attention
to the advertisement of F. M. Sims for new carriage trimmings etc.;

to the advertisement of the Sulphur Fork packet, *Julia*, R. C. Hutchinson, Master;

to the notice of N. P. Clark that he is a candidate for District Clerk of Fannin County.

died
a few days ince, D.C. Van Derlin, of San Antonio, formerly an able member of the State Legislature.

missionaries/abolitionists
The Cherokee Nation has authorized their Chief to open up correspondence with the different Missionary Boards for the purpose of remonstrating against sending abolitionist among them under pretext of being missionaries.

continued Indian Depredations
As we predicted last fall, the northern Comanches are upon us and, we doubt not, in considerable force, though only seen in

small parties. The federal and state officials were warned in time but heeded not the warnings. Our Legislature turned a deaf ear to the prayers of our exposed frontier settlers for protection and refused to provide for the calling into the field of a volunteer force. There is an awful responsibility resting on the western member, who defeated the Rangers Bill.

Last week, we announced that the Indians were down on the Cibola, near the Austin crossing, and had driven off a large number of horses belonging to Mr. Brown and other settlers in that vicinity. A party of citizens started in pursuit, on inferior horses, their best horses having been taken off and overtook the Indians, four in number, near Bandera Pass, attacked and killed three, wounded the other and recovered 50 head of horse. It is said that the citizens from this city in pursuit of the same party of Indians were within four miles of the fight. Several of the party were wounded.

On Wednesday of this week, the Indians attacked the house of Messrs Hill, near Cedar Brake, about 18 miles west of this city [San Antonio] and killed a man named Robinson and a Negro boy. It appears that one of the Messrs Hill, together with Brown and two others, had gone to where a German boy had killed an Indian the week previous. The Indians had evidently been awaiting the opportunity to attack the house. The mother of the Negro boy saved her life by crawling under the house. Robinson and one of the Hills were working in the garden, near the house, when they were surrounded. Hill escaped by jumping into a stream nearby and swimming to the other side. The Indians then sacked the house, destroying what they could not carry off, took two American horses and four mules and then departed.

On receipt of an account of this, General Smith dispatched several companies of mounted troops in pursuit to intercept the Indians in retreat. But, we fear that these Indians will have had too much the start. We have also heard that the Indians were below the Seguin crossing of the Cibola committing their depredations. We fear our isolated settlements will be overrun by this savage hordes.

The driver of the Austin stage saw an Indian on Thursday night on the other side of the Cibola.

Bowie Court
Bowie County District Court opened on Tuesday morning, the 11th, Hon. Wm. S. Todd presiding and adjourned on Friday. But little business was ready for trial. A defect in the organization of the Grand Jury of the previous term rendered all the criminal indictments null and consequently there was no criminal docket for trial.
The weather during most of the week was disagreeably cold and damp and not many person were in attendance at the Court.

tidbit
During the year 1854, 165 men were hung in the United States for murder. Of this number, only 7 could read and write.

price of slaves
The New Orleans Crescent of the 7th says that Messrs J. Beard & May auctioneers of his city, sold on Tuesday last, 32 Negro men for the sum of $47,450, or an average of $1,482, and 15 of all descriptions for $15,630, making an average of $1,042 each.
****
From *The Standard*, March 29, 1856

navigation of the Sulphur
We were pleased to learn that, while the main Red River was so low that the *Runaway* had gone aground on her downward trip; the Sulphur afforded excellent navigation and for the first time a steamer passed up to Epperson's Ferry, within ten miles of Boston. This boat, the *Julia,* advertises in this issue to make regular trips during the season to Elliot and Hays Landing four miles above Epperson. The captain has ascertained what we have known for many years that, whenever a boat can get to Jefferson, it can get up Sulphur with less obstruction than it would to Jefferson. As he has tried both experiments, he is satisfied. A boat of moderate size - say an 800 bale boat - can get up to Sulphur without inconvenience whenever the bar of the main river above the mouth of the Sulphur, would not allow the same boat to get to Fulton. There is a period of the year where our merchants bring freight to Jefferson and haul it 95 miles to Clarksville. They might just as well bring this freight within 55 miles, have better

roads to haul it over, and avoid the crossing of the Sulphur bottom. The whole truth is that they may bring it to the mouth of White Oak, within 22 miles of town, if our citizens would turn out during the dead low water season, and, in conjunction with a force from Bowie, cut away all obstructions such as snags and leaning trees. There is probably not a partially obstructed stream in the world, whose navigation could be more easily and permanently improved than the Sulphur. With a narrow bed, a deep channel and a sluggish stream, it gets up ordinarily early in the fall and remains up for several months, affording, when cleaned out, better navigation than on any part of the Red River. Yet in mid summer, it runs down to a few inches depth, allowing the convenient removal of all obstructions. The citizens of Bowie have exhibited some public spirt in cleaning it out nearly to the Red River line. Bowie is already profiting from its labor and boats have already taken cotton from Moore's Landing a week or two before they got to Rowland.

we are authorized to announce
the candidacy of John M. Bivins for Clerk of Fannin County.

we call attention
of the citizens of Fannin county to the advertisement of John O. Austin, daguerreotype;

to the advertisement of Stiewig's Steam mill in the southwest corner of Titus County.

tidbit of wisdom
To rejoice in the happiness of others, is to make it our own; to produce it is to make it more than our own.

the weather and the river
The weather has been fine for two weeks and our farmers, we believe, have been making the most of the opportunity for getting in their crops. The river at the date of our last issue was high enough for any class of boats that comes here but only one little trading boat came up. Others that were on their way up turned back probably before they learned of the rise. The *Victoria,* with

freight for several persons in this place, was expected Wednesday of last week and from then until Tuesday, when it was concluded she must have turned back. The river at our landing is now too low for boats of any size. There is a rain impending, however, and we may have another rise shortly. The Sulphur is still high (has been all over the Bottom) and pours a heavy body of water steadily into the main stream. This will keep all full below and give us the benefit of all the water may fall her on the river line.

new court schedule
The Eight Judicial District has been severed and part of what comprised it is now in the 16th Judicial District. For our convenience to determine the conflicts of courts as to govern our own movements, we have referred to the law and to the calendar and made the following chart which might be of a convenience to others.
Collin & Titus, both two weeks begin on April 12th
Grayson (two weeks)
Hopkins (one week) begin April 26th
Hunt, one week, begins May 3
Cooke is one week and Fannin is two and both begin on May 10.
Denton one week begins on May 17th
Lamar is two weeks and begins on the May 24th
Tarrant is two weeks and begins on June 24
Dallas is July 1, until business is disposed of.

Democratic Convention
An intelligent friend, living in an adjoining county, writes to us that he deems it important that a Democratic convention be held to nominate candidates for Judges and District Attorney. He says "The fact can no longer be disguised that there are two partes in the country and that both parties will be in the field. I think it best that a convention be called and that the Democratic party makes nominations for Judge and District Attorney."
Our correspondent suggests Tarrant in Hopkins county as the place and the first Monday of June as the time. All interested can consider the matter and express themselves as they deem proper. The Know Nothings will doubtless have representative candidates –whether secretly or openly. Those who think the administration

of law should be of even handed Justice and that there should be no secret ties contravening the high duty an official of the law owes to the whole community, had better calmly consider what course will be the wisest to ensure the election of those who have no secret ties superior to their public duties.

****

From *The Standard,* April 5, 1856

advice

Dark seasons are never pleasant to us, but are always good for us. A cloudless sky could never produce a good harvest.

we call attention

to the candidacy of S. H. Morgan for Judge of 8th Judicial District;

fresh articles for sale by Barry & Moore;

the advertisement of jewelry by B. J. Sneed. We have examined the stock and found many rich and tasteful items. One fine Duplex Lover watch, worth some two hundred or more dollars, attracts as much attention for its richness and peculiarity of two timekeepers in one case.

election still undecided

We hear from McKinney that it is still unsure whether Easton or McCoy has been elected District Attorney of the 16th Judicial District.

new church and Masonic Hall in Clarksville

The new church and Masonic Hall United, or rather the new building with a distinct hall for each purpose, is now raised and progressing on the lots immediately facing and west of our office. It is a large building for this part of the county, with fine altitude, which will render its appearance imposing. It will be finished about the 15th of June.

storm party

On yesterday evening, about half past eight o'clock, the worthy hostess of the Eagle hotel was aroused from her reveries by the approach of Fair Women and Brave Men, who upon their arrival, announced their intention to take the house by storm. They had not more than made known their design that the roaring sound of the violin, warned all that they were ready for the charge.

The assemblage was small, but the enjoyment of both sexes were unbounded. About half past one o'clock, the scene closed and the ladies, accompanied by their gallants, were conveyed to their respective homes.

slaves escaping

It is said that about 50Negros have escaped during the past two months from the Counties of Kenton and Campbell in Kentucky.

****

From *The Standard,* April 12, 1856

newspaper business

John H. Cullum of Corsicana will be *The Standard's* agent there.

we call attention

to the circular of N. P. Clark as candidate for Clerk in Fannin County.

thanks

We are indebted to Rev. Scruggs for a copy of the *Richmond Examiner.*

Cooke County report

Major DeMorse:

Dear Sir: Thinking that you or your readers might be interested in what is going on in the free state of Cooke, I have concluded to drop you a few lines. We have had a very hard winter here and a backwards spring. Farmers are going ahead and have better prospects for a crop this season than they had for the past three seasons. Considerable immigration has come in from different parts of Texas and, while speaking of immigration, let me say that I know of no other part of Texas that holds out greater inducement for immigrants than Cooke county, if fertile lands, good water in abundance, good health and a scenery beautiful in appearance as the far famed California with a population of honest and intelligent men. Our ladies, God Bless them, are as beautiful as the fable houris of Mahomett's heaven and good and wise as beautiful. If all these combined with the advantages of cheap soil so that every man can get a home. If these are not sufficient to induce immigrants to come, then I know not what will induce them.

Our Town is improving rapidly and bids fair to do well. There are two good taverns kept in the place, two stores, two groceries, two limbs of the law and two M. D.s, all of whom are doing well, save the professional gents and the grocery keepers some of whom look worse than Hamlet's Ghosts and the balance are too poor to cast a shadow. To vary the monotony of the scenery, we have an occasional dance in which the votaries of terpsichore amuse themselves: gentlemen, dressed in buckskin and the ladies I know nothing of their dressing, save whatever they wear looks beautiful, bloomers or not.[11]

We have preaching regular and an occasional wedding.

new invention

(from the *Jefferson Herald*)

We were shown on Saturday a cotton picking machine recently invented. It is very simple. Mr. Martin, the agent for this State, will be at Linden during the early part of this week, when the machine may be examined. It is warranted to pick a thousand pounds a day and we are assured that an active hand can pick 1500 pounds per day with one of them with entire ease.

District Court

(from the *Jefferson Herald*)

The District Court for this County was opened in Linden on last Monday week. An eloquent charge was delivered to the Grand Jury by the Hon. William S Todd. We have never heard anything of its kind more impressive or appropriate. We are happy to state, however, that few bills were found by that body, which is an indication of the improvement in the morals of the County. The criminal docket was taken up and disposed on Thursday. The District Attorney, *pro tem*, acquitted himself in a highly credible manner. But little of importance was done during the week. Parties were not generally ready to try and most of the cases were continued.

humor

The individual who perpetrated the following choice stanza, was a genius and a man of observation.

Men scorn to kiss among themselves

and scarce will kiss a brother

Women oft want to kiss so bad

They smack and kiss each other

horse thieves killed

We learn from the Nueces Valley that horses and mules had been stolen from Corpus Christi, at various times, and driven to middle and eastern Texas. A party of three, which had recently stolen a lot of horses, were pursued. At San Patracio, the pursuers were joined by citizens of that county and the thieves overhauled as they were going in the direction of San Antonio. A letter from the Valley says the thieves were taken and are dead. It appears that they showed fight and this was the result. Ten horses were recovered.

died

at his residence near this place, Gen. James O. Record, son of John Record.

****

From *The Standard,* April 19, 1856

we call attention

to the card of Malcolm Bolin of Mount Pleasant, Titus county; Commissioner for Alabama and Notary Public;

to the advertisement of the Mt. Pleasant Hotel, kept by Elam Riddle, our old friend, a clever man and attentive host.

weather

After a long dry winter followed by a considerable period of wet weather, Spring has arrived and the weather has been unusually dry for the past several weeks. But little farm work has been done until a period unusually late but, by close attention and perseverance, most of the spring crops have been got in the ground. In some places the ground has been so hard that it is impossible to plow to advantage and corn planted two or three weeks ago have made little progress in growing. The wheat crop, of which a large quantity has been sown, looks unusually well. Oats look well too and, if we are blessed with refreshing showers, our rich lands will soon give our farmers the prospect of an abundant harvest. We notice that in the sugar region, the severity of the winter has had a most baneful effect on the prospects of the sugar planter. The injury may be partial but from the unusually cold winter so far south of us we are apprehensive that the damage done to the sugar cane may be extensive.

Red River

The river, our only dependence as a means for getting cotton to market, is now at the low water mark. Our merchants and planters have been suffering severely of the past 12 months by the unprecedented continuance of low water. Had boats been in readiness to take advantage of the rise in the river, which we have had this spring, our cotton may have all been at market, but this not having been the case, our cotton still lies at the various landings or stored in gin houses. We understand that some of our merchants and planters are determined to wait no longer on the steam boats. Preparations are being made to build flat boats with a view toward of shipping them to Shreveport or the Mississippi. The state of things will continue until we get the railroaded within a reasonable distance. The present prospect is two railroad with our eastern boundary will be completed in two years. One will go from Gaines Landing, via Camden, to the cut off at Fisher's Prairie in Washington County Arkansas and thence to our eastern boundary. The other, the Vicksburg road through Shreveport to Jefferson. Both of these roads are progressing rapidly and we understand that the grading of the former from Camden to the Cut off has been let to very responsible contractors. The eastern part of the road from Camden to Gaines' Landing is in a very forward state nicely. Should our Legislature at the adjourned meeting in July adopt a wise policy – loans to railroad companies with proper security from our school funds to enable them to procure the rails and other equipment, after the grading has been completed, we shall soon have cause to delight in the improved condition.

imprisonment for debt

The Massachusetts House of Representatives has rejected a proposition from the Senate to amend the Constitution so as to abolish imprisonment for debt.

****

From *The Standard,* April 26, 1856

thanks

We are indebted to Isaiah W. Wells and Heald, Massle & Co. for the late New Orleans papers.

we call attention

to the announcement of Wm. H. Johnson for Judge;

to the advertisement of a meeting of the Democrats of Red River. A very full attendance is earnestly desired in order that there may be a reliable expression of the will of the majority of the Democracy of the County;

to the advertisement of H. Rhine and Bros who have really an elegant assortment of goods for sale.

resignation

Judge Reagan has resigned as judge of the 9th District and is again a candidate for that position. The reasons for the resignation are the increased salary which it is perceived will be paid to judges and which he cannot receive except in a reelections and the remodeling of the district by which he is the judge of half of the voters, who have no vote in his election and who might prefer someone else.

Judge Gray of Hopkins has taken a similar course.

May Day

The floral anniversary is approaching and the young ladies of the schools, we believe, have made ample preparation for the celebration. So, on the first *proximo*, there will be inducement to draw visitors to town. Bright eyes will reign supreme for one night and one day before the little world around here turns again into the pathways of business and beauty, blessing the gazer which will in itself be blessed in the ecstacy it imparts.

rain

Our farmers and gardens have long been in need of rain and on Thursday it came plentifully. This morning we have had light showers and vegetation will spring up magically under the congenial influence. Wheat and corn both look well.

vote of thanks

at the close of the session of the White Rock Presbytery of the Cumberland Presbyterian Church, commenced at McKinney on the 11th of April, the following resolution was passed:

On motion, the thanks of the Presbytery are unanimously extended to the citizens of the Town of McKinney and its vicinity for its kindness and hospitality during the meeting;

N. R. Smith, Moderator, R. R. Dunlass, Clerk.

died

at his residence yesterday evening at an advanced age, Capt. William Becknell.

The above announcement will cause great regret to the first settlers of this county as all are acquainted with the deceased. Capt. Becknell was the first who crossed the Plains to Santa Fe; was elected Captain of the first Company formed in Northern Texas in 1836 and while in the military was elected Representative to Congress.

We knew Capt. Becknell well for many years. He was a man of decided character and firmness, a model of a pioneer. [12]

****

From *The Standard,* May 3, 1856

we call attention

to the advertisement of Darnall & Hunt regarding dissolution;

to the advertisement of Allwood Academy;

to the advertisement of the Jefferson Hotel by N. J. Moore.

river traffic

We understand that two steamboats, the *Victoria* and another, passed our landing yesterday and the day before with full loads for New Orleans.

weather

We had a rise in the river of between four and five feet, before the rain which fell on Tuesday and we think it highly probable that now there will be a sufficient rise to permit large size boats to visit our landing at Roland. We had a most copious rain on the evening of Wednesday and all Nature is rejoicing in beauty. Crops are all beginning to look remarkably promising. The timely showers which we have had, followed by the genial warmth of the sun, have greatly improved the prospects of the farmer. Wheat promises now to be an abundant harvest. We had a rise in the river of between four and five feet, before the rain which fell on Tuesday, and we think it highly probable that now there will be a sufficient rise to permit large size boats to visit our landing at Roland.

Saturday Morning - Since writing the above, we have seen a gentleman who returned from Roland yesterday evening. He states that the river has risen more than 15 feet with considerable drift wood running. A Gentleman from Bonham, who arrived in town this morning, reports that a vast quantity of rain had fallen in that section on Tuesday evening and night, so that the prospect is now very favorable for a good rise in Red River, sufficient to let boats come up and take off the accumulated cotton of two years crop from the different warehouses along the river and at such rates as planters can afford to pay.

bridge is disrepair

We call the attention of our Corporation[13] to the state of the Delaware bridge, east of C.P. Thompson's. A small expenditure now would save the ruin of the entire bridge and may possibly save the life of some valuable horse or perhaps the life of his rider. We should think that, after the accident of the other bridge west of town which happened so recently, our Corporation would keep a sharp out for such horse traps.

county Democratic meeting

A large meeting of the citizens of this town was held at the Court House, J. W. Sims in the Chair.

The following delegates were elected unanimously to attend the convention in Paris for the purpose of nominating candidates for the office of District Judge and Prosecuting Attorney:

L. D. Henderson, H. R. Latimer, Thomas L. Cowan and W. Guest, all esquires. Dr. Gordon and Judges Fulbright, Wooten, English and Dillahunty. After speeches from H. R. Latimer and J. C. Burks, the meeting separated.

tragedy

An account of a group of more than a hundred men on the Blanco, who took a father and son from jail and killed them by multiple shots. They had been in jail for shooting a couple of citizens. *The Austin State Gazette* was outraged: "If, as in this case, a mob could put a man to death without benefit of trial -- a right guaranteed to every white man in the land --they may assert the same right on any other occasion. Who is secure?"

May Day

Our town was on Thursday the theater of festivity and joyousness. The young ladies of the Institute and Seminary kept up the time honored custom of celebrating May Day. The young ladies of the seminary, under the charge of Mrs. Gibson, crowned their Queen in a grove adjacent to Town, after which they returned to their Academy where they had prepared for the entertainment of themselves and their guests a sumptuous dinner, after partaking of which the company separated, many of them to join with the young ladies of the Institute. Long before the appointed time for the ceremony of the crowning of the Queen had arrived, the Town was filled to overflowing, by strangers from a distance - the friends and relatives of the pupils - and those of our citizens who wished to feast their eyes, ears and inner man. The young Ladies had prepared an elegant dinner, of which all who were present, were invited to partake. The young ladies who took part in the ceremony of crowning the Queen, performed their parts with a gracefulness of ease and dignity rarely to be equaled, but never to be surpassed. As for the favorite on whom the choice of the ladies centered to presided on the occasion, she looked "every inch a Queen." We would not be surprised if not the hearts of many a young man as well as some of the old bachelors, will remain in a kind of tremor for some time to come. It would be invidious to mention names, but we who were among outsiders, heard many a well mentioned compliment passed on individuals, and were we not already satisfied that those on whom they were passed, were already sufficiently conscious of their fascinations, we would particularize. On the whole, the day went off with great eclat and the citizens of our town and the surrounding districts were highly delighted with the celebrations of both schools. Long may their young hearts have nothing more to trouble them than on May Day. We have heard but congratulations to those young ladies who acted as managers on behalf of their fellow students.

In the evening, we understand, that a party was given at Mrs. Donoho's at which those who wished to join in the festivities of the dance had an opportunity of indulging. Our town during the day presented quite a lively and animated appearance and delight and satisfaction seemed to reign in every bosom.

more Indian Depredations- varied reports about Lipan Apaches

The *San Antonio Texan* reports that, on the 28th ult, several horses were stolen from the ranch of Mr. Wyatte, some ten miles below Castroville and also five from his father's ranch, by Indians. It seems that they had a drove with them at the time and they left two horses tied together as they had been driven until they were nearly dead. Some persons immediately started in pursuit and soon overtook another party of men coming down the country who were also in pursuit of the Indians. Both parties took the trail together and followed it until Thursday night. They found on the trail mocassins, Indian ropes and several hogs killed with arrows. On the pack horses that were tied together was a supply of pork rolled up in a panther skin.

Major Neighbors reports that the hostile Indians are threatening to kill the Indians in the vicinity of his reserve under his protection and he finds it necessay to keep a large number of soldiers to protect them from danger.

The Texan also says horses, cattle etc. have been stolen by the Indians on the Olmus, a few miles from our city, during the last week.

humor

"Patrick, my dear, where on earth have you been?"

"The Widow Maloney's Ball and what an elegant time we had at it. We had four fights in 15 minutes and knock downs with the watchmen left one whole nose in the house – and that belonged to the tea kettle. Faith! The likes we have never seen since we waked old Donnelly."

the blind vocalists

"These "children of misfortune" gave concerts in this place [Bowie] on Wednesday and Thursday nights last week. Their style of singing is truly exquisite and their power of voice full and remarkably sweet. These qualifications alone suffice to attract large audiences, wherever they go, but when added to these, it is remembered that so great an affliction as that of utter blindness is attached to them, their appeal to the warmest sympathies of a generous public cannot, it seems to us, go unnoticed.

The readings of the scriptures by Miss Brush is beyond comparison, affecting and touching. It seems but to breathe life into the world and make its meaning audible."

We call attention to the above communication from our correspondent at Boston, Bowie County in relation to the performances given by the blind vocalists in that place. We have noticed frequent observations of their performances during their tour through Arkansas and in several other places they have visited in this State. They are to appear this evening at the Baptist Church and from everything we have heard of them, we are satisfied, we will be highly entertained.

****

From *The Standard,* May 10, 1856

we call attention
to the advertisement of C. C. Alexander, wagons wanted;

to the notice of W. B. Stout, watch seal lost;

to the candidacy of J. W. Sims Jr. for Collector and Assessor;

to the professional card of Lorenzo DeKing. Esq., Tarrant, Hopkins County;

to the advertisement of the Union Hotel at Bonhan by James S. Parks;

to the advertisement for the Clarksville Hotel by Proprietor Wm. B. Sims. My house is large and commodious with as good of stables as any in the state;"

to the advertisement of John West of lands to sell.

hurricane

Hempstead county Arkansas has been visited by a tremendous hurricane leveling every opposing obstacle. Trees, fences, houses have all been prostrated and the deadened lumber in the cultivated sections have done extensive damage. We have heard of the ravages of the storm from several other districts south and east of this, although we are not in possession of the details.

We had the same evening a heavy fall of rain accompanied by very loud thunder and vivid lightning. We understand that the county west of this bordering on Red River was also visited by heavy rains the same evening. We should now suppose that there will be very good rise in the navigation in the Red River for some time and at last between steam boats and flat boats, our planters will soon get all their products off to market.

We hope that some ease in the pecuniary markets will be the result for, because of a combination of circumstances, money has been scarcer in this region than we have ever known it and from the difficulty and expense of bringing in supplies, the price of all imported goods will be ruinous to the consumers.

Hopkins County

The District Court opened in Tarrant, Hopkins county, Judge Todd presiding, and continued four days. There was little business before it and the court was only partially occupied and adjourned on Friday afternoon, the appearance docket being disposed of. There were in attendance from other counties: attorneys E. G. Benners and Martin Rogers from Cass; Wm. H. Johnson and T. J. Rogers, John P. Hill and B. W. Gray from Titus County; John A. Summers from Red River; W. H. Bonner and W. N. Peacock and S. R. G . Mills from Lamar; besides the resident attorneys T.L. Greene, E. D. McKenney; Russel & Rice, Ben Von Sickle, B. W. Musgrove and L. DeKing.

On Monday evening, a meeting was held of the Democrats and delegates were chosen for the convention to be held in Paris,

Lamar county. A regular organization of the Democratic party has matured and regular nominations made for every office in the county to be elected in the August election. The general feeling on this subject was praiseworthy. The party in Hopkins is united and the true Democracy of this gallant county will make a report of itself in August.

On Tuesday evening Mr. Benners and Mr. Montgomery, candidates for District Attorney, addressed the people in the Court room.

On Tuesday and Wednesday nights, the blind Vocalists gave two concerts, the first very fully attended, the second not so fully because it was interfered with by a heavy storm of rain just preceding the time of commencement.

Hopkins steadily increases in population and, although it has lost a large number of citizens some two years since by removal to new counties on the Heads of the Trinity, it now has about 800 voters.

Hopkins, as is well known, is a heavy cattle raising county. The last winter was more severe upon stock grazing on the wire grass prairies, than during any previous season. Some of the stock raisers lost largely by death of cattle from the severity of the weather. There may not be another such season for many years, yet it would seem to us that those who raise cattle, mules or sheep had better prepare themselves with machine mowers and lay in each summer a large supply of prairie hay. It would be a measure of precaution that would not be very expensive, could do not harm and might do much good.

Two gentlemen named Smith are building a flouring mill at Tarrant, the building is up, the machinery nearly ready and the Stones at some point of the Lake on their way up. They are preparing themselves to manufacture on a large scale flour of good quality. The locality is a good one for the business.

The Academy for Males, commenced last year, is not quite finished. It is a neat frame structure of two stories, in a commanding situation and is a commendable enterprise. It has been built by subscription.

The site of Tarrant is decidedly an eligible one for beauty - in a high point of high rolling prairies, with water and wood convenient. The rains run off so quickly so as to prevent the continuance of mud for any considerable period of time after the heaviest showers. The country, north and west, affords most splendid roads for pleasant riding. The Town has however grown very slowly since its first location, but will, we are told, improve materially this summer. It affords at preset two taverns, two dry goods stores, one Drug Store, one Family Grocery and one Drinkery. Lawyers, it has several, as our columns show; physicians two.

Further than this, it is the residence of some of the finest gentlemen as are to be found on the circuit of the 8th and there is no county town in the district away from home, where a non resident can pass his time more pleasantly.

Concert by Blind Vocalists

Our citizens were delighted on the evening Saturday and Tuesday with the concerts given by the blind vocalists Mr. Coe and Miss Mary Bush, who were educated at the Institution of the Blind in New York City. We can cordially recommend them to the favor of the public, wherever they may direct their course.

The Know Nothings of the South

That any man with the least pretensions to political information can concede to Millard Fillmore the remotest chance of being elected to the Presidency is a proposition we utterly deny and repudiate. Why, the party which affects to support him is split into so many factions that nobody can ascertain its identity. The bulk of the Know Nothings is under the control of the Black Republicans[14] and they are in open rebellion against Fillmore, not so much because they distrust his feelings on slavery as because of the desperate condition of his fortunes. It is barely possible that he may carry a single Northern State.

In the South, the prospect is even more cheerless in the eyes of the Fillmore supporters. They cannot count on the support of the

Whigs to whose alliance they are indebted for their partial successes in the South. Their own party is melting away by defection and tumbling to pieces under the heavy blows of its own members. The terror of its disciple is now derided and its organization has lost all of its strength and consistency since the public had a glimpse of its working. Between an inveterate Whig of the Federal school and a Democrat who owes all his consequences to a personal and political subserviency to Andrew Jackson, there can be no identity of opinion or interest.

Democratic meeting of Red River County

At a large and respectable meeting of the Democracy of old Red River County held in the Court House in Clarksville on Saturday the 3rd instant for the purpose of appointing delegates to attend a conference to beheld in Paris on the last Tuesday in May next to nominate candidates for District Judge and District Attorney for the Eighth Judicial District, on motion of the Hon. A.H. Latimer, Major James W. Sims was called to the Chair and William P. Cornelius was appointed Secretary.

On motion, Judge Latimer was called upon to explain the object of the meeting. The object of the meeting being explained, Judge Latimer moved the appointment of a Committee to draft resolutions and the following gentlemen were appointed: Smith Ragsdale, Nelson Doak, Dr. Hart, James J. Ward, Dr. Ware, George W. McCarley, Henry Rhine, Col. J. H. Burks, Edward West, Levi G. Childress, William P. Cornelius and Robert Neathery.

Resolved that it is the undivided sense of the meeting that L. D. Henderson, H.R. Latimer, Thos. L. Cowan, George Gordon, Judge Fullbright, Wm. Guest, Judge Wooten, Judge English and Judge Dillahunty be appointed delegates to attend said convention at Paris;

Resolved that we will support the nomination of the Convention.

                                                      Nelson Doak

Democratic meeting of Hopkins County

At a meeting of the Democracy of Hopkins County, it was resolved that L.G. Harman, Wm. T. Blythe, T. L. Green, James Hooten, R. L. Askew, Johnson Wren, J. E. Hopkins, John Woods, John Jarrett and A. G. Melton be appointed delegates to the convention, a majority of whom shall cast the votes of this county on all important measures.

Resolved that we recommend the favorable consideration of the convention, as a candidate for District Attorney, our esteemed fellow citizen Col. E. D. McKenney.

Resolved that this mass meeting of the Democracy of Hopkins County nominate candidates for the various county offices to be elected in August next. A committee of L.G. Harman, James Hooten, Wm. W. Goff, Wm. Hargrave, J. D. H. McRee was appointed who selected:

Precinct No. 1 - J. E. Hopkins, W. N. Dawson, - Sinclair;

Precinct No. 2 - H. Sanders, J. P. Goodman, Sam Sellers

Precinct No. 3 - Joel Blackwell, John Wood, Peter Visar

Precinct No. 4 - Johnson Wren, J. W. Matthews

Precinct No. 5 - James Hooten, J. G. Hamilton, Wm. Evans

Precinct No. 6 Central - A.G. Melton, E.D. McKenney, H. H. Hargraves, Eli Vass

Precinct No. 7 -Wm. A. Wortham, Wesley Johnson, –Thresher

Precinct No. 8 - John Garrett, William Wilkins, T. Proctor

Precinct No. 9 -William Paff, Thomas Young, Jesse Odom, Jonathan Fowler

The following persons were nominated for county offices

Chief Justice - A. G. Melton,

County Clerk - R. E. Matthews

Assessor and Collector - L. Vaden

County Treasurer - H. Russell

County Surveyor - L.G. Harman

Sheriff - W H. Pore

County Commissioners: John Garrett, Jas. B. Simpson, E. M. Posey, J. D. Miller and H. H. Hargrave.

The business of the convention over, the meeting closed with great harmony.

R. L. Askew, Chairman

Wm. M. Ewing, Secretary

died

It is with regret that this day we have to record in our obituary list, the name of our late friend Capt. John A. Bagby, aged 66 years and seven months after a protracted disease of the heart which he bore with much submission. Long a resident of this Town, he was born in Virginia on the 4th of May 1789 and in early youth removed to Alabama in which state he remained to the fall of 1844, when he came to Texas and resided here the rest of his life.

During his residence in Alabama, he was chosen Captain of a Volunteer Company and with it did faithful service to his country while engaged in the Creek War.

A man of retiring habits and an unobtrusive man, he rarely sought distinction but when his fellow citizens called upon him, he was always found ready to comply with their wishes. His brother Arthur P. Bagby was Governor of Alabama.

millwright and machinist

Advertisement of W. G. Dollar, millwright and machinist in Jefferson. He will build or repair saw mills, corn mills and merchant flouring mills of all kind, put up the machinery to wheat threshing machines, cotton gins etc and will construct all mlll dams, bridges, trussel work etc. He is at present engaged in putting up a flouring mill for Messrs. S. L. McFarland and Co. near Jefferson.

****

From *The Standard*, May 17, 1856

ventriloquist

On Monday and Tuesday evenings we had the pleasure of listening to the performances of E. Wilber in this Town. His songs were well sung and, as a ventriloquist, he is no mean performer of his art. We can therefor recommend him to the patronage of the public.

we call attention

to the advertisement of C. C. Alexander in this issue. It will be seen that he has everything desirable in the Mercantile line;

to the advertisement of N. W. Townes; of town property for sale in Sherman.

thanks

We are indebted to W. H. Milwee, Esq. of Lamar County for late New Orleans newspapers. Our thanks are due also to the Hon. J. Rusk and the Hon. L. D. Evans for late public documents.

the late storm

From all directions we learn that the hurricane which swept portions of this state and eastern Arkansas has taken a much wider and longer range than such storms usually take. Our western exchanges speak of its ravages and in all directions to the Mississippi, so far as heard from its destructive effects have been experienced. In the neighborhood of Dallas nine persons were killed. The particulars of the storm we have not seen.

Rowletts Creek, Collin county

Dear Major, I am aware that since you have not visited this region within the last 12 months and have not been kept posted in the current matters of the Trinity country, you can have but an inadequate idea of the vast improvement upon the wild and desert prairies you once rode over in this portion of the country. I am situated in the neighborhood of Plano on the lower division of the Rowlett survey, about 12 miles south of McKinney on the Dallas Road, on a beautiful and rich tract of land - abundantly supplied with timber and water. The situation selected for my Mother's residence is really beautiful and romantic and well worth graphic description. But as this kind of scenery is so common of North Texas, it would be of no material interest to most of your readers.

Five years ago, the country lying between McKinney and Dallas was a vast plain of sparsely settled prairie, traversed only by the traveler and the hunter. Lands were at that point comparatively worthless and the fertility of the soil not known or appreciated and the now luxuriant wheatfields were the lairs of panthers and deer. But it was not His Divine Will that this state of affairs was to be eternal. Now, those same prairies that were only know to the huntsmen are being cultivated in extensive fields of corn, wheat oats &c. This same county which only five or six years ago was the scene of wilderness and solitude it now checkered with heavy fencing and impenetrable bois d'arc hedge. Frame dwellings and "White Rock Spires" are springing up at every grove and eminences, as if by magic. Those very lands, which 5 or 6 years ago were bought for 50 or 75 cents an acre, are now held for between 5 and 15 dollars an acre. The emigration from Kentucky, Tennessee, Mississippi, Alabama and Louisiana is centering on this immediate neighborhood, with large lots of Negroes, mules and strong wagons &c, with a settled determination to make Texas their permanent home and cultivate her soil. There is no country in this world susceptible to greater improvement.

At present, this county is comparatively healthy, there being very little sickness except on the plantation of Messrs. Truman and Hopkins. They have recently lost 9 or 10 Negroes of a disease which has appeared in the form of an epidemic, denominated by the physicians as "Typhoid Pneumonia." The sick are convalescent and hope is entertained of the abatement of the disease without further loss.

The wheat crop is very fine. The corn crop is not so favorable.

Many farmers have their entire fields to replant in consequence of the continued cold weather in the early part of the season which destroyed the seed in the ground

I have no local news of importance. I heard yesterday in Plano that Cedar Hills, a small village about 12 miles west of Dallas, was entirely demolished on last Thursday night, 29th ultimate by a hurricane.[15] Nine or ten persons were killed and several seriously injured. Fragments of houses, merchandise and human bodies were said to have been found 5 or 6 miles from town. I have none of the particulars.

Meeting of Democrats in Lamar County

The central Democratic committee of Lamar County met at the Courthouse in Paris. On motion Wm. M. Williams was called to the chair and delivered a fluent and eloquent address explaining the object of the meeting to be for the purpose of sending delegates to the Democratic convention for nominating candidates for District Judge and District Attorney.

Hon. H. Wortham was requested to act as secretary. On motion in W. H. Bonner, the chair, then appointed a committee of nine: W. J. Bonner, Chairman, Joseph Baker, Daniel St. Claire, T. J. Dickerson, John H. Fowler, W. H. Hobbs, James Mosely, Isaac Newell and Sen. Logan Stevenson for the purpose of reporting on resolutions expressive of the sense of the meeting. Said committee retired and a call was made on William B. Wright, who delivered an eloquent animated and soul stirring address, marking, in a vivid style, the rise and progress of the parties, showing the inconsistencies of the self styled American party and loudly calling upon the democracy to unite and conquer. The committee also recommended the appointment of a committee whose duty it shall be to make a selection of persons to become candidates for the several county offices: E. J. Helton, Henry Long, Thomas Dennis, and Thomas Gaines.

The committee then added the following persons, to wit: Robert Price, James Skidmore, Dr. A. J. Nelson, John D. Thomas, Joseph McCarty, Bartley Pitts, Dr. R. T. Jones and John Guffee.

Meeting of Democrats in Hunt County

The central Democratic committee of Hunt County met at Greenville. The meeting was called to order by A. T. Howell. On motion, James Hooker was called to be chair and J. D. McCamant was requested to serve as secretary. On motion, a committee was appointed to draft resolutions. After a brief absence, the committee through their chairman, Sherwood McBride appeared and presented a preamble which was unanimously adopted.

Resolved: that A. T. Howell W. G. Mills, James W McCamant and John Richie are appointed delegates to represent the Democratic Party at Paris at the Democratic convention. The committee also recommends the appointment of a committee of 15 whose duty it shall be to make a selection of proper persons to become candidates for the several county offices, to wit

W. G. Mills	J. D. Webb
Lewis W. Moore	B. L. Richie,
D. Bromley	J. Wilson
James Lynch	William H. Thayer
J. F. McLaughery	Samuel Moore
W. T. Weldin	Sherwood McBride
A. Garr	
Money Weatherford	
J. G. Smith	

The Committee proposed for the following offices:

Chief Justice - Wiley A Mattox

County clerk - James W. McCamant

Treasurer - Charles Dougherty

Assessor and Collector - Nathan Anderson

Surveyor - A. S. McCamant

Sheriff - T. A. Dagley

County Commissioners: William G. Mills, Money Wetherford, J. D. Nicholson, William Kitching. On motion, it was resolved that J. E. Wilson, Lewis W. Moore and L. Moody be added to the list of delegates.

railroad meeting

There was a railroad meeting in Paris where Travis G. Wright, President of the Memphis El Paso and Pacific railroad company, will speak of the purpose of organizing a new company.

On the motion of S. H. Morgan, Wm. M. William was called to the Chair who explained to the stockholders the purpose of the meeting. N. W. Townes was appointed Secretary. A Board of Directors was elected:. Simpson H Morgan, G. W. Wright, J. D. Thomas, S.D. Rainey, John T. Mills, B. S. Walcot, Thomas Ragsdale, H. G. Hendricks, Samuel Bogart and J. W. Fort.

partial list of letters at Clarksville Post Office

Brown, L.	Harris, J. B.
Bloodsworth, J. D.	Hays, Miss M. J.
Bradshaw, G.	Hyde, Jordan
Cummings, F. E.	Juge, Dr. J. M.
Cherry, N. A.	Johnson, Mrs. J.
Franklin, B. T.	Johnson, Mrs. M.
Gibbons, J. C.	Johnson, C. B.
Gibson, Robert	Jones, W.
Green J. W.	Smith, Mrs. D. F.
Hill, Wm.	Tinnin, William
Holyfield, C. P.	White, E. H.
Hogan, H. C.	Webb, Milton
Hill, W.	Woodbridge, J. C.
House, R. M.	Woley, S. J.

Young, Miss D. C.

Yeates, Dr. L.

James W Thomas, Post Master

humor

There is a man in Boston who walks so slow, he wears a pair of spurs to keep his shadow from treading on his heels;

"I ain't particular" as the oyster says, when they asked whether he wanted to be fried or roasted.

property in Sherman for sale

N. W. Townes, intending to move permanently to Paris, offers his property in Sherman, located on the southeast corner of the Public Square, for sale. The house is fifty feet in length; the lot is enclosed, has a well of pure water in the yard, good stables and corn crib.

notice of dissolution of partnership

Notice by L. S. Johnson and P. J. Johnson, doing business under the name of Johnson and Bro, that the firm has been dissolved by mutual connent. The business has been sold to G. W. Johnson of DeKalb, whom they ask their former customers to patronize.

****

From *The Standard,* May 24, 1856

The Carncross Family

These entertainers have passed through the northern line of counties to this point and have given two performance here to the special gratification of the people about town. Tonight, they appear again, singing dancing etc. Freyer, the violinist who accompanies the troupe, is an excellent performer, good anywhere.

The execution of Miss Carncross and Mr. Salter upon the guitar is also good. Mr. Henry, who fills the comic role, is a passable low comedy actor. There is nothing very new to people of the world in the range of performances, but they are novel to most of our citizens and afford gratification of a night or two.

humor

Why is twice eleven like twice ten?

Because twice eleven is twenty two and twice ten is twenty too.

tidbit of wisdom

Intellect is not moral power, conscience is. Honor, not talent, makes the gentleman;

Liberty and liberty of conscience are all one and inseparable.

Meeting of Democrats in Fannin County

The central Democratic committee of Fannin County and Democratic citizens of the county met at Bonham. On motion, R. H. Lane called to be chair and H. P. Dyer was requested to act as secretary.

Col. Lane opened with a few remarks and introduced Mr. Wright of Paris who delivered a very interesting address to the citizens on the various questions of political differences now in agitation throughout the country.

The following delegates were selected to go to the convention in Paris:

precinct 1 - R. H. Lane and A. E. Pace

precinct 2 - Cicero Brown

precinct 3 - W. B. Crocker

precinct 4 - B. C. Bagby

precinct 5 - B. Orton and A. J. Nicholson

precinct 6 - John L McKasson

The following gentlemen were appointed alternates: W.A. Routh, Robert Johnson and R. W. Madden

The following were nominated for the different offices;

Chief Justice - J. F. Crawford

County Clerk - S. J. Galbraith

Treasurer - A. H. Trueblood

Sheriff - A. J. Routh

Assessor and Collector - K. C. Henslee

Surveyor - R. S. Jones and A.S. McCamant

Commissioners: Anthony Brown, James Dyer, Wm. Gambill and A. J. McFarland

married

On the 7th of April in Greenville, by the Rev. A. L. Davis, Alfred T. Howell Esq. to Miss Sally R. Dickson, daughter of John B. Dickson

We greet with pleasure the announcement that our friend Howell, for many years esteemed as a bachelor gentleman of most excellent principles and amiable qualities, has at last found someone he liked better than himself, to acknowledge fealty to and resign his cherished independence for queenly government of his own choice.

****

From *The Standard*, May 31, 1856

humor

The Greatest Organ in the World ! The organ of speech in women, an organ too without stop.

stump speeches

W. S. Todd, a candidate for reelection as District Judge, lists dates and times where he will address voters in Red River, Bowie, Lamar, Cass, Titus, Hopkins and Hunt counties.

trouble in Kaufman county

A gentleman just in from Kaufman informs us that the county is in a state of open rebellion, and that serious difficulty is apprehended between a set of desperate characters, who reside there, and the legal authorities. Letters of a threatening nature have been addressed to Judge Reagan and the district attorney, warning them that, if they come into the county for the purpose of holding the next regular term of the court, that their lives will be taken. Some of those letters are anonymous and some are, we understand, from responsible men - one from the District Court Clerk.

We know that Judge R. and the Prosecuting Attorney are men of too much nerve and personal courage to be deterred from following the strict line of their duty, by the threats of personal violence emanating from such a source and we cannot but believe that there are a sufficient number of law abiding citizens in Kaufman to protect the court in the discharge of it duties.

Visit to Fannin County

The seat of Justice for Fannin county is improving. Among its citizens are several who have a perception of one of the first and a greatest springs of progress for a country village - schools. The Milam Masonic Lodge of that place, assisted by individuals, had put up a building for the education of females, much surpassing in size, appearance and commodiousness any other that we have ever seen in Northern Texas. The use of this they have given gratuitously to a highly competent instructor, who is assisted by two Ladies, teachers of Music, painting, embroidery and other female accomplishments and general assistants in the school. Already at the beginning they have 70 scholars and have no doubt of largely increasing their numbers soon. Indeed, they are fast coming in. To walk through the building, a large, handsomely built, well arranged structure of two stories, gives one the impression that something respectable was intended to be done.

We are glad to see the *education* and *accomplishments of* females is being appreciated justly. Men may, under adverse circumstances, form an education which the necessities and intercommunication of life impart, but mothers and trainers of future men must be natured carefully when girls or the women of the Republic and trainers of the future men, upon whom depends so much of the character of those men, will be stunted in their moral and intellectual development, not only for their own advancement but for the country of which they are to become important members. The men of Bonham have acted wisely and deserve well of their fellows and the people of all those surrounding counties whose newness would not permit the present establishment of such institutions.

Bonham is also fortunate in a male school under an able and learned teacher, of superior character and agreeable manner, the Rev. Mr. Aikin, educated at Princeton and for some years past Chaplain at Posts on the Indian frontier. This school is also promising and we imagine will soon afford him adequate return for his services.

The town is building up and does a large commercial business. Some idea of the magnitude of the trade may be formed by reference to the advertisements of C. C. Alexander in our column on Bonham advertisements.

the incoming wheat crop

We have been in Hunt, Fannin and Lamar and have seen some persons direct from Collin, Dallas, Grayson and Cooke. Some crops in Grayson were planted late because of the grasshoppers and some in Collin are indifferent, but generally the crops are thrifty and the yield will be very large, while the aggregate crop will be larger than ever before grown in Northern Texas.

The Democratic Convention at Paris, Lamar County

The District convention for the nomination of District Judge and District Attorney, convened in Paris at about 10 0'clock on Tuesday morning the 27th. The Brick Church was filled to overflowing with spectators.

On motion, unanimously accepted, Col. R. H. Lane of Fannin was made President and Johnson Wren of Hopkins, Vice President; Nathan E. Griffiths of Lamar was then made Secretary and Robert H. Ward of Cass Assistant Secretary.

Major W. C. Battes of Titus then moved for a committee to adopt a basis for voting at the Convention. The several delegates presented members as follows:

Lamar: Joseph McCarty

Fannin: B.C. Bagby

Hopkins: L. G. Harman

Red River: L. D. Henderson

Titus: Wm. C. .Battes

Cass: Robert H. Ward

Hunt: John E. Wilson

Bowie: Martin Glover

Judge Todd and S. H. Morgan were nominated as candidate for Judge and Messrs. McKenney, Mills and Summers for District Attorney. Jacob Long and C. R. Roland were appointed Tellers.

The delegates then voted - Todd 43, Morgan 17. Upon motion of T. L. Green of Red River, William S. Todd was unanimously declared the nominee for Judge. For District Attorney, on the sixth ballot, Mills 31, Summers 15, McKenney 14. S. R. G. Mills was declared the nominee of the Convention.

Fannin District Court

The District Court, Hon. W. S. Todd presiding, commenced and ended in Fannin during the last week. There was less business than usual.

From *The Standard,* June 7, 1856

we call attention

to the new law firm of Dillahunty and Wright, very reliable gentlemen and good lawyers;

The Paris Hotel, R. B. Francis, Proprietor; the house is well kept, deserving patronage and getting it. The stable attached is large and has had a long reputation which has assisted largely in making the hotel attractive to travelers.

thanks

We are indebted to James E. Allen of Bonham for late New Orleans papers.

rain

The ground was getting dry and the plants were feeling the want of rain, when, at about one o'clock, this morning a heavy wind which brought up from the North, a rain which lasted two hours and which and poured down briskly. We do not know how far the storm extended but are able to certify that it was heavy rain, enough to wet the ground in our garden three inches while the wind was sufficient to blow the corn down. We imagine, however, that it was not general.

Lamar Court

The District Court opened in Lamar County on Monday morning and ended on Saturday. The Democratic convention drew a large concourse of people, dispatch being a major object with the farmers who mainly comprised the convention. No "gas" was vented and the business, which drew them together, the maintenance of the organization which sustains their glorious and long respected principles, was completed by 5:00 o'clock in the evening. During the remainder of the week, not many people attended the court. The wheat crop harvest drew the close attention of the great mass of country people. Some pleasant social gatherings served to while away the nights.

On Friday, B. W. Musgrove, candidate for District Attorney, addressed the people for an hour and a half in advocacy of his claims to the office and in exposition of his political views, which he contended had no association with the district attorneyship. He was followed by S. R. G. Mills, the nominee of the Democratic convention, who enunciated his political views, to which Mr. Musgrove briefly responded.

Paris has improved during the last 18 months, more than any other town in Northern Texas, and is a pretty and in every way thriving town. It has excellent schools and plenty of them, and this has induced the settlement of river planters for the education of their children. It also has a full supply of artisans, who in the various branches of wood, iron, tin, silver work and saddlery add to the productive wealth of the place, and in turn, give occupation to the school teacher, the merchant and the professional man. The place has excellent hotels, one of which can be found advertised in our columns. Major Francis keeps a good house, is well attentive host and gave satisfaction to a large throng that crowded his house during the sitting of the Convention.

Paris has a handsome brick church, used, we believe, by all denominations, a respectable academy building and a substantial Odd Fellows Hall, now just finishing.

The Drug and Fancy store of Webb and Saufley, whose advertisements are to be found in our columns, is the best got up and most capacious establishment of the kind in the District and is an agreeable place for a stranger to frequent, the proprietors being accommodating gentlemen. The prices of articles sold at this establishment are moderate. The Red River citizens who may have occasion to call at the store, will find an old acquaintance in the facetious and always pleasant gentleman who does up the medical prescriptions.

In the mercantile line, Paris does a large business for an inland village, having several very respectable stores, one of which, that of Davis Bro. & Bayless, will be found in our column this week - others probably hereafter.

Paris has a substantial Brick Courthouse, the first of its kind built in Northern Texas. All in all, we know of no other village in North Texas which gives more evidence of continued improvement and had a better prospect for the future than Paris, Lamar County.

married

on the 13th day of May, by the Rev. Thomas F. Garrison, Mr. Charles Anderson of Kentucky to Miss Sarah A. Russell of Sherman, Grayson County.

at the residence of Thomas Willison of Hopkins County, on the second *ultimo,* by Josiah Smith, Esq., Mr. Hugh M. Stewart of Titus County to Mary Ann Willison.

died

In Grayson county on the 6th of May, Celestia Virginia Bone, daughter of John W. Bone and Elizabeth A. Bone, aged 4 years, ten months and four days.

damage reported on steamers

(From the *Washington Telegraph*)

The Steamer *Effort,* in coming down Red River, struck a log on the White Oak Shoals breaking about 40 feet of her timbers and injuring her machinery. The cotton was thrown off and some of it is still lying in the sandbar of the shoals. Her injuries were repaired and she was expected to start down on Sunday morning.

The *R. M. Jones* is still aground with no prospect of getting her off. Hands are engaged in wrecking the *Victoria* whose loss we noted in our last.

advice to men

If you doubt whether you should kiss a girl, give her the benefit of the doubt and pitch in.

*********** 1

From *The Standard*, June 14, 1856

tidbit of wisdom
When the heart is out of tune, the tongue seldom goes right.

we call attention
to the advertisement of Western Mares and Mules, just in from San Antonio and on sale by Daniel Martin and Geo. Johnson at Black Jack Grove, Hopkins County;

to the advertisement of examinations to be held in the Milam Masonic Institute at Boston, Bowie county;

to the advertisement of James H. Clark of land for sale in Clarksville;

to the advertisement of daguerreotypes by Mrs. Harriet E. Wheat;

to the change in the announcement of candidacy of E.G. Benners for District Attorney;

election speech
William H. Johnson, a candidate for District Judge, addressed our citizens on Tuesday night past, preparatory to the commencement of the regular appointments in DeKalb.

thanks
to James M. Allen of Bonham for the New Orleans papers who came up on *St. Charles* on her last trip and writes to us that the steamer, which draws five feet, had to run along slowly above

Grand Ecore.

****

From *The Standard*, June 21, 1856

we call attention

to the advertisement by the Jonadab Temple and its preparations to celebrate the Fourth of July; notice given by Wm. Crittenden;

to the card of Courtes B. Sutton withdrawing from the canvas for County Judge;

to the advertisement of Commissary Blair of the Army for pickled pork, bacon and flour. It opens an opportunity to our farmers to dispose of a surplus of these articles in 1857 and give them timely notice for preparation. It is commendable on the part of Captain Blair to afford our farmers such a chance to subsist the troops employed in the state and we believe that they will promptly avail themselves of it;

to the advertisement of a mare lost by W. Stephenson of Bonham under suspicious circumstances.

administration of estates

Notice to all persons who have claims against the estate of Charles W. Young deceased, late of Titus County, are requested to present them to David Bruton of Mt. Pleasant;

M. T. Barrier is appointed Administrator of the estate of C. N. Barrier, deceased, of Titus County;

William Bure is appointed Administrator of the estate of Romulus Ladd, deceased, of Titus County.

shingles and boards wanted

12,500 shingles and 2,500 two feet oak boards. Apply to the *Standard*.

****

From *The Standard*, June 28, 1856

we call attention

that a ball will he held at the Clarksville Hotel on the night of the Fourth at half past 7 o'clock . Tickets to be had at the house.

to the card of John C. Burks, Attorney at Law;

to the card of T. J. Brem, "house and ornamental painter and paper hanger. We can certify that Mr. Brem has done some good work upon our office and dwelling.

4^{Th} of July Ball

We call the attention of the votaries of Terpsichore to the announcement of a ball at Clarksville Hotel on the evening of the Glorious Fourth. Everybody and his wife is expected.

"Go it while you're young!

For when you're old, you can't."

candidacy of J. C. Hart for Treasurer

We refer our readers to the announcement and circular of J. C. Hart for candidate for County treasurer. The office is one of very little profit, scarcely any, but nevertheless requires business capacity, which Mr. Hart is well known to be possessed of.

notice

by Thos. McGill that his wife Sarah McGill has left his bed and board without cause and he will not be responsible for any contract she makes.

****

From *The Standard,* July 5, 1856

thanks

We are indebted to George H. Bagby for the late New Orleans, Memphis, Cairo, Louisville, St Louis and Chicago newspapers.

fireproof safes

We see that the Anderson County Court has two large iron safes for the protection of the valuable papers of the County. This is an example which should be followed by every other county in the State, not already protected by fire, of that concerns so many and which cannot possibly be replaced if destroyed.

public barbecue

There will be a public barbecue in Tarrant on the 16th inst and a Temperance procession, a reading of the Declaration of Independence and Public Address. A general invitation is extended to the public.

heavy court load

(from the *Austin Gazette*)

The District Court is now in session. It has 900 cases on its docket. This is a bad state of affairs.

stages

We are reliably informed that increased stage service will be allowed by the Post Office department between Clarksville and Jefferson via Mt. Pleasant and Daingerfield. Whether this is to be a hack or stage we do not know. Either way, it will be a convenience to this region of the country and, in connection with the route advertised in our columns between Jefferson and Shreveport, William Bradford Proprietor, affords convenient service to persons having business below. Increased service in the way of semi weekly horse mails is needed between this place and Tarrant.

Hunt County

Our friends in Hunt County write us and tell that the crops are somewhat spotted. Wheat fine, corn good in places. No rain needed.

Democracy is flourishing there and its banner is kept blowing in the breeze b A. T. Howell and John E Wilson, Esq. who are addressing the people on convenient occasions. The northern and southern portions of the County are almost unanimously Democratic. Hunt will be right side up at the next showing of hands.

report on Fourth of July celebration

The Glorious 4th passed off, hilariously, without any unpleasant event that we are aware of.

The Templars and citizens generally celebrated the day as advertised. An oration listened to with marked attention by numerous persons was delivered at the Presbyterian Church by the Rev. John Anderson.

At night a Ball, at the Clarksville Hotel numerously attended, held its votaries enchanted until the small hours of the morning and was productive of much enjoyment notwithstanding the intense heat. The day and night were the hottest of the season, the thermometer at 4 o'clock p.m. being 98 in the shade.

we call attention

to millenary and dress making by Mrs. S. Look.

thanksgiving

As a people, we have more of the essential elements of the prosperity. We are the recipients of a kind Providence and should not forget to raise our anthems of Thanksgiving, praise to the Supreme Architect of the Nature, to whom we are indebted for all these blessings.

land for sale

Notice by W. W. Giddens and John Terry, Executors of Joseph Reed, of land for sale in Fannin county under head right originally issued to A. Butler; also to be sold land in Hunt County purchased by Joseph Reed from the Rev. Sorrell.

runaway

from A. L. Arledge, living four miles south of Bonham on the Greenville road, a Negro, name Ananias; about medium height, very black; very Roman featured; about 27 or 28 years of age; quick spoken and generally of quick motion.

Hopkins county

We are gratified to observe the prospects of a bounteous harvest. The wheat, the harvesting of which has just been completed, was universally good and the amount cultivated is no doubt twice that of any previous year in the county. Corn, notwithstanding the continuing drought, is very promising, and, should the farming community be blessed with genial showers soon, will be cheaper next fall than has been since this country was organized. We have been informed by gentlemen, passing through this county, that the corn crops are better in this county than they are in any of the surrounding counties. Emigrants would do well to be informed of these points and then "govern themselves accordingly."

Fruit is abundant more so than we have seen for many years. The peach trees are literally breaking down with their burdens and not the least tempting are the fine wild grapes for which this county is so well celebrated and which are in great quantities all over the woods.

letters left at Clarksville Post Office

Abbot, M. P.
Burcher, Mrs. Mary F.
Batemen, M.
Ball, George B.
Bryan, Mary Ann
Bryan, Benajah
Bryan, Mrs. Sarah M.
Blooodworth, Jesse D.
Burke, E.
Bagby Edward
Calhoun, James
Cook, William A.
Clark, John T.
Carter Robert
Canaday, Mr.
Collier, Mrs. Isabella
Cleveland, Gen. Benjamin
Collin, James
Cruce, William
Chaffin, Green
Dudley, W. N.
Evans, Miss B.A.
Evans, Lucinda
Foreman, M.
Fleming, W.D.
Farley, Mr.
Floyd, James B.
Ford, M. F.
Gaines, Henry H.
Gibbons, John
Gill, W.A.
Hale, John W.
Hackett, A. A.
Holafield, C. R.
Jones, J. P.
Jamison, Davidson
Kelly, Harry
Lester, Mr.
Moore, H. T.
Moore, A.
Moore, Martin L.
Murphy, William
Millstead, John
Murray, Joanna
Naylor, W. L.
Nelson, John W.
Oliver, Edward
Oneal, D.
Pennington, Samuel
Phelps, Alpha
Price, D. O.

Roland, B.	Walker, James
Ratcliff, Benjamin	Walker, John
Roberts, L. M.	Whitaker, Robert F.
Smith, D. F.	Wright, M.
Smith, Col. Robert W.	Van Zandt, W.
Sharp, Abram	Wade, O. M.D.
Sharp, A.	Welles, B.S.
Stevens, F. M. & Co.	Wimberly, G. S.
Shaw, Susan	Warren, Jacob
Taylor, William	Wardlow, Mary
Turner, John	
Wofford, John	

James W. Thomas, Post Master.

****

From *The Standard*, July 12, 1856

we call attention
to the examinations at Clarksville Female Institute;

to the examinations of the popular McKenzie Institute. They will doubtless well attended as usual, including by many including visitors from other counties;

to the advertisement for sale of dry goods, groceries etc. by Wilson and Jackson who are just receiving fresh supplies;

to the dissolution of a partnership S. Boynton and Co. in Mt. Pleasant, Titus County;

to the dissolution of Berry Rodgers & Rust, J. D. Berry to continue.

thanks

to Berry & Wallis of Gaines Landing for the New Orleans *Picayune* by steamer *John Simonds.*

Cooke County

We learn from Gainesville in Cooke County that they have fine crops. Both the Town and the county are improving.

Dr. McLane's celebrated vermifuge and liver pills

Two of the best preparations of the ages. They are not recommended as universal cure all but simply as their name purports. The vermifuge for expelling worms from the human system has also been administered with satisfactory results to various animals subject to worms.

The liver pills for the cure of liver complaints, all bilious derangements and sick headaches; sold in Clarksville by Wooten and Lyons.

****

From *The Standard,* July 19, 1856

we call attention

to the examinations at Paris Female Seminary; notice by Trustees Isaiah W Welles, Geo. W. Wright, Jacob Long and William H. Milwee.

Kaufman County

from Rockwall, Kaufman County, we learn that health is good, that the wheat crop turned out first rate and that corn looks very fine.

thanks

to L. D. Evans for Washington papers.

crops

The crops of corn, which were suffering somewhat before the generous rains of last week, have taken strength and color since and now promise to yield fairly. Cotton has looked good all the time. Yesterday, we had a fair shower which again refreshed the vegetation on good time.

We think this will be a year of plenty and that it is well that it is so as there is promise of extensive immigration this fall.

choice apples

We are indebted to Mrs. John Kimbell of DeKalb for her present, by mail rider, of fine juicy apples.

judicious

Young Boy: "Stand on my head for a penny, mam?"

Old Lady: "No little boy. Here is a penny for keeping right and upwards."

railroad

Dear Major De Morse:

Everything on the 4th passed off quietly. A considerable railroad meeting, a speech by John T. Mills and several thousands of stock taken. The meeting adjourned to be resumed on the 18th, when there will be a barbecue here [Bonham] and we expect to have speeches from Mills, Wright and Morgan fully explaining all the difficulties to overcome as well as setting forth the general plan of operation to construct the great national railroad. There are but few citizens in this county who doubt for a moment the great practical advantages accruing from such an enterprise but there are many who doubt its entire practicability at the same time. I think we should first build one to Galveston and, after that is completed, we can build as many from time to time as the country should need to carry off its surplus commodities.

We have an abundant crop of wheat this year and if we had a way to bring it directly to New Orleans or Galveston, we could realize a handsome profit. A better quality of grain can be grown nowhere in the Union and, had we the manufacturing mills, we could successfully compete with the northern states in the production of an article of flour, second to none.

report on drought down south

On the evening of the 3rd instant, I reached this place called the Mountain City [in Hays county], but it should be called at this time as the "city of heat and dust". The thermometer at this point, 106 degrees. On my way to this place, the crops looked fine, until the Trinity was crossed and, from there to here, and all the way to the Gulf, a dreadful drought prevails. The grasshoppers have wholly destroyed the vegetable gardens and, it seems to me, that the people must suffer.

Douglassville

On the direct road from Boston to Linden and five miles from Sulphur, on a somewhat elevated ridge, is located the embryonic town of Douglassville, environed by a dense forest, which, at this time of the year, presents all the beauty of rural nature. [At the Fourth of July Celebrations there], we had orations and a barbeque defined by some of our Lexicographers as "a feast in the open air", good feeling and friendly intercourse.

As yet few shops and mercantile establishments enliven the busy scenes of Douglassville. However, the carpenter's hammer is heard and the industrious population are variously engaged in preparing the foundation of the future town of Douglasville.

A mercantile establishment, known as the firm of Cole and Williams (the latter late of Bowie County) will no doubt give animation to the trading business of the place, one of the firm having already left for Philadelphia and New York, will import such articles as the county may demand.

Secluded and apparently as shut out as Douglassville is, it is surrounded by an industrious, enterprising and highly moral community. Education and Christianity claim much of their time and attention. A Baptist Minister of talents and learning, he conducts a school for boys and girls and occasionally may be heard the vibrating keys of the piano. Beautiful fancy work, such as painting, drawing and embroidery (now considered an indispensable part of a young lady's education) is taught by an accomplished teacher from the North.

****

From *The Standard,* July 26, 1856

Harris county

On Monday the criminal docket was taken up. Austin Burnett was indicted for cattle stealing. The jury found him guilty of petit larceny, the penalty of which is confinement in the state penitentiary for a period of one year. John K. Hyde, the murderer of Charles Butler, received the sentence of death yesterday. When the sentence was pronounced on him, the Judge, together with nearly the whole assembly, were deeply affected - some to tears -- but the prisoner evinced little emotion. He has a haggard and emaciated condition and is very weak from sickness and long confinement. On Friday the 11th of July, he will suffer his penalty under the gallows.

thanks

to Mr S. Helman, of McKinney, now abroad, for a copy of the *LaSalle County (Illinois) Sentinel.*

stage line

Advertisement for a new mail stage line from Washington Ark to Gaines Landing on the Mississippi through in 54 hours; the fare is $18 and the Proprietor is Beman & Co.

religious gathering

The third quarterly meeting for Clarksville Circuit will begin next Friday through Sunday. Preacher and people are respectfully invited to attend; notice by J. R. Bellamy and J. A Scruggs.

Donoho Hotel, Clarksville

This well known hotel, which has been kept by the same proprietress for 17 years, has been lately rebuilt and enlarged, until it is now one of the largest and most commodious in the state, affording a large number of single rooms. It is pleasantly situated on the public square and and is a very comfortable house.

A large and well filled stable, a horse lot and carriage house adjoin the hotel and the horses of travelers will be well fed and attended to.

Mary W. Donoho

crops and politics

Bonham

Dear Major:

As I am somewhat at leisure, I will give you an idea of the current affairs in Fannin and counties west.

I have recently returned from Collin and Dallas, by way of Grayson, and have taken some pains to post myself upon the agricultural and political conditions of those counties.

The recent rains have fallen in a few localities to the great enjoyment of the famished farmers. I believe I have been over pretty much all of Fannin and can say there will not be more than half a crop of corn raised. Corn will be worth 50 cents a bushel in this county. Wheat is selling at 60 cents to 75 cents a bushel.

The election gathering the most interest in this county is for County Clerk. Fannin is decidedly Democratic in its views and we therefore have no apprehension of our successes there.

In Grayson, politics are creating little interest among the citizens.

In Collin. the Democrats will have an easy go at it. For county office, the candidates are all incumbents without opposition – all Democratic. There is nothing said of politics in Dallas. No local news of importance.

celebration in Cooke County

Gainesville, Cooke County

Dear Major De Morse

We have just closed our festivities for the celebration of the Fourth. I sit down to give you an inkling of our proceedings. The day was one of the warmest we had this summer yet our village was filled with throngs of men women and children by far the largest concourse of people ever assembled in the County of Cooke. At half past ten in the morning they assembled at the large and commodious building lately erected by Aaron Hill for the Church and Masonic Hall, where the exercise was opened by an appropriate and eloquent prayer of the day from the Rev. William Bates, our chaplain, the preacher in charge of this circuit. The Marshall of the day, K. M. Wadsworth then introduced to the audience R. W. B. Oliver who preceded to read in an impressive manner the Declaration of Independence, Mr. William Howeth, to whom such task had been assigned unavoidably absent. Afterwards, Mr. Oliver gave an oration enchanting the attention of the audience for more than an hour. After a brief dispersion of the audience in the village, a procession was formed at the Cottage Inn by W. L. Fletcher with ladies in double file in front, gentlemen bringing up the rear to the patriotic air of *Hail Columbia* and then marched to the grove in the vicinity of the town where a profuse and excellent dinner had been prepared by our townsmen, Messrs. Fletcher and James, not forgetting their good ladies who shared largely in the preparation.

During dinner, we were all entertained by two amateur gentlemen on the violins. They were followed by Mr. H. and sister J. who performed on two violins and sang.

There were two large dancing parties in town and, when the rosy dawn was blushing in the eastern sky, the flying of many twinkling feet had just ended. The revels of the dance were only suspended for breakfast when it was resumed and kept up to dinner today, the 5th.

May you live to enjoy many such days as our Fourth and may your shadow never grow shorter.

adios senor

P. S. Crops good, heath good and doctors starving.

died

at Paris on the morning of the 28th of July, James S. , infant son of Lewis S. and Annie V. Wells, aged 8 months and nine days.

house for sale in Clarksville

James H. Clark of Sherman, Grayson County, has for sale in Clarksville a residence on one of the main streets leading into Town, 200 yards from the public square; four comfortable rooms, fireplaces in each, kitchen, smoke house and garden.

administration of estates

Notice that Geo. H Bagby, Executor of the estate of Isabella Talbot, will be filing an accounting;

Thomas J Mayo appointed Administrator of the estate of Eliza House of Hunt County.

****

From *The Standard.*, August 2, 1856

we call attention

to the advertisement of choice Yorkshire and Southdown breeds of sheep for sale by Captain Lewis Shirley, seven miles north of McKinney in Collin county. A good investment for the farmer and stock rancher;

to the advertisement of Messrs. Alexander and Jackson, long known as merchants in Grayson county, of their new and well filled store in Sherman;

to the advertisement of the firm of Darnall and Dickson, a popular house some years ago and desirous of testing its business capacities again under a new auspices. We have purchased some goods there and know the stock is large and well selected.. Mr. Darnall is one of the most tasteful purchasers who has ever bought goods for this market

thanks

We acknowledge receipt of a bountiful and varied supply of choice cakes from the hostess of the Donoho House.

to Gen. T. L. Green for late documents from the Legislature.

the election

"We have met the enemy and they are ours." [16]

Never has there been a more complete overthrow than the late elections has accomplished in this Judicial District of the combined forces of ignorance, intolerance and proscription and the entire defeat of the band of bigots, who appropriated to themselves the name Americans *par excellence* and denounced their enemies as anti Americans. When names correctly designate the objects represented, they have power but to call a thistle a rose, we opine, would scarcely elevate it in the botanical kingdom. From every county in the District, except Cass, we have heard enough to know that the Know Nothing representatives have been turned out of positions of trust which they occupied and that their places are supplied by the representatives of Democracy.

the canvas

Today, Judge Todd speaks here, also, we presume Mr. Mills and

Mr. Benners. Our information on the progress of the canvas everywhere in the district is most flattering to the hopes of the Democracy.

Bonham Female Institute

We insert in this number the advertisement of this excellent and well provided institution. Its promises will be performed and what it proposes to do is well worth the serious consideration of all parent who have daughters to educate and a re convenient to Bonham

The weather –the storm

We have had some showers lately and crops will be fine.

On Thursday evening at about ten o'clock, came on a rain, which had been for some days portending. And a rain it was - or almost a deluge - for two or three hours accompanied by startling peals of thunder and brilliant flashes of lightning. An immense quantity of water fell.

Some damage, we are sorry to say, was done by the storm. The barn of Mr. James Ritchey, near town, was struck by the electric fluid and fired. It burned down, destroying his crop of oats, wheat, four horses and his farm wagon, ploughs etc. This was a serious loss and should be made up to him by the voluntary contributions of our citizens. The community should act as underwriter to all such calamities, which bear heavily upon the individual sufferer but which would tax lightly each household in the vicinity to repair the loss.

Mr. Isaac Fishback, as we learn, had his stable unrooofed by the wind and a valuable mare killed.

Cisterns, we imagine, judging by our own, were filled with a rush, where there was any conduit for the water.

examination week

The annual exercises of the schools have drawn into our town, during the week now closing, many strangers. Everything has gone off well as we learn.

The examination of the Clarksville Female institute, having been adjourned after the first day to the new church opposite our office, we saw something of it, and must bear testimony to the general excellence of the pupils in the exhibition of their scholastic accomplishments. The activities were diversified at intervals, with performance upon the piano forte, by the Young Ladies and the Intermediate with a concert by the whole musical strength of the Institute. On Tuesday night, the large building was crowed to overflowing by a gratified auditory and the performances continued to nearly midnight. On Thursday, after th examination of the classes in Geometry, French, Latin and Chemistry, the Young Ladies read their compositions. These generally were so good that it would seem invidious to make special mention of any but there was such unusual excellence, strength and evident originality in the effort of Miss Martha Bagby, the daughter of the late Capt. John A. Bagby, of our town as to command notice. The composition of Miss Sarah Epperson was also superior, poetical in composition and finely expressed.

We must not omit to mention the very excellent supper set by the hostess of the Donoho House, who evidently made an effort for this occasion.

The examination of the McKensize Institute, which also commenced Monday morning, continued until Thursday evening, closing with addresses by several of the young gentlemen.

died

Dr Lemuel Peter at his residence in Boston in Bowie County at the age of 37.

administration of estates

R. H. Graham appointed the Administrator of the estate of Willis Dean, deceased, of Red RiverCounty;

notice by George H. Bagby, Clerk, that Joseph Wagley is the Administrator of the estate of William Lawrence, deceased, of Red River County;

Milton A Young is named the Executor of the estate of Harriet M. Young of Bowie County.

****

From *The Standard,* August 9, 1856

thanks

We are indebted to the Hon. L. D. Evans for copy of the *Daily Union*.

we call attention

to the advertisement of that excellent institution, the Milam Masonic Institute at Boston Bowie County;

to the advertisement of that long established school, Clarksville Female Academy.

taken up

by Geo. W. McCarley and posted before John P. Dale, a Justice of the Peace and appraised by John Ware and Chas. Durfee; notice by Geo. H. Bagby by his Deputy J. M. Bivins.

taken up by Mrs. Jane Bagby by Geo. W. McCarley and posted before John P. Dale, a Justice of the Peace and appraised by H. Stevens and T. H. Dale; notice by Geo. H. Bagby by his Deputy J. M. Bivins.

****

From *The Standard,* August 16, 1856

we call attention

to the advertisement of the McKensie Institute the next session commences the first Monday in October;

to the advertisement of Lewis Wells & Bros., Merchants at Paris, Lamar County. Our numerous readers in that county are doubtless well acquainted with the establishment of the Messrs. Wells but may not be with their late supply of goods. Their stock always embraces a great variety of articles, purchased with taste and purchasers will hardly find a more agreeable place at which to make their selections. The house has been long established in Northern Texas and may be considered a permanent fixture. Withal we have found them liberal and liberal people are the sort we always prefer to deal with, both as a matter of satisfaction and of profit. Their motto is "Quick sales and small profits";

to the advertisement of Barry & Moore;

to the advertisement of Webb and Saufley of Paris, dealers in wholesale and retail drugs;

to the notice to the stockholders of Memphis, El Paso and Pacific Rail Road Company.

Come to Texas[17]

In Northern Texas, as far as we have heard from it, the crop of corn is likely to be reasonably good and the supply of wheats and oats a re super abundant. This being the case, our section of the country invites immigration of those who have determined to move. They cannot in the entire southwest find another such grain groing region as North Texas and nothing superior for cotton. country. Our Red River and Sulphur bottoms are rich black and chocolate colored prairies, our choice sandy timbered lands, all invited the different classes of cultivators and promise rich returns for labor.

Come on then all of you, who are tired of worn out lands and can sell at high prices, which quadruples the number of your acres in the unbroken richness of the virgin soil, rank with fecundity.

We have lands in North Texas and plenty of them, vast wastes which, when properly cultivated, - that is to say, well cultivated by deep ploughing - never fail in drought or in excessive wetness. These lands are yet cheap, although yearly rising. Rich unimproved lands may yet be bought for a dollar or two an acre, convenient to prosperous towns, affording a market for supplies and selling of products and affording for the education of the children of the settler, schools which he could not find surpassed in any part of the United States. A man need not bury himself in the woods for a term of years to get the advantages of a new country. Right here in Clarksville, and in the adjacent counties of Bowie, Titus, Lamar, Fannin, Grayson, Collin, and Dallas, he can find all he wants in rich land at low prices, and, yet, be immediately adjacent to thriving towns, with their social and educational advantages. Or, if he would push out a little further for grazing facilities in Hunt, Cooke, Denton, Wise, Tarrant and Parker, he might find the verge of the grand prairies of the almost illimitable west, and yet be near enough to schools of very high character to send children, where they will be well instructed, educationally, morally, socially and yet near enough to communicate with or see in the three or four days of travel.

We want but one convenience to give us a position almost unequaled and that is a railroad.[18] That we are sure to have in four years and to have near us in less time.

river

We call attention for meeting at the Court House on Monday next, to take measures to clean out the Sulphur, a most important object. Attend everyone!

thanks

We a re indebted Hon. E. Clark and Gen. T. L. Green for late papers from Austin.

Dalby Springs

Our readers will see a notice of this place for resort among our communications.[19] At present the spring is the retreat of a gay company of Ladies and Gents from our Town and from sundry other localities not far distant. We had hoped to be with them at one time, but whoever knew an editor to have any spare time for recreation. The best part of us, our heart, is down there now. Perhaps, we do just as well, for there are few joys in life the reality of which is equal to the anticipation. Nevertheless, those who have time and, with it, retain the capacity for pure heartfelt enjoyments, might do worse than to while a few days away at Dalby's.

married

in New Orleans on the 17th day of July by the Rev. Dr. Harmon, Miss Mary T. Case to Capt. George H. Disley.

list of letters left at Clarksville Pot office

Armstead, B. H.	Knox, F.
Blair, John	Franklin, John, M.D.
Crabtree, William	Gambell, Joseph
Chapman, Edward	Griggs, D.C.
Calvin, W.	Gregg, Mrs. Virgina A.
Cornell, Watson	Gould, Miss Virginia
Crutcher, William	Henry, William F.
Carter, D.	Head, John
Davis, Miss Narcissa	Herdnon, Jacob W.
Evans, Jesse	Hennings, F.

Hargrave, Glen
Hardin, Mrs. Sarah M.
Johnson, H. D.
Jones, H.
Jones, William
Inman & Bros. Messrs.
King, James
Langford, Maj. A. R.
Long, Thomas
Ledbelly, J. W.
Norton, George B.
Park, William
Portey, Matthew
Reynolds, Mrs. Sarah
Skelton, D. K.
Scallon, John
Shumaker, J.
Steele, Miss Ellen

Thomas, W.
Titus, R. B.
Thebo, C. H.
Vance, Miss Mary
VanZadt, William
Whitacker, Mrs. Nancy
Wynn, John C.
Wyse, John B.
Wheeler, Ambrose
Wordlow, Miss M.
Winn, John
Wiggins, Dr.
Walker, William G.
Wilson, John J.
Young, James
Young, H. F.
Young, W. T.

James W. Thomas, Post Master

lawsuits filed

Notice of order by Malcolm Bolin, Justice of Peace, given by Constable Isham Russel of Titus County to William Hensley that he has been sued by Archibald V. Darby on a promissory note for $ 16.50 and interest at 10%; by Andrew J. Duke and August J. Turner for the sum of $69.04; and by Silas Huskey for $72.91.

****

From *The Standard,* August 23, 1856

rain

We were favored with a refreshing shower of rain on Thursday afternoon. It will benefit the cotton by slowing the dropping of its squares.

turnips

Those of our readers, who have not sown turnips, should do so at once. There is no crop which our farmers grow that yields a better return

we call attention

of the parents, guardians and others to the advertisement of Transylvania Female Academy in Mt. Pleasant. Miss C. A. Allen and Miss E. Cody, Principals.

Buchanan nominated for President

"What cannon is that?" asked a person hearing the 100 guns at one place because of the nomination salute

"Bu Cannon" of course was the response.

"Well, it has the right ring to it."

married

By Chief Justice Harman of Hopkins County at the residence of William Strother, Mr. John M. Ewing, to Miss Sarah E. Strother, all of that county.

hot weather

The weather has been on a bust for ten days and the thermometer too high to be spoken of publically. We may refer to its conduct during some northern next winter. But now conversation on this point is not endurable. Men "as thin as two of Cassidy lard the lean earth as they walk along."

crops in Upshur and Cass Counties

We learn from the *Herald* that corn and cotton crops in Upshur and Cass Counties are very fair and that corn will be abundant and that there will be a large increase in the cotton crop.

Dalby's Springs

We learn that there is quite a crowd of visitors at this summer resort. Several of our townspeople have taken themselves thither within the past few months, among them the Editor of this Paper who left for the locality on the outside of a sorrel horse, on Sunday night last.

bet on upcoming presidential election

We are authorized by a gentleman of Greenville, Hunt County to say that the following bet is offered to anyone disposed to take it up – to wit, that Buchanan will get a majority of either the popular or the electoral vote over Fillmore in the coming presidential election and that any person desiring to make such a bet can call at the office of J. E. Wilson, Esq. of Greenville, who can inform him where he can be accommodated.

Judge Todd injured

Judge Todd, who was seriously hurt by being thrown from a mule on Saturday last, has so far recovered as to be able to sit in a chair and to walk about the house without a stick. He still suffers severely with a pain in the spine and back of the head but he hoepes to be able to hold court which commences Monday next.

we call attention

to the advertisement of the new Steam Saw Mill by Snell and

Milwee. These gentlemen have a large tract of pine, fresh, from which they should be able to get good materials and, having a new saw mill and several competitors to contend with them for the trade, we have no doubt that they will do their best for those who may purchase of them.

Dalby Springs

We passed some three days and nights most delightfully at Dalby's, in drinking the amber water, dancing, promenades to the Spring with music and sunning ourselves generally. We found there pleasant spirits that had thrown off for a little time the cares of life. Some were angelic and *spirituelle* and scarcely touched the earth with their dainty feet; others were not so much so, but they looked of the earth, and had a solid substantiality which made a sensible impression upon the sand as they pressed upon it, yet they were light hearted and most entertaining. As to the male bipeds, there were some of them there too, agreeable gentlemen but we can not waste ink and space upon them. Quite a number of ladies and gentlemen came in from about Boston, while we were there and more were expected.

We found the atmosphere surprisingly cool and the accommodations, though plain, quite comfortable. Various amusements varied by the occasional walk to the Springs, varied the occupation of the day and at night the dance was unfailing and ever fresh. Charlie Leigh's violin was worth its weight in gold.

The amber colored water of the springs is the richest looking fluid we ever saw and has a vivacity of appearance that approaches sparkling. It has a healthful, though not rapid, action upon the stomach and bowels.

There is a sour spring at this place which has gone dry during the drought or affords so little water as to be useless.

The locality is pleasant looking, somewhat broken, sandy and presents large rocks that have undergone volcanic action. If a little money was judiciously expended in improving and clearing up the place, with the advantages of its waters, and the fish and game adjacent, it may be made a regular and most pleasant summer resort.

****

From *The Standard,* August 30, 1856

expulsion

Tranquit Temple of Honor at Fannin County, at a regular meeting of this Temple, held on the 21st of July at the Temple Hall, Wesley C. Walker was expelled from the order for violating Article two of the Constitution. Notice given by Greenberry Davis.

we call attention

to the new advertisement of Clarksville Female Institute; also to the relatively old establishment of the Clarksville Male Academy, formerly carried on by John Anderson. The eminent qualifications of Mr. Anderson as a teacher and the prevailing need for a male academy in this town, render any commentary on out part entirely unnecessary.

District Court

Court commenced on Monday. Since then, business has progressed moderately, the attention of some of the lawyers and most of the public being given to the contested election case between the County Judge and Commissioners, the contest being one of the magistrates and the constable of this precinct.

From Mt Vernon, Titus county

We learn that it is distressingly dry there. Corn crops very good, but cotton will not make more than 300 to 500 pounds to an acre.

administration of estates

James Gilliam has been appointed Administrator of the estate of Edward Hughart of Red River County.

From *The Standard*, September 6, 1856

tidbit of wisdom

All that is good and beautiful in life, blooms around the altar of domestic love.

the weather, the river and the crops

Wednesday morning a light rain. On Thursday at about 1 o'clock, the clouds which had been lowering for some days and surcharged the atmosphere with dampness, began to deliver their contents after the manner of a regular Northern autumn rain. This lasted for no more than an hour and the clouds cleared up. On Friday morning, however, it again looked dark and at half past one in the afternoon, it again commenced raining and lasted an hour or so.

For several days prior to this, rain had fallen heavily on the north side of the Red River over a large extent of country. The consequence of this is that Old Red has risen 17 feet in two days and was booming. The river has dropped considerably since then, but we think from the present prospect that the Sulphur, before many days, will send down a tributary stream that will give body and current to Old Red.

On yesterday evening, all night and this morning, we have had a cloudy sky with a slight rain during the night. At 9 a.m., as we write, it has commenced raining sharply. We believe from the signs above us that navigation below Shreveport will be assisted materially which is the reason why we write so particularly about the weather.

We have inquired about the crops of our county. There is an abundance of corn. Cotton has suffered from drought, more on the river lands than the prairies. The river lands will yield about half average, the prairie lands two thirds.

From an examination of our exchanges, we are confident that the cotton crop across the United States is to be a short one and prices necessarily, as we conceive, must be enhanced.

Will our planters, now that the shortness of the crop allows them an excellent opportunity, give extra attention in handling and get a better price in consequence. When we first came to Red River fourteen years ago, the cotton raised here, from bad handling ranked barely "ordinary". It was charged to the black ground, but since then it has advanced to middling and we know one crop raised on the black prairie last year, which was sold as "fair": at 12 cents a pound. Now is the time to begin a better handling system and raise the credit of our product. We are in best cotton latitude – not too warm or too cold – with rich lands. We can raise "Fair cotton all the time." Will our planters see to it and profit themselves?

thanks

to David C. Russell for New Orleans papers.

District Court

The court has adjourned and formal adjournment only awaits the writing up of the minutes.

On Monday, the Court will begin In Bowie.

It has been a term of some interest and there were some cases of which brief note may be made with gratification to our readers, but, as the decision of a jury in a late case makes it difficult for the press in this region to report anything of the sort, without giving all the evidence and argument at length. We omit any statement of the case our paper, being a new paper and not a law reporter. People wishing to learn anything of our cases can inform themselves in the primitive manner it was done before the Flood - that is to say, they can stand by and hear for themselves.

died

on Friday morning of sporadic dysentery, Miss Margaret A. Doak, aged 18, daughter of Nelson Doak, Esq.

runaway

Notice by Col. S. T. Hanson, living six miles above Pittsburg, Upshur County, of a runaway Negro boy named Henry; 20 years old; six feet high; dark color, spare made, weighs about 150 pounds.

administration of estates

Notice by P. M. Duke, Clerk of Bowie county, that J. P. Alford, Executor of the estate of Presley Maudling has file his petition for fees at the courthouse in Boston.

****

From *The Standard,* September 13, 1856

thanks

We are indebted to Mr. G. W. Johnson of DeKalb for St. Louis newspapers.

we call attention

to the advertisement regarding a runaway Negro by L. C. Elliot of Bowie; also to the runaway from of Col. H. C. Hanson from Upshur County;

to the advertisement of a strayed horse by David Bruton.

river

After an unprecedented continuance of low water, Old Red is back to itself.

lost land certificate

Notice by Kezziah Thompson, Executor of the estate of Josiah Thompson of Hopkins county, that he has lost or misplaced a certificate issued to him for land in Henderson County.

no mail from the East

The river being out of its banks at Mill Creek so that the stage cannot cross, we are without late items from the East.

****

From *The Standard,* September 20, 1856

we call attention to

Notice by Carrol Grant of Fannin County regarding a strayed or stolen horse.

thanks

to L. D. Evans for copy *Campaign Democrat* from New York;

to Henry Nathan for a copy of the *Delta* from New Orleans.

no eastern mail last night

The ferry at the mouth of Mill Creek has been carried away and, as a result, the stage did not leave on Thursday night as usual and consequently we were without the usual return on Friday.

Red River

We hear from Col. Cooper, Choctaw agent, that the Red River was low at the mouth of Kiamitia yesterday, although it was still 15 or 20 feet more than the low river mark at Roland. The sky looks dark and sullen, as though the elements were preparing for a settled rain. If so, it might raise again. If not, we think that there will be three or four more weeks of good navigation for second class boats to Shreveport. One of our mercantile houses ,which had expected to haul from Gaines Landing, has ordered its goods by way of Shreveport and is starting wagons to receive them.

The four flat boats belong to Rhine & Bros left our landing day before yesterday, freighted with cotton.

examinations at the Bonham Masonic Female Institute

Dear Major De Morse:

On Friday night the 5th instant our town [Bonham] was enlivened by a large crowd assembled to attend the first examinations at the Bonham Masonic Female Institute. The citizens of the town and county are taking great interest in the cause of education and the examination did much to excite their interest in that case. On seeing what can be done in five months, they are buoyant with hope of the future. The principal and the teachers have much to take credit for and the students from their various curriculums from the ABCs to Latin and French showed that they had been guided by skillful hands. The music and singing were such as to satisfy th most fastidious taste. You may well feel that our country is fast emerging from its frontier condition when we see such school in operation as we also find in Clarksville and Paris. Onward and upward shall be the motto of our northern counties and schools.

taken up

Three Negro men were taken up at Fort Towson about 10 days since – Emanuel, Edward and Tom - one of which has the forefinger of his right hand taken off. All three of them are black, medium size and represented as belonging to Hanson Paxton living in Arkansas, on Red River opposite Spanish Bluffs.

cash store revived

A. M. Alexander would respectfully announce to the citizens of Grayson that he is again opening at the Red Store in Sherman, a large and elegant assortment of new goods.

court in Bowie County

The editor of this paper was in Bowie county most of last week. Court opened on Monday but did not accomplish much until Wednesday, the lawyers being involved in the principal suits not being there until then and the court being without any business on which it could act. On Wednesday, the trial of John A. Summers and James Clark on a charge of assault with intent to kill came on and, after hearing witnesses, the court adjourned until next morning. Arguments of District Attorney S. R. G. Mills and defense attorneys John Mills and S. H. Pirkey were then heard, the case going to the jury, which after a short withdrawal returned with a verdict of "not guilty". The prosecution by the District Attorney were vigorous and well considered but his witnesses did not make out much of a case. The defense of Mills and Pirkey were ingenious and forceful.

On the other indictments which were tried before we left, the District Attorney proved himself an efficient prosecutor and obtained verdicts for the State in nearly every case.

The case of *Waddill vs. Waddill* was decided in favor of defendant C. K. Waddell.

The attendance of people at court was not general. Indeed, it was the dullest court week we have ever seen in Bowie.

report from Bowie County

A very excellent movement in Bowie against the Overseer of the Roads and a judgment obtained against one infinitely less culpable will do good. Cannot the strong arm of the law be brought to bear upon some of our overseers who habitually neglect their duty?

The hill crops of Bowie are short. Some of the river crops are not good but some of them are better than common. Three or four gentlemen told us the cotton crop was the best in five years. The general crop of the county, however must be considered short. The same may be said of the Arkansas border, although some of the crops on that side are excellent. We are told that Col. Hatmaker on the old Hawkins place will make 800 bales on 960 acres, 500 of it bringing a bale to the acre. Crops of R. M. Jones and Henry Hawkins are also said to be fine.

Boston has improved some and the steam mill near DeKalb is making a showing upon that place. Some good houses have been erected and more are contemplated. De Kalb is looking up. A good friend of ours is bringing from the North a large and choice stock of goods.

One of the new buildings is con joint structure, of which the upper part is a handsome Masonic Hall

The excellent school of Mr. Featherston, opened on the first of the month with flattering prospects. It had, when we left, 92 scholars with prospects of increasing to 125. The institution may now be considered permanently established. The Principal has attained an enviable record as a teacher and, although strict in his disciplines, acquires the confidence and affection of his pupils.

Bowie is determined in conjunction with Cass and Titus to clear out the Sulphur to its upper lines. Will Red River and Titus continue the work to Hart's Bluff or to the bridge on the Turnpike road?

lost

by J. N. Ledbetter of lost note for $300 somewhere between Jefferson and DeKalb.

married

by Chief Judge Harman of Hopkins County at the residence of Wm. Strother, Mr. John M. Ewing and Miss Sarah E. Strother, all of that county.

****

From *The Standard,* September 27, 1856

thanks

to G. W. Johnson of DeKalb for St Louis papers

river

The *Washington Telegraph* reports a boat passing at Fulton and another expected. We have made inquiry and learn that at Rowland, it had got too low to let a boat up, but on Friday night it rose 8 feet and continued rising.

We learn from the mouth of the Kiamitia that on Thursday and Friday the river rose 15 feet and today is on a stand.

monuments to the dead

We call attention to advertisement of T. M. Coulter, stone cutter at Honey Grove in Fannin County, much of whose work we have seen and do not hesitate to declare it superior than any other we have seen in Northern Texas. Mr. Coulter executes lettering and ornamental work upon tomb stones in a very good manner. Some of our citizens have already received work from his yard and others have placed orders. Our grave yard may be very much improved in appearance and a fitting testimonial given of our appreciation of the departed by the expenditure of a little money this way. It is full time that something be done to relieve the uninviting despoliation of our place of burial. Uncovered hillocks of ground of the occupier have long since discredited our sense of the Christian virtue of remembrance for objects of affection taken from us. Necessity has been somewhat an excuse for this, but it does not remain now. We can enclose our burial grounds and we can put up some neat monuments or simple head stones, commemorative of an existence once prized by us.

Insurrection of slaves in Colorado county

(from the *Houston Telegraph*)

We learn of Mr. Howes of this city (Houston) who returned from Columbus on Wednesday evening that a plot was discovered to be afoot in that place amongst some 400 Negroes, to rise against the white population, to murder and to rob them. The Negroes intended to commence their operations tomorrow and probably would have completed their designs, had not a Negro belonging to Mr. Toake informed his master of the fact. When Mr. Howes left, a number of the Negroes were in custody and some two or three were to be hung today. One was whipped so severely that afterwards he died. Two or three Mexicans were arrested who were supposed to be the instigators of the insurrection. The Negroes had a large quantity of arms and ammunition and everything necessary to render themselves formidable.

Ladies Fair and Concert at Paris

We have received a neat little missive inviting us to be present at the Ladies fair and concert at Paris, Lamar County during the first week of November. The object of the fair is to procure funds for buying a bell for the Methodist church. So many famous *Belles* who have signed this invitation, will doubtless effect that object, with scarce an effort. We fear that our engagements will not permit us to be present; yet we may wish the goodly enterprise much success.

pay up

Notice by J. C. Hart, the third and last call. "I positively will not wait longer than October 1 to close up the business of the late firm of Darnall & Hart. Please take advantage of this time to settle. If not, I shall put the claim in the hands of an Officer.

died

Michel B Menard, one of the oldest settlers in Texas and founder of the city of Galveston died at this place on the 2d instant. The deceased was born near Montreal and settled in Texas in 1826 establishing a trading post among the Shawnees.

of gastritis at the family residence (Dr. Geo. Gordon's) adjoining Town on the night of the 20th, Frank H. Clark, aged 26 years old.[20]

The deceased was formerly the editor of the *Jefferson Herald* and, in his editorial position, known to many in the state. He was born near the mouth of Mills Creek (now Bowie County) in this state in April 1830 when this was an Indian border undergoing all the dangers and inconveniences of the frontier. His father, James Clark, the founder of this Town, was a man of active energy and influence and had been a member of the Arkansas Legislature for several sessions. Frank Clark was liberally educated, had fine intellectual capacity and had given promise of prominence, but disease held its heavy hand upon him for some years and he has at last, with unexpected suddenness, fallen a victim in early manhood.. As a slender boy of 15, he enrolled himself in the service of his country in the Mexican War and was elected corporal by the Company raised in this Town. Subsequent to this, he spent two years (graduating) at Transylvania Law School. He commenced the practice of law in this Town but the fondness for the editor's life, contracted in years of intimacy with the writer of this, induced him to associate himself with the *Jefferson Herald*.

C. De Morse

****

From *The Standard*, October 4, 1856

tin shop

We call attention to the Tin Shop, operated by Schackleford and Johnson, which fills an inconvenient vacancy. Messrs S. and J., we understand, are good workman.

administration of estates

Notice by J. M. Bivins, Clerk of Red River County Court, that Robert S. Hamilton, Administrator of the estate of James M. Hamilton, deceased, has filed a final settlement of the estate.

taken up

notice by J. M. Bivins, Clerk of Red River County Court, that a stray taken up by Isaac Luallen and posted before Courtes Sutton, Justice of the Peace, has been appraised by Henry D. Glass and Elias H. Darien.

concert and tableaux for the benefit of the Methodist Church

Some of the Ladies of our Town have organized an association for the finishing up of the Methodist Church, which lacks all the inner appurtances of a House of Worship. In pursual of their object, they propose to give on Wednesday next, a Supper and a series of *Tableaux vivants*[21], to which the admission fee is fifty cents - too little. Of course, we presume that all the beauty of the vicinity will be present and that not a small portion of it will be presented in the shape of scenic pictures, at which the Spectator will have the privilege of staring at intensely without being subject to the charge of rudeness. The object to be carried out is entitled by right to everybody's fifty cents - the supper will be worth fifty cents, the concert a dollar and the tableaux - the value of these is illumitable to each admirer of any one of the beauties who will be placed in view on that occasion. So that any Speculator in rarities can easily see that he will save somewhere from a dollar up to a nameless amount, by paying out a paltry half dollar. It is certainly a great chance to save money by paying out a little. And Franklin has told us that a penny saved is two pennies earned.[22] Consider it in any light you chose. It is a great opportunity. An invitation to attend was left at our offices, during our temporary absence, by some of the Fraternity. We shall cheerfully do so but shall claim the privilege of paying for it, as others do.

****

From *The Standard,* October 11, 1856

tidbit of wisdom

It is impossible to love one in whose truthfulness, we cannot confide.

humor

An old lady of Pennsylvania had an unaccountable aversion to rye and never ate it in any form.

"Till of late" she said "they had got to making it into whiskey and I find that I can now and then worry down a little."

Cooke County

                Gainesville, Cooke County

Major De Morse

We have a fine country [Cooke], not excelled for stock raising in Northern Texas and, when seasonable a generous soil that pays the farmer well for his labor. The grass on our prairies is now knee high and growing rapidly. Horses, cows and hogs are as fat as they can be. We will kill tens of thousands of pounds of pork, as good any in Texas which has fattened the range. We count cattle by the thousand, more often than by the hundred. Of horses, we have the Mustang, the Indian pony, the Thoroughbred American. This year an abundance of corn.

Times are looking up a little, in this part of the "Moral Vineyard", good crops of corn with late rains securing a fine winter range with an almost entire exemption from sickness has given somewhat an impetus to business. There is only one thing needed to make this the most desirable portion of Texas –navigation. Oh, for a rail road.. Well, we will have it someday, just as certain as we possess a salubrious climate, a luxuriant soil, pure water and the native material for a Paradise of a Country. We will have a railroad and that too in the not so far distant future.

I must add we are all, with the exception of about six, for "Buck and Breck".[23] Hurrah for the 4th of November and the Gallant Buchanan!

the concert –tableaux etc.

The promised entertainment was given on Wednesday evening at the Methodist Church. The attendance was good, but not so crowded as we had hoped. We are told a handsome sum was raised for the internal improvement of the building.

newspaper news

The regular editor of this paper will be absent from home for some weeks during which times the columns will be under the direction of a competent writer and supervisor.

Slave troubles of Colorado County

(From the *Galveston Civilian*)

On returning from Austin, our junior spent a day or two in Columbus and sought the most reliable information relative to the recent trouble with the Negroes in Colorado county. The facts necessary to a proper understanding of the whole matter are substantially as follows.

In Colorado county, as in many other sections of the state, slave owners have yielded, for two or three years, that strict oversight upon the conduct of Negroes, which all experience proves necessary to their good government and happiness. Favorite servants had been allowed enlarged privileges and large crowds of Negroes congregate with impunity at nights and on Sundays, resorting to various sports and vices. The legitimate and unfailing result followed, in the conception of crimes endangering the property and lives of the whites.

One of the plotters, whose conscience became sore under his treason, revealed the whole conspiracy to his master. This lead at once to a prudent, but thorough, investigation and this investigation revealed facts that startled the whole community. By the confessions of over perhaps a hundred Negro men, it was fully established that most of their number in the county, extending up and down the river for some 33 miles, had held regular nightly meetings in the Colorado bottom for some time; that they had resolved that, on a given night, after having stolen all the arms and ammunition possible, to meet in a body and attempt to reach Mexico. Two military captains were chosen, one on each side of the river, Alic and Mose and a shrewd old villain, Jim, were selected as political chiefs. Passwords and signs were adopted. As the time approached, the field of operations, under the advice probably of a white man named Durden, was extended. It was determined to kill the owners, rob the houses of money and valuables and, as many of the scoundrels confessed, to carrying off a portion of the young ladies. This man Durden, by the word of the Negroes and by some strong corroborating circumstances, was fully committed to the scheme. He was to receive the money, make his escape and meet them in Mexico. He fled on these revelations and has not been taken, an event that would be followed by his immediate execution. With these facts before the people, it is indeed remarkable that counsels so moderate were adopted. Those who owned no slaves insisted that slave owners be placed on all committees, as the most conservative mode of action and the suggestion was substantially adopted. The authorities thus appointed by the people took the whole matter under advisement. The final decision was to hang Jim, Mose and Alic and to punish the others, according to the measure of their connection to the plot. These three were hung from the same gallows in Columbus, after a final and unanimous vote of an immense crowd, each one on the gallows unreservedly confessing all and professing regret at the enormity of their crimes. Jim belonged to a widow lady who was paid eleven hundred dollars, raised by subscription. The other conspirators were whipped, some severely, but generally not as to break the skin. One only of the number proved so refractory that he caused his own death. The object plainly was to sting but not to injure their bodies and, for this purpose, broad leather straps were used instead of whips.

Another white man, named Mehrmann, or Merriman, though not implicated in this general conspiracy, was subsequently accused in tampering in some manner with a couple of the guilty Negroes and he was ordered at once to leave the county and the state, on pain of punishment. This man appeared ignorant and trifling.

It is believed by discreet men in Colorado County that behind all this dreadful conspiracy lies the murderous plotting of some secret emissary from northern abolitionism and men acquainted with all the facts and Negro character, will continue to entertain that opinion.

When we left Columbus, all was quiet. Throughout the whole affair a spirit of wise discretion seemed to preside -- no riot, no confusion took place, but the people managed everything with a dignity, moderation and solemnity.

notice of lawsuits

Notice by William Moore, Justice of the Peace of Red River County to Lewis Tanner that he has been sued by H. S. Janes.

Notice by M. Bolin, Justice of the Peace of Titus County, by A. P. B. Mayfield , Sheriff to H. Page that he has been sued John W.Withee.

runaway

from L. L. Harrison, of Hunt County living on the west side of the Sabine river, a likely Negro boy, George; 34 years of age; weights about 175; 5 foot 11 inches.

Clarksville Classical Mathematical and Mercantile Academy

Rev. John Anderson MA and J. A. Huff, BA principals. The school has been closed two years but will reopened in November. Mathematics allows men to become civil engineers. That this profession is a profitable one for those engaged in it cannot be denied and that it is likely to give employment to many of our interesting young men for an indefinitely long period is now beyond question. We are glad that the principals of the Male and Female Academies in our town have determined to give young men the opportunity for rendering themselves so eminently useful. As a mathematician, we do not believe he has an equal in the state. Our youth can now received a science education without being sent to the North.

****

From *The Standard,* October 18, 1856

how women veil the truth

When a woman says of another woman "she has a good figure" you can be sure she is freckled or that she squints or that she is marked with the small pox. But if she simply says "She is a good soul" you may be morally certain that she is both ugly and ill made.

tidbits of wisdom

Great souls attract calamity, as mountains do the thunder clouds, but while the storm burst upon them, they are the protection of the plains beneath.

steam boat sunk

The *White Cliffs* reports that the steamer *R. M. Jones,* Capt. McWilliams, bound from Fulton to New Orleans, with a cargo of cotton, struck a snag, eight miles above Campte, keeled over and sunk. The boat will prove a total loss.

frost

We have had several frosts, although as yet none heavy enough to kill the cotton. Yesterday we noticed a field of cotton in better bloom than a month ago.

meeting of Democrats in Jefferson

A mass meeting of the democracy is to take place next week in Jefferson, Cass county. The editor proper of this paper has been invited to attend accompanied by all his anti Know Nothing friends and a sample of the Know Nothings as will attend. Plenty of room has been provided for all.

murder in Mount Pleasant

We learn that a general row broke out at Mount Pleasant, on Monday last, which resulted in the immediate death of Mr. Ben Porter of Titus county. Our informant states that two Keenans, charged with the murders, are now in custody. We have not learned the particulars. Mr. Porter leaves a wife and a large family of children.

a new pistol

The *Albany Times* states that a new pistol which shoots 90 rounds a minute, with the ball carrying 140 yards farther than any pistol now in use, and that it is also much lighter and is in every respect superior to Colt's celebrated pistol.

****

From *The Standard,* October 25, 1856

Milam Male and Female Academy

We call attention to the new advertisement of the Milam Male and Female Academy under the supervision of William B. Featherston. This institute now numbers 110 students and the principal says he has room for 40 more

Our corporation roads and our bridges

We again call the attention of the corporate authorities of our Town to the condition of both of the bridges leading from Town. The labor of a Negro for a couple of days or less six months ago would have fully repaired the upper bridge; while had the plank lying on the lower bridge been put into place, when brought, it could have been put into repair for a trifle. As it is, the action of the summer on the unpiled plank has nearly rendered it unfit for service. We notice that a barrier was thrown across the bridge last week and a notice to travelers warned of its unsafe condition. So long as the weather is dry the traveling public suffers no great inconvenience, but let a few days of rainy weather come on and the present crossing of the creek would be almost impractical for loaded wagons.

In other matters, we learn that our corporate authorities are bestowing becoming zeal in the enforcement of their law. We trust that when the interests of the whole traveling public heading west of town are at stake, some immediate steps will be taken to have both bridges so repaired that there will be no longer any apprehension of crossing them. Were the bridges for any other part of the county under overseers in such disrepair they would have been sued.

While on the subject f improvements in our Town, we conceive it to be our duty to call to the attention of the authorities to some other matters which seem to us to fall within their province.

The late fire, which at one time threatened to burn up the Town, should be sufficient warning to guard against such contingency for the future. We would instance, for example, an old house that we believe belongs to ono one, adjoining the post office which, if it took fire, might be followed by disastrous consequences. Why not tear it down or sell to some one to remove for fuel? Does not the Corporation have sufficient power to do so? Let the Corporation do its duty and we doubt not but that they will be fully sustained by the citizens of the Town.

our jail

We would the attention of our county commissioners to the unsafe and unsightly building in our town known by the name of the "jail." It is well known to the inhabitants of our county that it is unfit for service, which, at any time, it is liable to be called upon to render. Owing to its insecure condition, our county, during the past few years, has been put to considerable expense in guarding prisoners, both before and after trial. Prisoners had to be sent to the jails of other counties for safe keeping, thereby imposing on this county additional expense. The time has arrived for making the effort to get a jail, which, instead of being a disgrace to the county, can be an ornament to our town.

Presidential election

Never, since we became a nation, has a more important election taken place than that which is to come off on the 4th of November. The permanency of our glorious Union is involved in the contest. Should Fremont be the successful candidate, we have no other notion but that this would be the death knell of the Union. The position of the South would be that she could not in justice to herself, her interests, her institutions, submit to the licentious domination of Northern fanaticism and the aggressions of Abolitionist and Black Republicans must be met either by separation or civil war.

lawsuit over title to Red River lands

The District court has been in session here (McKinney) since Monday of last week, Nat. M. Burford, presiding. Some troublesome cases have been under consideration, the most important of which is the heirs of Babb against Pulliam and sundry claimants under him, who reside upon the league of land which is the basis of the controversy. The land lies with its nearest line near six miles of Town [Clarksville] is rich black prairie with some 14 farms and residence upon it. It is now worth about $50,000. The jury decided in favor of the occupants as against the non resident claimants. The case goes up to the Supreme Court upon exception to the ruling of the judge. The claimants are children of E. W. Babb to whom a grant of a league and a labor of land was made by the Land Commissioners for Red River County in compliance of his claim as the apparent head of an residential family, living some seven miles below Clarksville upon the place well known to most of the citizens. The depositions which are numerous and from persons in Virginia and Tennessee where Babb and a person here claimed to be his wife formerly resided, show without any room for doubt and without conflict, that the woman not only was never married to him, but that he had left a wife in Virginia, who now lives in Ohio, and that he had emigrated d to Texas to live without disturbance with Edie Collier, or properly Edie Hardy, cohabiting for several years with Shandrich Collier, she never having been married to any one . Her own sons by Collier testify that she was never married to Babb, as did several others. Babb sold one half of is prospective right, before issuance of a land certificate to Richard M Hopkins. Edie sold hers to William M Pulliam. For the recovery of this land , as the legitimate family of Babb, this suit is brought. Plaintiffs' claim was to disregard the sale by Edie, who had no real right to the land, not being Babb's wife and consequently entitled to nothing and could sell nothing.

The case was very ably and industriously conducted during three days, by S. H. Morgan, Harbinger and Higby for the plaintiffs. John T. Mills, Tomilson, Lewellen and H. G. Hendricks for defendants. Court will adjourn this evening.

During the first week of court week, addresses upon the railroad subject were delivered by S. H. Morgan, Judge Mills and Dr. Throckmartin.

There have been present during court, attorneys from other counties: Messrs Grider, McCoy, Stone and Good from Dallas, O. G, Welsch from Denton; Faris from Ellis; Hendrickson, Everts and Clark from Grayson; J. T. Mills, Townes and Williams from Lamar; S. H. Morgan of Red River, Roberts, Lane and Marshall from Fannin; Hardin and Martin Hart from Hunt.

McKinney improved

McKinney has improved some, since my visit last year. There are eight mercantile establishments here. The leading business is done by Rhine & Brothers, who have a large store and are in receipt, through Houston, of a heavy stock from the north. Money is said to be scarce here, although the wheat crop was abundant and a good deal has been hauled off to the south western counties. Corn is sufficient for the supply of the county and sells for between 50 to 75 cents a bushel, not much at less than the latter price. Wheat rates at 75 cents a bushel. It is a fine wheat country. Mr. Michael Mallow, residing six miles from Town, had 28 and one half acres measured, upon which he made 973 bushels, weighing 73 pounds to the bushel or 1183 bushels by the mercantile standard, being 41 and ½ bushels to the acre. Mr Mallow conceives that nearly 100 bushels were lost in the field by the careless mode of harvesting. This sort of crop will do well to boast upon. from native soil, not enriched by any sort of manure.

On the road here, I passed many wagons going out of state. The occupant were mainly from Hill, Coryell and Parker counties. They made very short crops in most of the new counties the past two years and it is telling on some of them. Sone of them, however, can lose population and still outnumber some of the older one. What do you think of Wise and Parker counties, settled less than a year and a half ago, and already containing seven and eight hundred voters? Northern Texas will vote heavily in two or three years more.

I have been staying at a very excellent house of S. D. Skidmore. We have all fared well, had pleasant rooms, quiet and have been charged moderately. I shall go from here to Dallas.

married

On Thursday evening, the 16th instant, at the residence of Martin Glover, in Bowie County, by His Honor John W. Leigh, Mr Edward A. Estes of Sevier County, Arkansas to Miss Mary E. Richardson of Bowie County.

****

From *The Standard,* November 1, 1856

did you know

There are in the United States122 colleges with more than a thousand professors and having more than 12,000 students. They have extensive laboratories and astronomical equipment and libraries containing more than a million books. There are 44 theological schools with 127 professors and between 1,300 and 14,000 students. There are sixteen law schools and about 600 students.

our jail

In our last when we called the attention of our County Commissioners to the jail in our town, we little anticipated it would be soon a heap of smoldering ruins. We rather think that a very little effort could have saved the graceful old structure, but it seems that most of those present at the fire had no greater veneration for the building than we expressed. We hope now, as a new jail must be built, means will be adopted for erecting a building which will be creditable to our County.

Collin County shoppers take notice

We the attention of our readers in Collin and the adjacent counties to the advertisement of a large stock of goods received by Rhine & Bros at McKinney *stage through to Shreveport*

We are glad that, at last, a direct line of communication has been opened between this place and Shreveport. We are satisfied that this line will repay well the enterprising proprietors. Our citizens, going and returning from New Orleans, can now, with little fatigue, accomplish the journey in three days. Letters and papers will travel that route in about half the time.

new goods

The Messrs. Rhine have been daily receiving goods for the past two or three weeks. Their stock is by now the largest and best assorted that has ever been opened in Clarksville. When all their goods arrive, they will have enough to fill three such store houses as they now occupy.

Dallas County

On Wednesday morning, the District Court for Collin having adjourned, the Judge and myself started for Dallas, all the members of the Dallas Bar who had been in McKinney, having preceded us. . Small farm were frequent along the route, yet the improvement of the last three years has not been as great as I supposed from description and from the increased prices at which land is sold. A vast domain of unsurpassed richness in all our Northern region still invite the attention of the agriculturist.

On the way we observed a wagon like vehicle, which upon examination, I found to be the Emery Wheat Thresher, highly recommended in the region for portableness and by their competitive performance, being worked by two horses and threshing 250 bushels a day. There are said to be about forty of them in this County.

The City of Dallas has improved considerably, although it is all scattered about, as not to be all visible to persons passing through. On the Square, a new court house has been constructed of brick, fifty feet square. The windows are too large, proportionally, for the size of the building, giving it a rather an unsubstantial appearance. The top has a flat roof hidden entirely by a low parapet. The arrangement of rooms below is similar to our court house, being one at each corner of the house. Less space is wasted than in ours. The court room above occupies the entire square of the house with no room cut off for jury rooms as in ours.

A large brick hotel is also in contemplation by Mr. Cockrell, an enterprising and valuable citizen, who has built a large brick double house for stores, nearly finished. Dallas is a pleasant locality at this season of the year, not so much in the summer when the sand gets moved to the square to a depth of six inches and the heat of the sun reflected by it, is intense. The mercantile business of this place, once considerable, has deceased with the spread of population and the establishment of new centers of trade, by the creation of county seats. There is still, however, one heavy establishment in this place and three of moderate business, besides a respectable drug establishment. The Crutchfield house, always an excellent tavern, is the only one now kept open. The river here seems to have shrunk to one half the size it was when I was here last. Then it looked like a still narrow lake.

Dallas is one of the most agreeable places Northern Texas to a visitor who is acquainted with its choice spirits. It is one of the first points of settlement in Northern Texas . Dallas county is one of the best in the state - has probably a voting population of 1,000 residents in it and has developed as rapidly as any of the old counties in Northern Texas, perhaps more rapidly than any other.

Tomorrow, in company with Judge Burford, whose guest I have been for the past to days, I start for Sherman.

died

at Lockhart on the 14th October, Mrs. Anne S. Oldham, wife of the Hon. W. S. Oldham of this city.

destructive fire in Clarksville

Our citizens were thrown into a state of great alarm on Wednesday evening by the breaking out of a fire in the cabinet shop of Mr. J. B. Shanahan, which soon extended to the cabinet shop of Mr. Wm. C. Gaines, both of which were entirely consumed. In Mr.

Shanahan's shop, we understand that over $500 of fine furniture, together with a large quantity of valuable materials, all his tools, etc. were entirely destroyed. From the nature of the materials, the fire had broken out for only a few minutes, before all chance of saving anything was lost. Mr. Gaines saved all the furniture from his showroom and a few of his tools, but lost a large quantity of valuable lumber and materials for making fine work. The loss falls heavily on both. It is estimated at not less than $3,000. Mr. Shanahan has lost most of his savings from several years of persevering industry. To both of the sufferers, we sincerely extend our utmost sympathy and we earnestly recommend to those who are indebted to either party to come forward and settle their indebtedness. Promptness on the part of their patrons would be a true manifestation of their kindness and it would afford lost material and essential aid.

On this occasion, our town was most providentially saved. Had the wind continued as it had at the commencement of the fire Mrs. Donoho's large fine hotel would have inevitably been consumed by the fire. The burning of this building would have occurred, despite every effort which could have been used, been communicated to the Court house and thence to the other buildings around the Square. Had our town been supplied with a fire engine, the fire could have easily been confined to Shanahan's shop and all danger to surrounding buildings would have been obviated. We sincerely hope that our merchants will make an effort to be prepared against any future contingency.

During the progress of the fire, we were struck with the idea that some regularly organized fire company should forthwith be got up. There should be some one to take command at such a time. Was it not the duty of our Mayor and constable to appoint as many assistant constables as the exigency of the case demanded? Let the whole affair be a warning to us to be more careful about how fires are secured in our houses and let the gratitude of our heart be offered to God, who holds the winds in his Hands, for preserving our town.

emigration

Those who seek rich soil which they might own - they and their children - are daily to be seen now, winding their ways through the counties [of North Texas]. They enter a country, which pleases the eye and gladdens the heart by its beauty. No man can look upon it and ask if it is rich. That is a proposition self solved at a glance. If, however, they are critical and would know of its products, they see, by the size of the corn stalks, by the yield of the cotton, that they have seen no such country before. And, as they move on, they see thousand of acres of virgin soil into which no plough has ever been thrust, still green with the garment of verdure which Nature has given it and wooing with a promise of rich fruitfulness that cannot be doubted. We have the garden of the world, rich enough for millions, now wasting their energies in unproductive regions. Come to it! There can be no more propitious time. The price of land is yet so low that a citizen of an old state would smile derisively at the mention of it. Grain is plentiful and cheap and, in another year, the land will certainly be higher. Food may or may not be as low. Texas is the last field of the Southwest. In all of Texas (we know it well) there is no fairer or richer lands, than in the Red River counties. We disparage no other, for the state has an immensity of fertile lands, but we say, ignorantly or from prejudice, that we believe the Red River counties to be the choice of all Texas, for all purposes. Yesterday 40 wagons passed through our town.

****

There was no issue published of *The Standard* for November 8, 1856.

****

From *The Standard,* November 15, 1856

tidbit of wisdom

He who marries for beauty only is like the buyer of cheap furniture. The varnish that caught the eye will not endure the fireside blaze.

If you wish to cure a scolding wife, never fail to laugh at her with all your might, until she ceases, then kiss her. Sure cure and no quack medicine.

Fannin Court

The *Bonham Enquirer* reports 815 cases upon the docket in their district. The session commenced on the 6th instant.

wanted

A journey man printer wanted at this shop immediately.

no paper last week

The sudden lost of two of our hands and the necessary withdrawal of our foreman for a few days and the impossibility of our immediately filling the places, has caused a week's omission of our paper. We hope to fill the vacancies and issue hereafter regularly.

Hunt County Court

Greenville, Hunt County

Judge Todd arrived here yesterday morning in a heavy rain which ceased in an hour or two and the Court was opened and the juries empaneled. Today, the Court opened for an hour or more for the issuance of Colony certificates, then adjourned until tomorrow morning; and the [Presidential] Election was held at the Courthouse. There has been no excitement, but much interest manifested.

Two of the editorial profession, besides myself, are present, A. J. Fowler of the *Palestine American* and Ron. A Vansickle of the *Prairie Eagle*. Attorneys from other counties present are Judge Dillahunnty of Red River, Wilkinson of Cass, and W. H. Johnson of Titus; Musgrove of Hopkins, Peacock of Lamar; Col Durant of Leon; Gen. Good of Dallas; Col. Lane and Roberts of Fannin and Mr. Lemons of Smith.

Greenville has not improved since last Court. The County has perhaps gained a little. Wheat is worth a dollar a bushel here ; corn 50 or 60 cents. They have a most indifferent apology for a court house, a little frame house of one room, but they have about $3,500 dollars in the County Treasury and, with the two year state taxes allowed them, should be able to put up the wall of a good Courthouse which may be finished by special tax.

victory for the Democrats

Beyond all doubt, Buchanan and Breckenridge have been elected to the offices of President and Vice President for the next four years by an overwhelming majority.

election celebration

The loiters about the streets yesterday evening witnessed the first insinuation of the election by the arrival of a stage ornamented with a huge set of Buck Horns. A cheer was immediately raised for Buchanan, which went around the Square in good earnestness. The symbolic language was easily understood even before the driver had the chance to announce the news or the postmaster to open the mail. We understand that some four or five of our citizens had considerable bets pending on the results in Kentucky and whether they or the friends of Buchanan generally signified their pleasure at the news we cannot tell, but this we know that cheering did not cease occasionally till late in the night.

Mayor's power in time of emergency

In our last paper when giving an account of the fire, we called attention to the fact that there was not much of concert on the part of those who were present in their efforts to stay the progress of the fire. In connection with this, we inquired were it not the duty of the Mayor to take command and give such directions as to him seemed best under the circumstances. We have never seen the Act of Incorporation of our Town and are therefore in total ignorance of the power of the powers of the Mayor. We simply asked the question of the duty of the Mayor for the sake of information, but it appears we were misunderstood. That the *pro tem* Editor of the Democratic *Standard* should be guilty of such a breach of Democratic principles as to insinuate that the Mayor should [have] taken control in such a situation.

Now we throw out no such insinuation. We asked in our ignorance of the law, a simple question. We suppose we may gather from it that the Mayor has no such authority and very properly abstained from the exercise of any doubtful power.

Sherman

This is the last day of the first week of Court in Sherman which will continue to Wednesday of next week. Judge Burford, who is presiding , gives general satisfaction here.

Got here from Dallas on Sunday evening by the direct route, through a high prairie region and, on leaving Cedar Springs two miles from Dallas, we passed through no timber until we got close to Sherman, except very thin skirts on the margins of small creeks. The country between the two places is pleasant to view and almost all rich.

Saturday night, we stopped at the place of an old friend, John Hoffman whose farm I have had occasion to note before. It is in Collin County on high rich prairie some six or seven miles from any body of timber and shows what might be done without much timber. There are about 300 acres within the fence, which is mostly posts and planks. The land is in a good state of cultivation and the appearance of things is such as always follows attentive industry and thrift. I went over the field with Mr. Hoffman to look at his wheat and his bois d'arc hedges[24]. The wheat has been drilled in and presented a most beautiful appearance with the regular interstices produced by the mode of seeding. The land was as mellow and as finely pulverized as a garden – a rich chocolate colored soil with which the bright green of the young wheat (about six inches high) made a beautiful contrast. Most of the wheat was in straight lines but part had been checked for the purpose of trying comparative productiveness of the two modes, the same quantity of seed per acre, being allowed in each way. We examined the drilling machine, which is of Michigan manufacture, and it seems a good one. Mr. Hoffman informed us that there are some half dozen of them in Jefferson which he was authorized to sell at cost and carriage, on 12 months time, to any solvent person wanting one. With two horses and one hand, it will seed eight acres in a day . I should be glad to see them generally introduced into the wheat growing portion of our state, believing they will lead to better cultivation and increased production. Mr. Hoffman also showed us his hedge, plants high he set out last spring and which are doing fine.

From Cedar Springs onward to the line of Collin county, farms were not numerous, but immediately on getting across the Collin's line, we found them more frequent and they so continued nearly all the way to Sherman. On our way, we passed quite a number of Arkansas apple wagons, wending their way southward.

The County has made good crops this year. Wheat has been sold for a little as 50 cents a bushel and is now to be had at 75 cents. I have heard of a crop in the county which average 43 bushels an acre. Corn sells at 50 cents a bushel. There have been more persons in Sherman this week than I have ever before seen during Court week. The county has not gained much population this year.

Sherman has improved somewhat. It has several stores. Mr. A. M. Alexander, who had met a serious fire a few weeks since, has a new store house and a new and large stock of goods and is doing a business that will soon renew the value of what the fire destroyed. Grayson, as I have frequently remarked before, is one of the best counties of Northern Texas and one of the most attractive from the variety of soil and beauty of scenery. It must also be generally healthy. Since I have been here I have seen a great number of immigrants pass through on their way to counties south west of this.

This evening I shall start for Greenville.

There are present here from other counties quite a large number of gentlemen of the Bar among them Judge Mills and N. W. Townes of Lamar, Judge Dillahunty and Capt. John A. Summers of Red River, Gen. Good and J. C. McCoy of Dallas; Messrs. Stone and Armstrong of Collin, and Lane and Roberts of Fannin.

From *The Standard,* November 22, 1856

Fannin Court

The District Court, Judge Todd presiding, opened in Bonham on Monday and will adjourn tomorrow morning, all business ready for trial being disposed of and the Court only partially occupied at the present time. There were few cases on the docket.

Attorneys present from other counties were Hervey Dillanhunty from Red River; John T. Mills, William B. Wright and S. R. G. Mills from Lamar; H. G. Hendricks from Grayson and Martin Hart from Hunt. Bonham has been very dull during the week.

I learn that two wagoners, who hauled grain for Colonel Butt in Grayson County to Fort Belknap, were killed on the return trip near the west fork of the Trinity, by Indians supposed to be Kickapoos. The men were named Brown and Washburn. The father of Washburn was killed on the Bois d'Arc about nine miles from here about 15 years ago by Indians. The men had no weapons and declined to take any under the impression there was no danger. They were scalped but not robbed. Nor were their teams disturbed. The Indians, a day or two afterwards, made an attack on 8 or 9 wagoners but these were armed and they drove them off. A party of citizens and small party of soldiers went in pursuit but, when two days out, a rain erased the tracks of the savages and the pursuit was necessarily abandoned.

I am told that the forces at Fort Belknap are not mounted, while Fort Chadbourne have three companies of mounted men. This seems like an unwise distribution of cavalry and is complained of for leaving all these portions of the frontier with only an unreal show of defense. The foot soldiers are very useful for the wheat and corn raisers hereabout in consuming a part of their surplus production, but it is presumed that they were not placed on the frontier by the War Department for that purpose. If depredations are committed and the soldiers are left in an inefficient condition for pursuit and punishment of the foe, the result will be hurried reprisals by the settlers at the border, which may not be sufficiently discriminating and may light a general war. This is to be avoided.

The county is gaining some strength by immigration. Corn is plentiful at 50 cents a bushel and wheat between 70 and 75 cents. Pork is worth about three cents. Northern Texas is able to feed cheaply all who come to it for settlement and to furnish much more for other counties nearby not so fortunate in crops.

The schools here are doing well. The Female Institute has about 70 scholars with more in the immediate prospect and Mr. Fuller's Male Academy has about 60 scholars.

Bonham has improved but a little within the past six months, but promises some substantial improvement in the Spring.

to the Medical Profession of East Texas

We, those who names are annexed, believing that a thorough organization of a "medical society in Eastern Texas" is imperatively demanded, take this method of urging all regular educated physicians in each county to hold a meeting and select delegates to represent them in a general convention of physicians to be held at Tyler, Smith County on the 18th of May next.

That such an organization would not only elevate the standard of the profession in our land, but also inspire the individual members with a laudable desire to emulate the rapid strides of scientific reformation in the older states, must be evident.

Geo. Gordon, MD,	J. R. Lyons, MD
John McDonna, MD	W. L. Gammage, MD
J. A. Barry, MD	
E. S. Look, MD	
G. H. Wooten, MD	

Rally Democrats!

A grand Ratification and Glorification over the election of Buck and Breck will take place in Clarksville on Friday next, the 29th instant. Come one, come all!

we call attention

to the advertisement of L. D. Weisner, broom manufacturer. "Encourage Home Industry!" We have seen some of the brooms in his store in Bonham and can certify they are a good article;

to the advertisement of A. M. Glass, watch repairer and jeweler in Bonham;

to the advertisement of Parish's Steam Mill in Fannin County.

list of letters at Clarksville Post Office

Agers, Eli
Annis, Mr. J. T. L.
Billingley, Henry L.
Butler, John
Benningfield, Willim
Browder, David
Bateman, Jonathan
Covey, John W.
Dean, J. A.
Davidson, Mrs.
Dodd, Mrs. Elizabeth
Evans, H.C.
Edmondson, Eli
Franklin, John
Fulsom, Susan
Freeman, Henry

Fleming, Adaline
Glass, Alexander
Hancock, Joseph P.
Huppers, George W.
Hall, Miss Mary E.
Hollum, Ira
Higright, Richard
Haley, William
Huskey, L. C.
Jones, Colin E.
Kerbey, Joseph
Kosciosco, G. D.
Lindsey, J. C.
Laughlin, C. H.
McCrorey, John
McDonald, Mrs. E.

McCall, Marshall
Murphy, Hugh
Mosby, Fortunaus S.
Oliphant, W. D. and J. B.
Owens, James
Poe, Alexander
Padrick, John
Revels, James C.
Richards, J. Virgil
Sparks, Hardy
Shelton, Miss Mary
Sherry, Barney

Scott, R. H. MD
Sims, Josh
Thompson, Miss Rett
Whitaker, Mrs. M.E.
Ward, Asa
Wilkinson, J. P.
Woolam, Rev. J. C.
Ward, R.A.
Wasson, A. C.

Jas. W. Thomas Post master
****

From *The Standard,* November 29, 1856

Democratic jollification

The Democrats of Red River county have postponed their grand jollification until next Wednesday, December 3. All are invited to attend who rejoice in the elections of Buchanan and Breckenridge to the highest offices in the gift of the American People. We expect many Democrats from surrounding areas.

Come one and come all and let us rejoice together, for our country is saved from those who would tear down our great Temple of Liberty.

we call attention

to the Administrator's sale of land on the Red River in Bowie county by Margaret Janes of the estate of Jarret Janes, Bowie county, 1500 acres, 400 cleared and in a fine state of cultivation with gin houses and other necessary out houses. Inquire of Mr.

W.C. Janes and John Wasden for particulars and to inspect the property;

to the advertisement for the sale of Negroes by H. C. Lightfoot, Bonham, Fannin County;

to the advertisement by L. W. Arnold, living three miles Northwest of Alton on Hickory Creek, Denton County, of a stolen mare mule.

Editor will return

Before the next issue, the Editor will be at his post and relieve us from a pleasant but rather onerous, burden when borne with other avocations, which are far from being light. Let who will, eat the bread of idleness. We know it is far from being our lot.

rain, a rise in the River and visions of Christmas delicacies

We have had considerable rain during the last four days and should the storm have extended far west, we anticipate such a rise in the Red River as will enable steamboats to get to our landing and bring up some goods before the Christmas holidays. How often have we in our hearts envied those who are within a reasonable distance from the coast where they are supplied the rich production of the Earth and the Seas. Apples, yes, will have in abundance in a few years. With peaches, melons and sweet potatoes, we are as well supplied as our hearts could desire. Our supply of winter vegetables is generally scanty but salt water fish are totally unknown. Those who have enjoyed these luxuries, lament the want of them. How a fine salmon or turbot or a barrel of fresh oysters would delight our eyes with the anticipated pleasure of satisfying our longing desires.

Our townsmen, Rhine & Bros, are the owners of the *Fanny Fern*. We hope the first trip she makes to Roland that her enterprising owners will have a corner, well stored with oysters, a few fish, salmon stowed away in ice and such a supply of Irish potatoes as that this county can get, at least an abundance to plant at an early season.

The Democratic Rejoicing at Paris, Lamar County and the Fair

On Monday evening came off the celebration of the constitutionalists – we will not say merely of the Democracy for with us in the late contest were mingled old line Whigs who love their country better than their prejudices.

We feared, when we saw the placard at Bonham on our way home that there was to grand rally for "Buck and Breck" and a torch light procession, that the affair would prove a failure. Not so. The Sovereigns were out in their strength, the crowd was a crowd in number properly speaking and amid the glare of the torches, the inspiring addresses of the Speaker and thrilling inspiration of the fifes and drums, the rally was an event for Paris. The transparencies, with appropriate mottoes, were all got up, the illumination of the Paris Hotel and the partial illumination of other buildings, the wild glare of the numerous pine torches and the continual discharge of anvil artillery, a very fair substitute for four pounders, with the enthusiastic shouting of the individuals composing the procession, as they passed around the town, made up the first attempt at a genuine political celebration that we have seen in Texas. Brief addresses were made by Judge Todd, Judge Mills and our fellow townsman John C. Burks, which were well received by the audience. To Messrs Wm. B. Wright and S. R. G. Mills we believe much of the credit of the preparatory arrangements is due.

Among th transparencies was one in the upper window of the store of Wells & Bro., over which was a canvas brightly illuminated on which were recounted in round tabular form, the Democratic majorities in the several states which cast their vote for Buchanan and Breckinridge. On the bottom, under the numbers, was the inquiry "Who cares?" Truly not those who were celebrating the victory.

On the same evening, the long promised Fair for the benefit of the new Church was held in the Church building. In attendance were a large number of persons crowding the building Three tables, the length of building, were waited upon by numerous ladies, inviting edibles, beverages and articles of taste to the visitor. In addition to this was musical entertainment. The ladies looked as beautiful and bright as possible and fascinated a very handsome sum out of the pockets of the gentlemen who went there to be smiled upon and pay for it liberally. Both parties, we believe, the bewitching and the bewitched, are satisfied and the church and the community benefitted. So all is well. We understand that the amount realized was something over $400.

Denton and Wise Counties

The District Court has been in session here, Judge Burford presiding, since Monday morning. Court is held in an open log house, without fire, and the sessions during the cold weather prevalent during the week might be considered uncomfortable, but here, where a part of the attendants on the court sit up around log hearths because rooms cannot be got, no one grumbles much.

I suppose accommodations at Alton for travelers and visitors is especially limited now because the county has decided by the public vote to move the seat of justice and a part of the very few houses which constitute the town. The new town to be called Denton is about six miles east of this place in a neck of prairie which connects with the grand prairie, the town site running up into the timber. It is a pleasant looking place and probably healthy. Most of the citizens here will now move to it. Denton has about 600 voters and is gaining some little by immigration.

Denton, as many of the readers of *The Standard* already know, has unsurpassed grazing facilities.

The wheat crops have been cut short by grasshoppers and money is very scarce partly because of that. The last corn crop was a tolerable one and the young wheat is promising. Pork is worth here 4- 6 cents, corn 65 to 70 cents, wheat 75 cents to a dollar; flour $3.50 per hundred. There are here a good many strangers. Birdville had sent a large delegation partly of attorneys and partly of others interested in the county seat controversy between that place and Fort Worth. The citizens of Birdville are intent to contest a contest lately had which declared in favor of Fort Worth by some 25 majority. Much ill will exists on the subject.

I find here some gentlemen from the new county of Wise. It has a large incoming population from Hopkins county. It has no county town, except in name. It has no court house for the District Court to be held in and it may be held under a tree as it has been before this on our circuit. There is, however, little to nothing to do except to organize a Grand Jury and let it inquire into the offenses against the peace and dignity of the state. Wise County has on its present border fine bodies of bituminous coal, which is now hauled for many miles of use in forges. It has also suitable rock of grindstones. Wise is said to have a large body of rich land in it.

The following attorneys were present Messrs. McCoy, Nicholson, Stone and Guest of Dallas; Easton, Armstrong, Throckmorton and Lewellen of McKinney; Everts and Weaver of Cooke; Sisler, Boyle and Bell of Tarrant.

Passing from Bonham to Alton, I went through Kentucky Town which is a rich and beautiful country, a little southwest from Bonham and nearly all good prairie lands between the two places.

From Kentucky Town to Alton, the land is very high, beautifully broken into eminences and rich. For about six miles, farms are frequent upon the road, then they become scarce, until at 12 miles from Kentucky town, the last house is left, until the traveler gets near to Pilots Point in Denton, a distance of 25 miles. For several miles of this distance the road leads over the "Elm Flats", a kind of valley surrounded by prairie hills in which cattle delight to winter, the grass intermixed extensively with the Mesquite is said to afford superior winter range and, I suppose, there is in the comparable depression in the ground, a partial protection from cold winds. The land, which was described to me as rich, did not appear so to me, although I may be deceived having been so long accustomed from residence in the rich black prairie region to think strength of color and richness to be co existent and inseparable. I did not go off the road to examine, but along the road the land seemed to be a kind of gray soil and in some places I am certain a decidedly whitish poor soil. The flats are comprised, I think, in some extensive surveys originally made for Dr. B.F. Hall to the amount of 20,000 or more acres, but these surveys doubtless cover much of the highland adjoining.

Pilot Point, aspiring to be a town, has one or two stores, a blacksmith shop, several log residences and a good flouring mill. It is a beautiful location for a town, a cluster of gentle hills, quite elevated, covered with sprawling oaks and commanding a prairie expanse of miles of good lands. Some day there will be a pleasant town here. It is one of Nature's designations for that use. One of the heaviest settlements in Denton is adjacent to the [Pilot] Point and five miles carry one to Zillaboy Creek and onto the Elm Fork of the Trinity, by the margin of which I rested over night with Daniel Strickland, the assessor of the county. Riding across the Elm the following morning, I was surprised to find water only in the holes and learned from Mr. S. that the stream had not run for any length of time for two years, during which there had been an unusual drought. The Elm at this point has a large bed and its condition evinces that is must be dry indeed. This drought has existed westerly to the sources of the color and many persons have moved out of Corywell, Hill and Parker, which are new counties actually driven out by the scarcity of foodstuffs. Some of the ejected settlers have moved to [other parts of] Denton, Collin, and Fannin counties, where all the elements of sustenance are plentiful. And they will be apt to remain there.

The truth is that the Northern counties of Texas are agriculturally the finest in the state. As we go southward, we may find the same quality of land but the country is drouthier and has not the capacity for growing wheat profitably. For the cultivation of cotton, there is no better region that the parallels which comprise Northern Texas. Our grazing facilities are fully as good and yet thousands of immigrants pass through Northern Texas to settle is less desirable country farther south. I have notice though that, if they stop with us and rent, and then make personal examination beyond, they seldom move but they purchase among us and stay.

lawsuits pending

Notice by John M. Bivins, Clerk of the Court, that George M. Pennypacker and Julia E. Pennypacker (formerly Julia E. Wortham) have filed a suit in the District Court of Red River County against Travis Wright and James D. Wortham, Executors of the last will and testament of Timothy Wortham also against Mary J. K. Wortham and Augusta C. Wortham, children and minor heirs to said Timothy, seeking distribution and partition of the estate;

Notice by C.B. Sutton, Justice of the Peace of Red River County to N. O. Miller that he has been sued by Rowland Bryerly on a debt on open account.

****

From *The Standard,* December 6, 1856

we call attention

to the advertisement of a Tin Shop at Paris by R. C. Sherril, who understands his business;

to the notice that the shareholders of Memphis El Paso and Pacific Railroad company of another call for payment;

to the notice of a dancing school opened by Sam Williams, widely known through Louisiana, Arkansas and Eastern Texas, as the prince of dancing masters. Those parents, who appreciate the importance of giving this polite accomplishment to their children, either for the purpose of making them dancers or for the more important object of improving their carriage of person, and improvement in the matter of association, will do well to avail themselves of the present opportunity without delay;

to the new and well kept Livery Stable of Turner B. Edmondson at Paris, Lamar county. The accommodation is extensive and the stable well kept.

newspaper business

A. Bishop, Esq, County Clerk, will act as our agent in Wise

County and John H. Prince, Esq., County Clerk, as our agent for Parker County.

thanks

We are indebted to our friend R. W. Nesmyth of Jefferson for sundry favors, in the way of election news during the past few weeks.

immigration

About two months ago, the people of North Texas had made up their minds that the incoming to the State this Fall would be small. Within the time since elapsed, it has become apparent that this impression was erroneous. Crossing at Mill Creek and passing through this county and crossing at the Indian ferries above, a very large immigration has come in, a considerable part of which has settled in Lamar, Collin and Grayson counties in Northern Texas and many have passed farther south. It may also been that some of the Northen counties here have also received some new settlers, but of this we are presently not advised. Red River has got few. Offering inducements inferior to none of the others, with land unsurpassed and timber plentiful, for some reason they pass through and look for an El Dorado beyond. We cannot complain of their choice for anywhere in a dozen counties of North Texas, they may do well but whether they can do better for quality of price of and for convenience of any sort, we doubt.

The Democratic Celebration in Clarksville

Very rich rare and exuberant was the Clarksville Democratic rejoicing and at the same time in good taste and not offensive to the most determined opponent. Of course, we do not mean to compare it with a City Celebration. It was the first class of a new style of rejoicing in this region and the attempt fulfilled the sanguine hopes of it proponents.

In Paris, there were more people, great number of strangers and as much enthusiasm as human nature can generate. Our numbers answered the purpose and, considering the intense cold, were more than we expected at nightfall when the streets looked nearly deserted. But before night could full assert her dominion, four platforms at the corners of the Square and some at private residences had bonfires upon them and the thundering sound of the explosives commenced. A little later, as the people poured out of their house, numerous transparencies got up in excellent taste, each surmounted by a large eagle were brought out in line. Upon therm were mottoes of democracy in large letters and choice expressions from the writings and speeches of Jefferson, Pierce Buchanan and Breckinridge were printed upon them. Intermingled were national flags of silk and Buck Horns, of course, played their part.

The foremost transparency was a large one in red with the name of Washington and all his Democratic Successors in large letters. This was carried by four bearers and watched over with paternal anxiety by its projector. Something of this sort was essential to the perseveration of these transient affairs from the incautious jollity of the torch bearers who rocked torches about in a decidedly Democratic way.

The performance commenced by the appearances on the Square of the transparencies heading the procession, all marshaled by J. C. Burks in chief and Major Edward West as assistant. Marching around the Square amid enthusiastic cheers and peals of artillery and the shrill sound of fife and drum, they halted in front of the Donoho House and were addressed from the balcony of the house eloquently by J. C..Burks. Then, *The Star Spangled Banner* was sung by a large corp of ladies, among whom were young girls carrying banners from all the Democratic states, tastefully decorated. This demonstration was received joyously and the voices were distinctly heard across the Square and beyond. Then followed an address by H.R. Latimer and then *Columbia the Land of the Free* by the Ladies. Then followed, successively intervened by marches around the Square, addresses from Courtes B. Sutton, Sumpter Mills, Judge Todd and the Young Democracy represented by John A. Bagby and Thomas J. Crooks.

Before all this was through with, the Ladies had occupied the ballroom and dancing soon commenced and continued till midnight. We have not heard of the slightest interruption to the general good feeling prevalent among all those present.

Paris and Lamar

District Court opened in Paris on Monday of last week, the Hon. Judge Todd presiding and adjourned on Saturday evening. There was not much business but attendance of people from the country was large. The Democratic celebration and Ladies Fair doubtless drew many from other counties.

Paris is improving rapidly - quite so. There is a mutuality of public spirit on the part of the citizens, which is pushing it forward. Paris has two good hotels; that kept by Major Francis, whose card will be found in our columns had a strong run of patronage during court and is satisfactorily kept. The other house also has the reputation of being a good one. Paris has eleven mercantile houses, some of which do a considerable business.

It has two newspaper establishments, one of which, that of the *Enquirer*, we visited. Under the escort of its dashing Editor in Chief and founder, the junior busily engaged among the types. The office reminded us of the locale of *The Standard* in days gone by, when in a house of similar, limited dimensions, we were in just about the same sort of fix. The Junior is a regular member of the craft, has gone through all the laborious gradations and was making a form when we called upon him. We trust that his labor of love may prove fruitful of profit and the striving against the general destiny of the brotherhood, he may rise above it and he may receive proper recompense for his untiring exertion.

A joint stock company is getting up in Paris for the erection of a large brick hotel, creditable to the place, to be rented to whoever will keep it on a scale suited to the rising fortunes of the place. A subscription for a new building for a Male Academy is getting up with an indication of immediate success. Three large brick fire proof stores are already contracted for to be built upon the Square and one is to be commenced immediately.

Lamar County is receiving large additions to its population from the grand army of immigration which for the past few weeks has been passing over the main line of travel through Northern Texas. It is a rich country and will support a dense population.

Paris schools tend much to its advancement. The Female Seminary under the charge of the Rev. C. J. Bradley, has 80 scholars. The Female Academy of the Rev. Jas. Graham and Lady about 70. The Male school of Mr. Carpenter is we understand is doing well. A subscription for a new building for a Male Academy is getting up with an indication of immediate success.

the wheat of Northern Texas

There is still a very large body of the wheat of this year's harvest remaining in the hands of the farmers of Northern Texas who, many of them, are losing the use of its value, which they need.. We have admonished them before that it would do well to grind and sack it and haul it to southeastern and southwestern Texas.. The price to be obtained pays well for the hauling in addition to the value here of the wheat of the wheat. At Hunt Court, we met an old friend who had gotten up is wagons and started to Houston with his flour. He sold it a hundred miles this side of Houston at $5 per hundred, got cotton freight for his wagons from the place of sale to Houston and invested the proceeds in groceries which pay a return profit. This is far better than idly sitting on one's hearthstone and regretting that there is no sale at home for large quantity. Southeastern Texas has no flour. Middle Texas has none. Bring up some of your sluggish cattle and make them and their sluggish master better themselves. The railroad will come along by and bye but it will not transport the present year's wheat to market.

school house burns down

Bonham

Dear Major De Morse

Last Saturday night our Female Institute [the Bonham Masonic Female Istitute] was set on fire by some incendiary and entirely consumed. The fire was first discovered at about nine o'clock at night, but the discovery was too late to stop it, as the whole roof was in a few minutes in a blaze. The building is an entire loss. Many of the books are lost too. The piano, by considerable exertion, was saved, supposed not to be materially injured. Considerable excitement among our citizens. No clues as to who was the perpetrators. It must have been the work of an incendiary as I learn that there little or no fire during the day previous. However, notwithstanding our great misfortune, the school will go on uninterrupted. The Baptist Church has been proffered and it has been accepted and not a day will be lost by the scholars. Tomorrow, there is to be a meeting of the citizens at the Courthouse for the purpose of raising a subscription for the immediate construction of a new house to be made of brick and covered with tin to be made fireproof. There is much enthusiasm manifested among the people and there is no question whatsoever that a sufficient amount will be raised to do the construction. One of our citizens has given $1000 and several other hundreds of dollars.

married

on the 27th *ultimo* Elder J. R. Clarke, principal of the Douglassville Male and Female Seminary, to Miss Josephine Favors of Cass County.

****

From *The Standard,* December 13, 1856

we call attention

to the advertisement of H. Rhine and Bros. Their stock is a large one and we understand that their prices are considered less than usual in the community. Not having purchased in person, we speak only from the representations of others.

the Bonaham Masonic Institute

Our readers will see that this handsome and commodious building has been burned and the fire is supposed to be the work of those demons in human shape who sometimes stealthily, bring misfortune on other people. We can imagine no offenses to prompt such malice and trust that it was work of accident

However this may have been, it seems that the citizens with a spirit, worthy of all praise, have again made arrangements to build another edifice, this time of brick with a tin roof. This is prompt, sensible and generous. The Institute is a credit and a positive pecuniary benefit to the place. It should be well sustained and the acts of the citizens show that it will be. The constructor of the late building, Mr. Lissenbee has made it a credible specimen of architecture. We trust that the new one will be put up also with reference to style as well as to use.

****

From *The Standard*, December 20, 1856

tidbits of wisdom

A great man will neither trample a woman or cringe before a king.

Vice stings even in its pleasures, but virtue console us even in pain.

we call the attention

of planters and others interested to the card of Steamer *Fanny Fern*;

to the professional card of John A. Summers Esq, attorney at law in Jefferson.

Negro stealing and Negro insurrections

There seems to be a mania present in Tennessee, Kentucky, Missouri, Arkansas, Texas partaking of these two peculiarities. It is time that it should cease summarily. It seems that plots have been germinating in our midst. The fault lies in letting Negroes, known to be vicious, to remain among us to degrade the general population at large and to corrupt other Negroes of naturally good tendencies.

The fault also lies in part in permitting slaves to hire their own time, become speculative, indolent and finally criminal. This has been done here for years in utter defiance of the statues and not a Grand Jury or District Attorney, whose duty it was to suppress and punish it for the protection of society. We hope to see all this amended . In the meanwhile, we hope to see the owner of every notoriously dangerous Negro will be required to take him away or have it done. We trust that the present warning in not permitted as a farce, until a more serious one may be given by the burning of houses and shedding of blood.. Every Negro in the least way implicated should be severely dealt with. As to whites, against whom there is positive evidence in connection with such a scheme, or with Negro stealing, the following little notice suits our views of even handed justice exactly. The *Georgetown Independent* says "In Belton last week a man named Walker was hanged by a party who arrested him for the stealing of a Negro. They found him some 150 miles from where he had taken him. To save further trouble, they hung him to a tree."

Servile insurrection and Negro stealing are two crimes that may be properly dealt with in a summary manner in our opinion and, if any white man puts himself in such association as to allow room for suspicion, he should be summarily dealt with. The fault lies with himself. No white who preserves the proper distance between the two races, can ever become liable to serious suspicion.

married

on the 15th *ultimo* at the residence of J. E. Hopkins of Hopkins County by the Rev. Mr. Webb of Lamar, Sam Moore of this place to Miss N. A. V. Hopkins.

lawsuit brought

Notice by T. G. Riddle, Justice of the Peace of Titus County to A. M.D. Rice that he has been sued by Benjamin L. Beaver on a $85 note; the summons was delivered by A. B. Mayfield, Sheriff, by E. Riddle, Deputy.

strays

Notice by K. L. Tuder of Paris in Lamar County.

****

No issue of *The Standard* was published for December 27, 1856

****

1857

From *The Standard,* January 3, 1857

tidbits of wisdom

"Knowledge is power" as the boy said, when his master floored him with the dictionary;

To some men it is indispensable to be worth money for without they would be worth nothing.

we call attention

to our readers in Hopkins County and the upper part of Titus County to the advertisement of the new mercantile firm of Wm. M. Ewing & Bro. We imagine that dealing with clever men, fair minded and accommodating, our readers in that area may find it profitable to deal with the Ewings They have a supply of staple and fancy goods; and in that area our readers may find it profitable to deal with the Ewings. They are on the southwest corner of the Public Square, under the Lodge rooms;

of our readers in Lamar County to the advertisement of Rhine Bro. & Co;

to the special announcement of David C. Russell for the sale of his goods at cost and carriage or thereabout. Perhaps some of our readers, who are in want of goods, might do well to look there, the stock comprising an assortment of winter goods;

to the notice of Drs. Barry & Moore whose partnership in the practice of medicine is being dissolved;

to the advertisement of the new boat, *Reub White*. She is entirely new having been launched only a few weeks ago; she was built expressly for the trade.

thanks

We are indebted to our young friend, John M. Jackson, now at Exeter, New Hampshire for sundry engravings, magazines and papers.

news paper news

We issued no paper last week because our printers thought they were entitled to some Christmas recreation, an opinion in which we concurred.,

We have to leave out all editorial of length and do well to get out at all. Christmas has been such a merry Christmas about here.

flour

Some of our friends in the country cannot be aware at the exorbitant price at which flour is sold in this town. We buy from wagons at $3 per hundred, but when w purchase it at stores $4 per hundred is required. This may be mysterious to people who know that wheat is plentiful through most of Northern Texas at 75 cents per bushel. Could not some of our country readers, either in this or in adjoining counties, do well by leaving a load or two of their flour for sale here at fair prices?

court house in Hunt County

We are requested by the Chief Justice and the County Commissioners of Hunt County, to state that they have determined to build a court house for the County, in Greenville, the plan for which is placed in the Clerk's office for examination and they will receive sealed bids for building until the third Monday in February, when the proposals will be opened and the one which most completely fills the requirements of the county court will be received.

burning of the Adjutant Generals office

We learn from the *State Gazette* that the trial of Blankenship, charged with participation in the burning, has resulted in his acquittal. Much interest was felt in this trial and the array of attorneys was extensive.

Christmas week

This week which has had a character of festivity for nine or ten centuries, has come and gone and the days of labor have commenced once more. We believe our citizens indulged in an unusual number of merry meetings and made the most of the festive week. Two balls at the Donoho House and dances innumerable in the country were a part of then enjoyment. We hope all have found the benefit of the recreation and are ready in good spirit to go on with the labor of life for another year.

To our readers, we tender the usual compliments of the season just past and we wish them "a happy new year", although true happiness is a rare felicity and we fear that few will realize it. Much of it must consist, of necessity, in doing to others justly and thereby securing a conscience void of offence. This portion we may all secure to ourselves and then, to the beneficence of Divine Providence, we must look to for the remainder.

Fair at Paris

We see that t the ladies of our neighboring town have had another fair, this time for the benefit of the Female Academy and raised the very handsome sum of $626. Praiseworthy! We are glad of their success.

Paris has had the "go ahead spirit" prevalent, just now and will do well.

Hunt County

From Hunt, we learn they have had a lively Christmas around Greenville, that the weather is cold and that many immigrants are settling in the county.

married

on the 14th of December at the Presbyterian Church at Marshall by the Rev Mr. Dunlap, Hon. William S. Todd of Red River County to Mrs. Mary T. Britt of Harrison County.

The Texas Almanac,

The *Texas Almanac,* published at the offices of the *Galveston News,* is the first attempt in Texas to get up an Almanac compilation after the style of the old American Almanac still published in Boston.

The Almanac has 160 octave pages, is well printed, contains an almanac at the beginning, calculated for the State of Texas, the post offices in the State; the newspapers in the State; statistics of the property of each county; statement of railroad charters; officers of each county of the State; laws relative to attachments, deeds, and wills; biographies of some old Texans and a brief notice of the early history of Texas.

It is well worth the price of 25 cents and every citizen should encourage the continuation and improvement of the work by buying one, aside from the fact that he will easily get 25 cents worth of information from it and will frequently find it convenient for easy reference.

Memphis, El Paso and Pacific Railroad Company

We learn from one o f the Directors that delegates from this Directory and from the Houston and Red River Road, met a few days since and determined the point of junction, within certain bounds and subject to ratification. This will be probably not more that ten or fifteen miles south of the Northern line of Collin County and not further east than the East Fork. Of course, the precise point will be determined by instrumental survey.

died

Judge Lipscomb of the Supreme Court in Austin;

at his residence in Lafayette County, Col. William Wynn in his 74th year, an old Planter, long and favorably known to many of the first settlers in Louisiana and Texas. He had been born in Dinwiddie County, Virginia and emigrated to Arkansas about twenty years ago.

administration of estates

Notice by John M. Bivins, Clerk of Red River County, that Benjamin H. Eppereson and Martin Guest, Administrators of the estate of Martin Guest, deceased, have filed an accounting of the estate.

Notice by John M. Bivins, Clerk of Red River County, that Ann Black, *Administratrix* of the estate of Alexander J. Russell, deceased, has filed an accounting of the estate.

strays

Notice by John M Bivins, Clerk of Red River County, that a horse was taken up by Thomas Harman, living about 16 miles southwest of Clarksville, posted before Henry D. Deberry, Justice of the Peace for precinct No. 6 of that County and appraised by Lewis C. Hancock and Elisha F. Smathers.

Notice by John M. Bivins, Clerk of Red River County that a horse was taken up by John Sexton, living nine miles from Clarksville on Burkhams Creek, posted before James W. Thomas, Justice of the Peace, and been appraised by John Robbins and Preston G. Phillips

From *The Standard,* January 10, 1857

tidbits of wisdom

Among all other features which adorns the female character, delicacy stands foremost;

Learn not to judge too rashly of anyone, either in respect to good or evil, for both are dangerous.

weather

We have had a real winter here. The snow on the ground is about four inches deep.

****

From *The Standard,* January 17, 1857

tidbit of wisdom

The man who is without an idea generally has the greatest idea of himself

we call attention

to the announcement of John C .Taylor as a candidate for Associate Justice of the Supreme Court;

to the advertisement of Dr. J. A. Berry;

to the card of Sutton & Sutton, Attorneys at Law.

river

The *Reub White,* which went up to Jonesboro a week or more ago, has since gone down, taking only 170 bales of cotton from that region, afraid that the depth of the water would not admit of more. We understand that four of five flatboats are getting ready about Kiamitia and Jonesboro to take off the cotton. Two keel boats and two or three flats are, we understand, nearly ready at Roland and we have no doubt that before long, we shall have our rise and the cotton will get off in good time as a fleet of the new steamers will be pushing up, eager to get loads.

the weather

Presently the Ice King holds his scepter over us, for several days and it was not until Monday evening last, that thawing commenced in earnest. The snow from the first was well crusted with sleet, very smooth and very slippery. For six or seven days there might have been good sledding and our boys, who went out, found excellent skating on the creeks.

Wednesday morning. The snow is thawing but is still covering the ground and the crust looks very light and slippery. Many are the falls that careless travelers have had on it. Our old friend, Wm. Tinnin of Lamar, who was down here on a visit broke his arm some two or three days since by a fall upon the crusted snow.

The mails have almost ceased to visit us.

list of letters at Clarksville Post Office

Ayres, Mrs. Caroline	Daniel, J. M.
Anderson, Samuel Bailey	Davidson, Miss E.
Boswell, William	Davidson, L.C.
Benson, Mr.	Elliot, G. F.
Bain, R. M.	Ewing, Dr. J. ...A
Buck, Stephen	Ellis, Stephen.
Carter, A. P.	Franklin, G. W.
Ceck, Valentin	Fleming, William
Dickson, Clement	Galbreath, Samuel C

Good, Rev Mr.
Goff, Thomas
Harris, Mrs. Elizabeth G.
Head, John
Hayes, William
Harris, H C.
Keener, J. M.
Lewis, William N.
Thomas, S. H
Thompson, William S.
Wilson, Miss S.

Welch, M. C
Young, Rev J. D.
Land, J. N.
Seales, Miss
Sherry, P.
Sims, William S.
Smith, D. C.
Shooks, Mr.
Young, W. H.

James W Thomas. Post Master
****

There are no copies available of *The Standard* for January 24, January 31, and February 7, 1857

****

From *The Standard*, February 14, 1857

Templars and Odd Fellows Festivals

By reference to our advertising columns, it can be seen that the Templars are going to have a grand rally, address, dinner etc on the 28th to which they invited the surrounding Templars; and the Odd Fellows are to have a procession, address and dinner on March 2, the Anniversary of the Declaration of Texas Independence.

Memphis, El Paso and Pacific Railroad

The surveyors passed here two or three days since, the line running about half a mile north of the court house. We have not had the time this week to notice the progress of the work.

jail escape

Our correspondent at Tarrant, Hopkins county writes Yuhance, who was committed to jail for killing A. Goldman, has given bail and is now at liberty. Holliday, who was committed on stealing a yoke of oxen and is Yuhance's bed fellow, broke the jail door a few nights since and made his escape to parts unknown.

we call attention

to the advertisement of J. B. Shanahan, long known to our citizens as a cabinet maker, who was so unfortunate as to lose largely by the late fire. Anyone who wants work in his line, will, we thinks find his prices very moderate.

Red River

The river in this part has risen several feet this past week. The *Reub White*, which had been aground just below Rowland, went down on Thursday. The *Union,* which got 800 bales at our landing and had been lying there some days, went down on Thursday and the *Erie* has been up and gone down within a day or two.

Democratic meeting in Bowie

At a public meeting was held at the courthouse in Bowie regarding gubernatorial election, John Loop was called to the Chair and Col. John H. Smither as Secretary. The Chairman then appointed a committee to draft resolutions [regarding the nomination of H. R. Runnels for Governor] composed of S. H. Pirkey, John A. Talbot, N. B. Patton, R. .J. Battle and Jacob McFarland.

The following gentlemen were named delegates to the Waco Convention: J. A. Talbot, D. M. Chisolm, S. H. Pirkey, S. H. Ellis, and William Moore.

conventions

In our columns this week will be found a call to the Public Meetings of the Democracy at the Courthouse of this County, on

Saturday the first week of Court, to send delegates to Waco and Tyler. This thing should be attended to and men who go who will express the will of the country.

****

From *The Standard*, February 21, 1857

small pox rumors unfounded

We understand that Mr. Fleming, living on Pine Creek in this county and lately returned from New Orleans is down with the small pox and that three or four other persons, living in that vicinity, have caught the infection. They have all been brought together and measures taken to prevent, if possible, the spread of the diseases. Nothing of this sort and no other sickness worth mentioning is prevalent in this Town. The place is entirely healthy and the doctors underemployed. The proprietors of the Donoho House has a notice in our columns, some report having gone ahead that the small pox was in the house or was likely to be. There is no truth in that rumor.

the river

Red River commenced rising last week. The *Reub White*, having unloaded at Fulton, went up to Kiamitia on Monday. The river is now bank full and said to be rising; there are reports of other boats up. If not now, we presume several will be up in a day or so.

come to the festival

All Surrounding Subordinate, Social and Degree Temples and all Templars in good standing are earnestly solicited to attend and take part in the festivities of the occasion.

Come One, Come All. Let us have such a grand demonstration as will not only make the Friends of Temperance proud of our great strength, but cause the votaries of old King Alcohol to tremble for the safety and stability of his Kingdom.

M. H. Partain

no small pox here

Understanding there is a rumor about, to the injury of my house, that a stranger stopped in infected with small pox and communicated that disease, I wish to state that the person who passed through town a few days since, and who has since been taken down by the disease at his house in Pine Creek *did not stop* at my house; nor is there any small pox at this place. I give this notice so that travelers may not be deterred by the report from coming to the Donoho House.

                      Mary W. Donoho

                      ****

From *The Standard*, February 28, 1857

we call attention to

the notice of S. J. Moore for County Treasurer;

to the advertisement of T. B. Hearn for two lost horses.

Red River District Court

On Monday next, the District Court for the County, the first of the Circuit, commences its session.

moving

the Hon. William S. Todd is about to move to Jefferson and wishes all communications be directed to him there.

tobacco planting

We have always believed that tobacco may be successfully raised here but have been told that the climate was not sufficiently humid enough in the summer. In Jasper county, we have been informed that a very fine quality of Cuba smoking tobacco has been raised.

In 1843, we think it was, the late Dr. Smith of Bowie brought from Cuba some seed, which his brother, Judge Smith, tried the cultivation of, but that did not come up. Year before last, some fine Cuban tobacco seed was sent to us by the patent office and was divided among several old tobacco raisers, who took much care in planting, but did not get them to germinate.

We are probably too far north for the successful cultivation of Cuban tobacco, but the quality raised in Kentucky and Virginia, it seems to us, should grow here.

the weather

After continued showers, Spring has set in very auspiciously; she comes after a dreary winter which in this region was unusually cold.

Our farmers can plant their spring crops early and the cattle upon the prairie which have which have suffered seriously from the severity of the weather and scanty herbage, will especially feel the benefit of the grateful change of temperature and the general warmth of the sun's rays.

The plum and peach trees are in flower and the weeping willow has its long graceful branches clothed with green.

the river

The river is within six feet of the top of the bank in Rowland and rising. Nearly all the cotton in this region is shipped. The *Erie* passed up to Kiamitia yesterday morning. A barge built by Captain Moore at Rowland during the summer leaves on Sunday morning for Shreveport loaded with cotton.

friendship among boys

It is very beautiful to see the friendship of little boys. There is more friendship at that time of life than any other. The grown up man is like a fortress angular shaped with a moat around it standing alone.

groceries

J. M. and J. C. Murphy advertise their large brick warehouse at the steam boat landing in Jefferson, where there is a large stock of groceries, bagging and rope always available.

professional card

R. W. B. Oliver. Attorney at Law, with his office in Gainsesville, Cooke County.

****

From *The Standard*, March 7, 1857

we call attention

to the legal card of Turner L. Green, late of Hopkins County who has removed to Bonham;

to the advertisement of C. C. Alexander, of Bonham for a two horse Allen power thresher and separator, almost new;

to the advertisement of C. A. Bulkley's new grocery establishment at Jefferson.

thank you

We are indebted to our townsman Thomas R. Wilson for the late New Orleans papers;

We are also indebted to our friend W. T. Thayer of Greenville for New Orleans papers.

District Court

The Court will terminate its session tomorrow night by lapse of time, the docket not nearly been disposed of by trial. Some tedious cases have been on hand and much new and some old business lies over to the next term. Bell charged with the killing of Jones has changed venue to Lamar County.

celebrations

The Odd Fellows and the Templars, have each had a procession, address etc. since our last issue. Both societies made a good appearance with respect to regalia, but both had small processions, compared with the size of the orders. There is a lack of zeal in these public celebrations in our community. We suppose it is not sufficiently aroused by a richness of display. Gorgeous dress and appointments and fine music, of which last we are very destitute, would bring out a more imposing display of numbers.

shooting

On Sunday last, after the issuance of our paper, we were informed that Parson Jones, a statement of whose elopement from Paris with another man's wife and fraudulent conduct towards his creditors we had previously copied from the *Lamar Enquirer,* had been shot on the street by Mr. Bell, the brother of the runaway wife. We went down to the scene of the act on the street before the saddler's shop adjoining the Clarksville Hotel. Here we saw the body of Jones lying as it had fell, a ghastly sight with eyes and mouth open upon its back with one leg drawn up. We had not before seen the man to recognize him. His glassy eyes had a bad expression and his color was not good. The features were those of a man without a soul. The reverend and hypocrite – the wolf in sheep's clothing - had gone to his last account without a word of repentance or time for a thought about the future. It was a ghastly and disagreeable sight and, as much as we condemned the man and his acts, for surely there is no lower depth to reach than he who debases the profession of religion to the basest worldly and carnal purposes, yet the impression necessarily forced upon the mind for several hours had a mixture of horror and disgust, anything but agreeable. The parties were all strangers here and we would have preferred if the act was to be perpetrated, they had found some other locality for its performance. For three or four hours the body lay upon the street to the discredit of our Town under the mistaken assumption that it should not be moved until the coroner could attend to it and hold an inquest and the coroner was in the country and did not get in until the afternoon. Then it was taken up decently cared for and interred at night, being put in the ground carefully and with all due attention.

The mode of occurrence as it has been authentically conveyed to us was as follows. Jones who had been acquitted by the District Court of any offence against our criminal laws had been ready to get off and had been with Judge Mills in connection with giving a power of attorney on his property and his indebtedness in Paris. He had just come down with Judge Mills from the room of the latter, in the second story of the Hotel, and was standing a moment before the saddler's shop talking with the judge, when Bell came out of the shop, passed around the Judge and, putting a pistol close to the back of Jones, shot him, the shot passing through his breast and probably taking the heart with it in its course. Just about the time the shot was fired, the miserable man discovered his assailant and prepared to run but had not time. He wheeled around and said "I am a dead man" and, as the Judge thinks, was dead before he hit the ground. The Helen of the tragedy – the woman who had eloped with him –and who was on the porch, hearing the gun shot came out and inquired the cause was answered and went back in tears and took to her bed. She has since left for Tennessee.

Bell ran out of town, was followed and captured in the field of J. O. Carter but a short distance out.

Jones has left a wife and children in Paris. His previous employment, as we have come to learn, has been checkered with misconduct, if not criminal, but he had succeeded in imposing himself upon the good people of Paris as a teacher of the word of God. Such a fate needs little comment to impress upon the mind that sooner or later, the avenging spirit in some form will have compensation for the evil acts that were done and, even in this world, bad men are made to feel that partially successful crime is closely followed by the mocking fiends of Scorn, Shame and Misery of the mind, if not bodily punishment.

Red River

The river is still high and a boat was expected up yesterday. From George Reeves, Esq., from Grayson County, we learn that the river was very full at Preston and that the water came from above Washita.

Red River County Democratic meeting

at a Democratic meeting at the Courthouse in Clarksville, Red River County, the following proceedings were had:

On the motion of Simpson H. Morgan, the Hon. William S. Todd was selected as Chair and, at the suggestion of J. C. Hart, he explained in a brief and concise manner the object of the meeting. C.B. Sutton was selected to be Secretary of the meeting.

Upon the motion of John C. Burks, a committee of seven were chosen to prepare resolutions of the meeting regarding nominations for Governor. The committee was comprised of L. D. Henderson, James W. Sims, James Gilliam, H. R. Latimer, John C. Burks, Dr. George Gordon and Edward West.

Delegates selected for the convention were John C. Burks, William Hooks, Col. L. D. Henderson, William P. Cornelius; Judge J. B. Wooten, R. B. Rodgers, J. C. Hart, David Fullbright, and James Gilliam.

The Committee requested that Major DeMorse publish the resolutions in *The Standard.*

****

From *The Standard,* March 14, 1857

women's rights

A women and four daughters, all residing in Northampton Massachusetts have had 17 husbands among them. The mother had four, one daughter also four and three each for the others three.

we have been requested

by the friends of Courtes H. Sutton to announce him as a candidate for the Lower House of the State Legislature

we are indebted to

the Hon. T. J. Rusk for sundry public documents and for seed;

to the Hon. L. Barbour for the *Congressional Globe.*

we call attention

to the advertisement of B. F. Thompson, Watchmaker and Jeweler;

to the advertisement for cattle for sale by N. B. Paxton of Bowie;

to the card of Sommes and Hill, New Orleans. Mr. Hill, the well known Texas member of the firm, has had a practice of 18 or 20 years in this state with the highest character for legal capability and integrity. Of course, any of our citizens, who my have legal business in New Orleans, would find him the very best person to consult with, or to act on the accomplishment of their objectives. Mr. Hill will in the future reside near New Orleans as he has an office in th City. No member of the Bar of this state has had a more desirable reputation and he will doubtless achieve eminence in the profession in his new home.

Bowie

The Editor has been in Bowie County nearly all week. Not much business was done for the reason that the parties to the most important suits were not ready. The weather became very cold at the close of last week and has remained so to the present time so that persons in attendance at the court were quite uncomfortable excepting on the inside. Most of the cotton of Bowie has been shipped.

Red River

The river is falling, but still sufficient for small boats. The *Hope* came up yesterday.

Grayson Democratic meeting

A large and respectful meeting of the Democrats of Grayson County was held at the Courthouse Tuesday the 3rd instant, for the purpose of appointing delegates to the Democratic State Convention to be held at Waco on the fourth of May next.

On the motion of Col. H. F. Young, B.P. Smith was selected as Chairman and G. W. Hobson as Secretary. In a few brief and remarks, the Chairman explained the objects of the meeting.

On motion, the following gentlemen were appointed a committee James H. Clark, W. D. Fitch, W. Thompson and William G. Reynolds.

After retiring a few minutes, they reported the following which were unanimously adopted by the convention:

Resolved, first, that for the office of Governor Col. M. T. Johnson is our first choice.

Resolved, second, that for the office of Lieutenant Governor, the Hon. M. W. Allen of Collin County is our first choice.

Delegates s selected to attend the Convention were H. F. Young, James Clark, B. P. Smith, James Ward, Coleman Watson, G. W. Hobson and William E. Saunder.

Cooke and Wise Counties

Dear Editor

To while away a leisure hour I give you some inklings of this locality (Gainesville)and the neighboring county of Wise. On Sunday morning last, we left the capitol of Cooke and wended our way westward. The weather, which had been for the last several days dripping, windy and stormy, was now calm clean and delightful.

From the crossing at Elm Fork, near Gainesville, to Clear Creek we rode over a firm body of prairie crossing several creeks and branches whose borders were covered with timber. On following the courses of the stream, the growth of timber is thick and what appears at a distance to be a narrow strip, upon near approach, proves to be rich valley, varying from a quarter to one or more miles in width. This particularly is the case of Clear Creek and its tributaries.

We saw a herd of beautiful antelope, ten in number, on a highpoint of prairie near Wadsworth Bluff, a romantic and picturesque eminence rising abruptly from the edge and a retired looking valley, to an elevation of some hundred feet behind which the broad and undulating surface of the fertile prairie extends for miles, are favorite feeding haunts for antelope. They seem to be ever on watch. We had not approached them nearer than half a mile, when they elevated their heads, moved restlessly about and gazed at us apparently smelling the "tainted gale"; then as we gradually neared, they trotted to and fro, arranging themselves in a line, fronting us and as our near approach, suddenly wheeled in line and in perfect order, bounded away.

We soon arrived at Cloud Spring, a clear cool delicious stream flowing from the side of a rocky hill out of a rock spout in the edge of the prairie.

Evening found myself and one fellow travelers (the other having pressed onward) stopped at the residence of Mr. Lowery on Hart's Creek where we were welcomed and cared for, both man and beast, with the hearty hospitality of an old Texian.

During the night, it rained and the next morning, I wended my way across the pathless, roadless and almost trackless prairie, until we arrived at Howels Store, or rather Taylorsville, the new county seat of Wise. There are no buildings as of yet, except a Courthouse, which is finely situated upon a rolling prairie. There has recently been a sale of town lots at Taylorsville at which 27 lots were sold, averaging $75 each. Pretty good for a new county. Night found me at the hospitable mansion of Col. A. Bishop, County Clerk of Wise County, where I was entertained in a style not usually found in a frontier country - physically at his beautiful table and mentally by his extensive and varied information about men and business. He informed that there has, as of yet, not been a term of the Probate Court in Wise County and says the reason is because no one dies and there are no estates to be settled up and hence there is no business for a Chief Justice in Probate. Wise is settling up and now votes some 300.

Today there was a severe hail storm here. A public meeting is to be held on the 8th of next month to nominate a candidate for the next Legislature and appoint delegates to the Waco Convention. Johnson is clearly the choice of this and neighboring counties. I will write again soon.

R.W. B.O[25]

****

There are no copies available of the *Clarksville Standard* from March 21, 1856 through August 29, 1856 although those issues were published

****

From *The Standard,* September 5, 1857

District Court

The District Court, W. S. Todd presiding, opened on Monday last and had preceded with the business which will occupy all the two week period allowed by law for the term at this place. It has mostly been taken up with old cases.

new postoffice

There is a new post office, called Spencer, established at the house of Moses Lipe in this county, twelve miles east of Clarksville on the Mill Creek road.

we are indebted

On Saturday night last, to Mr. Henry Nathan for New Orleans newspapers of the Saturday previous but too late to avail ourselves of its contents for that day's publication.

The Alamo Ranger

Upon our first page and running over to the fourth will be found in interesting detail the experience of the company raised in San Antonio for Nicaragua. We suppose it is a fair specimen of the Nicaraguan filibuster experience[26] – hard fare, physical suffering and continual mortification. The greatest hardship of soldiers life everywhere is not the result of battles but of camp disease resulting from bad food, filth and exposure. Disease in campaigns of much duration carry off four for everyone who dies in actual conflict.

beef packing

We refer our readers, especially producers, to the advertisement under this heading in our columns. Mr. Black writes to us that he is engaged in the beef packing enterprise experimentally at Shreveport last winter and satisfied himself that it could be done with success. We hope to see it success extensively. It will open a home market for beef which will lessen the dependence of our stock raises upon the New Orleans market. There will be less uncertainty in this. The producer can always know what his cattle will bring at Jefferson as sometimes prices are very seriously and unfavorably affected by a full supply in New Orleans and has to sell at prices not remunerative.

The Chinese sugar cane – promising.

The results already received from the cultivation of this crop in Texas are very favorable. In our own county, syrup has been so successfully made from it as to yield a large profit. We hope that some of our readers will report directly to us, stating everything in relation to the growth of the plant and the precise results in syrup where the juice has been extracted.

We have a small patch in our garden, which has grown well and d matured seeds. The quantity is too small for experimentation on the juice. We have cut some of the tops to let it seed again, as it is said it will, and we have planted two or three weeks since, from the seed of the first crop, to see how a second crop from seed would mature. This last planting is about 3 inches high.

crops

We learn since our last that the river crops in the upper part of the county are not yet injured and give promise of good product, if the season from this point forward be favorable. Further down the river in this county and in Bowie, they are already considered injured to one third of the crop. The stalks are as high as the head of an ordinary man on horseback and the branches of stalks in rows six feet apart interlink.

In the prairie, the rains have injured the prospects.

burglary

On Monday night, the grocery store of W. F. T. Hart was entered into and money robbed of about 450 dollars. The robber, in opening the box with the blade of his knife, left the point of the blade in the box. This was preserved and, on Tuesday night, the pocket knife of a carpenter named Hampton, who was suspected, being observed by a fellow workman with the point freshly broken off. Comparison was made with the point left in the box and they fitted. Upon this, Hampton was arrested, confessed, went to the place of deposit, dug up the money and delivered it, and was confined, on Thursday evening, and is now, we believe, indicted, in conjunction with the Negro man Jeff, the property of Reason Ragin, who is reported as the principal contriver and manager of the robbery.

we call attention

to the advertisement C. C. Alexander in Bonham. Their stock is the largest in Northern Texas;

to the card of Reece Hughes at Jefferson who offers for sale a very extensive stock of goods.

administration of estates

Matthew Armstrong and Sarah Mossington are appointed Administrators of the estate of Charles Mossington, deceased, of Hopkins County;

to be sold at the residence of the late Isaac H. Fishback, one half mile south of Town, 70 head of fine good horses of superior blood; notice by Elizabeth Fishback, *administrarix*.

married

on the 31st dy of August, at the residence of R. M. Hopkins by the Rev. A. M. Stone, Dr. Jasper A. Barry to Miss Mary A.. Hopkins.

not married any longer

Notice by James Crowder of Tarrant that his wife Mary Crowder has eloped and left his bed and board and not to trust said Mary Crowder on his account as he will not be responsible.

wanted

Notice by R. C. Sherril that he wants to employ two or three journeymen tinners at his Tin shop in Paris. Good wages will be given.

property for sale in Bonham

Notice by A. H. Trueblood of a desirable piece of property in Bonham for sale with nearly half a block on the south side of the pubic square. The house is large enough to accommodate 18 -20 borders and a good boarding house is much needed in that place. There is also a good stable and crib attached to the place; also an excellent garden spot.

professional card

Notice by Dr. Alfred Hall that he has opened an office in Bonham and that special attention will be given to all cases requiring surgical skill.

schools opening

Notice by E. F. Gibson, Principal and M. J. Gattis and M. R. Gattis, Assistants, for the Clarksville Female Academy that the twelfth session of the institution will commence on the 21st of September;

Notice by Wm. B. Fetherstone, Principal that the Milam Male and Female Academy resumed the first day of September and will end with examinations in the last week of June;

Notice that the Clarksville Male and Female Institute will resume under the direction of Rev. John Anderson, Principal and Mrs. M. M. Anderson, Vice principal;

Bonham Male Academy will begin its third session under the charge of B. F. Fuller as Principal;

The third annual session of ten months will commence at Bonham Female Institute on Monday, October 5. It is our design to have thorough instruction given in all the English branches, Latin, Greek, French German as well as vocal and instrument music, drawing and painting. For further particulars, address A. E. Pace, C. C. Alexander, S.A. Roberts. and S. E. Brownell, Principal.

new mail stage

from Washington, Arkansas to the Mississippi River at Gaines Landing. It will connect with the Clarksville and other stage lines; notice by Beman and Co.

builder

advertisement by S. Flemington, house carpenter and joiner and stair builder. He will also make running gear for gins, mills and cotton presses; his residence is five miles south est of Clarksville.

items for sale

advertisement by Davis Bro. and Bayless in Paris, that they have received for sale spring and summer goods;

by A. S. Kottwitz in Paris, groceries, shoes and boots, bagging and rope; also china, silks, brocades, tissue; carpenters and wagon maker tools, iron steel and castings and ready made clothing. Call and examine the largest stock in this region of the country of superior quality and make;

carriage and buggy harnesses for sale at Darnall and Dickson of Paris;

William M. Ewing & Bro, in Tarrant, Hopkins County have for sale staple and fancy goods;

W. M. Kelly of Tarrant has on hand and wishes to sell at low rates an excellent general assortment of merchandise;

merchandise for sale at Sulphur Spring, Hopkins County, by Bullion & Connally dealers in dry goods and groceries, whole sale or retail;

thoroughbred Hector for sale by T. F. Titus, in Savannah, Red River County;

advertisement by Bagby, Corey & Co. of staples, groceries, ready made clothing, hats, hardware. Call at the house formerly occupied by Darnall and Hunt

Just arrived - Gilbert Ragin has just received direct from New Orleans, per the steamer *Erie,* and opened on his old stand on the west of the Courthouse Square in Clarksville, a large assortment of dry goods and groceries.

advertisement by Wilson & Jackson cheapest goods sold in the market. Come and try us.

new drug store
in Tarrant, Barry & Moore are receiving complete assortment of drugs, medicines, dye stuff, paints, oils, tobaccos with every variety of perfume and family toilet articles, together with an assortment of fine wine, brandies, lemon syrup and other articles usually kept in drug stores.

house painter
R Wright, house sign and ornamental painter and plasterer; is located in Bonham, Fannin County.

tombstone maker
T. M. Coulter, tombstones, monuments and every article belonging to the stone cutting business.

sawing and flouring mill
Notice by J. C. Parrish of his steam, sawing and flouring mill at Eclectic Grove near Warren, Fannin County.

eye doctor
Dr. Lafayette Yates of Louiseville Kentucky is now located in

Paris where he will give his undivided attention to treating diseases of the eyes.

livery stable

advertisement by T. B. Edmundson of his livery stable in Paris. He has single and double buggies, hacks, horse wagons and saddle horses at a moment's notice at the establishment he has fitted up and is prepared to accommodate travelers and residents.

Cooke County land for sale

by Henry Morris, 400 acres on Red River in Cooke county two miles below James Bourland, 160 acres of which is in a high state of cultivation. The place was first settled and improved by Thomas Ragsdale.

house in Paris for sale

by John T Mills, his residence in the town of Paris, also 6 acres of land a mile east of Town and immediately on the Clarksville road. There are 8 acres in Town on which there is a fine dwelling house, two story and six rooms, kitchen, store house, well, cistern and stable.

****

From *The Standard,* September 12, 1857

Chinese Sugar cane

Our subscriber in Fannin county, Sam Johnson, sent us a vial of molasses by mail, which strikes us as being very rich and having the taste of the sugar house molasses. We have extracted notices form several of our exchanges of successful production of good syrup.

District Court

The Court got through all but the motion docket yesterday morning and was not held yesterday evening. Everything that was ready has been tried and next Court we shall have an easy docket.

Hampton indicted for robbery was found guilty and sentenced to one year in the penitentiary. The Negro Jeff, indicted as a conspirator, was acquitted.

Attorneys from abroad in attendance at the Court were William H. Johnson and Malcolm Bolin of Titus, John T. Mils, Wm. M. Williams, Wm. B. Wright and Wm. H. Millwee of Lamar; Robert H. Lane and Samuel A. Roberts of Fannin and S. H. Pirkey of Bowie.

Dalby's Spring

Advertisement by Warren K. Dalby that his place of summer resort has been lately much improved and visitors are invited with an assurance of comfortable quarter. The main house has been greatly enlarged and improved and several cabins will be constructed in the course of the month; for horses there will be plenty of feed.

The water of the Springs is already notable and has fine medical qualities for diseases of the skin, old sores, dyspepsia, diseases of the kidneys and the water has been sufficiently tried and proven invariably efficacious. It is a light yellow color, exceedingly pleasant to drink and can be drunk in large quantities.

Paris Hotel

notice by R. B. Francis, Proprietor. His house is large and commodious with as good stables as any in the State.

Sulphur Springs Hotel

Mrs. Price having recently taken charge of this establishment, has fitted it up and is prepared to accommodate travelers and residents.

strayed or stolen

from Daniel P. Moss living near Kentucky Town in Grayson

county, 15 head of horses;

from L. W. Arnold, living three miles northwest of Alton, on Hickory Creek, Denton County, a large brown mare mule.

a chance to double your money

D. C. Russell now offers to sell off, wholesale or retail, his new and complete assortment of goods in Clarksville.

****

From *The Standard*, September 19, 1857

crime

Crime is shockingly prevalent throughout the country. Our exchanges are full of the grossest outrages for which the perpetrators frequently go unpunished. The great defect is that there is none of the certainty in our criminal system which exists in Great Britain, whether the wrongdoing be by high or low, rich or poor, it will inevitably be punished if discovered and that the probability for the discovery of the perpetrators, would be very strong. Outrages of the gravest possible character upon defenseless women are almost daily occurring in the cities and we believe that great number of cases go unpunished.. The papers are filled with them. Killing is almost as common as any other exercise.

Bowie County

The editor of this paper returned last night from Bowie Court. Court opened on Monday. Hon. W. Todd , presiding and will adjourn this evening. Attorneys from other counties in attendance at the court were Col W.R. Hill of New Orleans, Samuel F. Mosely of Cass, John T. Mills of Lamar, S. H. Morgan and J. C. Burks of Red River. Most of the heavy cases were laid over, parties not ready for trial.

Crops of cotton in Bowie are in an uncertain condition, large, stalky but the amount of yield to be determined by the season. If it continues wet, the yield cannot be large. If it would cease to rain and there would be a prevalence of wind to dry the ground and the underparts of the plants, the cop may be very good yet. The corn crop has been moderate in quantity.

Boston is to have new hotel before next Court – a large new building and one is now erecting in DeKalb. DeKalb is improving and will be a neat little village in a year or two more. What houses there will be in two years will be all neat structures.

died

on the 9th inst. of congestive chill, Ida, infant daughter of B. F. and Flora Fuller, of Bonham, aged three months.

Bonham Female Academy

The third session of the Institute will commence October 5; S. E. Brownell, MA, Principal; Prof. Charles Pistor, teacher of Music, French, German and General Assistant. Mr. Joaquin Cuadras, artist, teacher of drawing, painting, Spanish and chirography; Messrs. Pistor and Cuadras were both educated in Europe.

Washburn's Southern Circus

The only legitimate circus of the season, embracing a variety of talent, will exhibit at Clarksville Tuesday the 22 of September and thereafter at Paris, Honey Grove, Bonham, Sherman and McKinney. Among the equestrian, acrobatic and gymnastic performers, the following may be found standing at the head of the profession and unequaled throughout the southern Country:

Jean Johnson the most wonderful somersault Rider of the Age, having at the present time no equal in America;

A.F. Aymar of the celebrated Aymar brothers will appear in daring and fancy acts;

Masters Washburn and William and several others in their acts of *La perch equipoise* [27] and on the Double bridge of Ropes;

Stump speeches by the clowns comics and local songs;
Doors open at 2 ½ and 7 ½ p.m.;
admittance: 50 cents; children and servants 25cents.

suit for divorce
notice by W. H. Christian, Clerk of Titus County, that a lawsuit has been begun by Nancy Anne Coffee, maiden name Nancy Lee Roder, for divorce. He alleges that she was legally married to Langston Coffee in the state of Alabama, but that he abandoned her in 1852.

horses for sale
notice by B. D. Alford that he has for sale a fine lot of mares, American, Spanish and California, some good horses and young mules, in all forty to sixty head.

runaway
Notice by Squire Stevens of Pittsburg of Upshur County of runaway Negro boy named Judge; about six feet; 20 years old; of a black complexion; rather high cheek bones, high forehead, slender built and will wight about 155 to 160 pound. He will probably deny his name and owner.

Clarksville Female Academy
12th session starts September 21. E. F. Gibson is Principal, M. J. Gattis and M. R. Gattis are his Assistants.

private piano school
opened by D. Danforth at the residence of Dr. J. R. Lyons in Clarksville.

professional card

Alfred Hall, M. D., permanently located in Bonham and tenders his services to residents of that town and the surrounding county.

****

From *The Standard,* September 26, 1857

Washburn's Circus

This establishment got here on Tuesday last and has been performing every night since, generally to good audiences. The performers are better than any that have been here before. The stable of horses is not extensive enough for great displays but the Equestrian, the Herculean and Acrobatic feats, and the witticisms of the clown, Jean Johnson, are excellent. Those who have not seen them would do well to attend tonight and those who have might lend assistance to some worthy men, who have been unfortunate of late. It is the last chance. Go and see them.

newspaper business

Mr. Hollis, Post Master, Comanche Peak, Johnson County is authorized to act as agent for *The Standard.*

party

A complimentary party was given by the ladies in vicinity of Roland in this county to our Representative Col. Burks and it came off with great zest on Tuesday night, at the Sulphur Springs near the river. It was a large party and good music and an inviting table. A large number of ladies and gentlemen went from Town.

valuable land for sale

by W. W. Marler of one of the most valuable tracts of land in North Texas, containing 325 acres, three miles south of Pine Bluff, Red River County. Every acre of the tract is good principal growth of Black Walnut, Sumac and large hickory; this land is well watered and healthy and situated in a good neighborhood; see the subscriber at Kiamitia or B. H. Perkinson at Pine Bluff.

taken up as strays

Notice by Josh Stephens, County Clerk, Titus county that taken up by J. G. Harris and posted before James Welch, Justice of the Peace of Titus County, a sorrel horse about 15 hands high; appraised by Wilson Bryan and L. Lawrence Scott; another, a 14 year old pony, also taken up by Mr. Harris, was appraised by E. W Terry and Wilson Bryan.

by N. C. Erwin and posted before W. T. Wite, Justice of the Peace of Titus, a mare and colt; appraised by L. Willis and J. S. Sheck;

by Wm. S. Riddle and posted before M.. Bolin, Justice of the Peace of Titus County, a work ox; appraised by John L. Riddle and F. G. Barnhart.

****

From *The Standard,* October 3, 1857

the crops

We imagine that at this point it is a matter to be determined by the rains and the boll worm, that the cotton crops in northen Texas and Arkansas will be hardly more than half crops. A very late frost and dry windy weather hereafter might do much to increase the crop, but we do not look for a full one.

With cotton at its present price and rising and the certainty of a generally short crop, we shall not have cause to complain. We have experienced the beneficence of Providence in generous grain crop and our Northern counties may be considered in flourishing condition. We presume there will be a large immigration this year. There never was a better time for it. Those who wait a year or two hence will pay largely increased prices for land. The upward tendency of the country and the progress of the railroad will push prices upward.

Star Mills at Sulphur Springs

We call attention to the advertisement of the Star Mills at Sulphur Springs Hopkins county. We have had occasion to notice them before. They manufacture the very best quality of flour and the establishment is a credit to the region in which it is located. For the country contiguous and the counties west trading to Jefferson, they must be a great convenience from the celerity as well as excellency with which they grind wheat. The advertisement is by Fathered & Bingham; with praise to D. W. Lowe and P. Brown "our engineer and chief miller."

died

On the 22nd of September, aged two years and eight months after a lingering illness at their residence near Bonham, Fannin County, William George, son of Alexander and Martha M. Johnson, formerly of Austin.

"And who shall receive one such little child in my name, receiveth me " Matthew chap 18, verse 3

"And when the Lord saw her he had compassion on her and said to her 'Weep not'" Luke chap 7, verse 13

Little Willie slumbers sweetly
in his lonely narrow bed.
Pelting storm and howling tempests
cannot reach his little head.
Sweet affection drops a tear
over the spot where William lies
Angels whisper "Look ye yonder"
Pointing upwards to the sky.
Put away his little playthings

Yonder lies his little whip.
On the table lies his whistle.
Oft he pressed it to his lips.
Oh, remove these sad memorials.
Lay them careful away.
Christ be thou our consolation
in the dark and gloomy day.
Little Willie slumbers sweetly
in his lonely narrow bed.
Pelting storms and howling tempests
cannot reach his little head.
On that bright and glorious morning
Christ will whisper from above.
Rise my child and let me dress thee
in robes of white and spotless love.

In Bonham the 18th instant T. C. F. Green, infant son of T. L. and M. L. F. Green, aged 10 months and 7 days:

"Why art you doomed sweet flower:
It is because thy beauty is too bright?
Thou has but one short hour
to spread thy fair leaves to the enamored light.
T' is the loved and loveliest first decay.
But there remembrance may not pass a way.

administration of estates
David B. Pritchett appointed Administrator of the estate of Blewitt Stewart of Red River County.

Beef packing

I will give liberal prices in cash for all good heavy fat beef cattle delivered to me at the town of Jefferson throughout the months of November, December and the first part of January ensuing.

Having made ample preparation for slaughter and packing, I shall be able to consume 40 to 45 beeves per day.

R. H. Black, Tarrant, Hopkins County

reward for capture of arsonist

$3000 reward will be paid by the Board of Underwriters of New Orleans for the apprehension and conviction of the person or persons who set fire to the store of Rhines & Bros. on the morning of August 1, 1857.

John Yournes

stray

from John Womble in Bowie County, south of Dalby Springs, two oxen.

****

From *The Standard*, October 10, 1857

moral advice

Blessings which we have slighted ,when in our possession, are more highly prized when we are in danger of getting deprived of them. And our hearts are more keenly touched by the anticipation of loss than by the fullness of enjoyment.

drugs

Purchasers will be careful to ask for Dr. M'Lean's celebrated vermifluge. They and his celebrated liver pills can be had at Wooten & Lyon sin Clarksville.

stray

taken up by Jonathan Jobe and brought before Joseph G. Dalby Justice of the Peace in Bowie, a bay mare; it was appraised by W. R. Dalby and William M. Wood; notice by P. M. Duke, County Clerk for Bowie County.

professional cards

Johnson Williams & Townes with offices in Titus and Lamar Counties;

Notice by Mills & Mills, John T. Mills and Sumter R. Mills, that T. L. Green has removed to Bonham and will in the future devote his time to his profession;

Dillahunty & Wright, Attorneys and Counselors at Law: offices in Clarksville and Paris; will practice in all the courts of the 8th Judicial District and in the Supreme Court; Hervey Dillahunty is at the Clarksville office and William B. Wright in Paris;

Hardin Hart, Attorney and Counselor at Law: office in Greenville, Hunt County; will practice in the 8th and 9th Judicial Districts;

John C. Magee, Attorney and Counselor at Law: office in Gainesville, Cooke County: will give prompt attention to all business trusted to his care. Particular attention given to collection; charges moderate;

James H. Clark, Attorney and Counselor at Law; will practice in 16th Judicial District and Supreme Court in Austin: office at Sherman, Grayson County;

John J. Good, Attorney and Counselor at Law; will practice in the courts of Collin, Grayson, Cooke, Denton, Wise, Parker, Johnson,

Ellis, Tarrant and in the Supreme Court of the State in Austin: office in Dallas.

R. H. Lane, Attorney and Counselor at Law: office in Boston Bowie; will practice in the 8th Judicial District; in the Supreme Court in Austin and in the Federal Court in Tyler;

C. A. Farber, Attorney and Counselor at Law: office in Boston; will practice in the 8th Judicial District; in the Supreme Court in Austin and in the Federal Court in Tyler;

R. W. B. Oliver, Attorney and Counselor at Law: office at Gainesville, Cooke County

Weaver & Weaver, Attorneys and Counselors at Law: office at Gainesville, Cooke County

William H. Johnson Attorney and Counselor at Law and General Land Agent: office at Mt. Pleasant, Titus County;

Bushrod W. Musgrove, Attorney and Counselor at Law: office in Jefferson;

John C. Burks, Attorney and Counselor at Law: office in Clarksville;

Thomas Lewellen Attorney and Counselor at Law: office at McKinney;

John C. Easton, Attorney and Counselor at Law: office at McKinney; will make collections and attend to land claims in Collin, Dallas, Ellis, Tarrant, Denton, Cooke, Grayson, Wise,

Parker and Johnson counties;

Thomas Willison, Attorney and Counselor at Law: office at Tarrant, Hopkins County;

Sutton and Sutton, Attorneys and Counselors at Law: will practice in 8th Judicial District; Norbonne Sutton and Courtes B. Sutton: office in Kiamitia, Red River County;

E. D. McKenney Attorney and Counselor at Law: office at Tarrant, Hopkins County

John A. Summers: Attorney and Counselor at Law: office at Jefferson.

list of letters at Clarksville Post office

Clarksville Advocate	Campbell, James
Austin, William K.	Campbell, D.
Avanta, Cary or John	Cummings, Rev.
Bankston, James	Condon, Jackson
Ballard, W. W.	Collins, J. W.
Ballard, Miss Mary	Clark, E. T.
Bible, L. T.	Crawford, W.
Baker, Gwen	Collard, W. E.
Bilge, Dr. J. H.	Cone, John
Brown, J. P.	Conner, Wesley
Bryan, Benjamin	Cummings, H.
Baggett, John M.	Chandler, E.
Butler, Miss Martha	Dunn, Miss Harriet

Daniel, T.
Day, Miss Clarinda
Day, Miss Mary E.
Doyle, James
Dickson, Miss F.
Duke, Col. William J.
Drake, Thomas
Elkin, P.
Evans, Henry
Evans, H. C.
Embry, H. J.
Epperson, William
Echols, Benjamin R.
Edmonson, K.
Ferrett, John
Rarrar, Edwin
Furlong, Dr. Luther K.
Fisher, M.
Fisher, M. W.
Fuller, John W
Gaines, Gen. H. H.
Gage, W. W.
Griffiths, Josiah
Hartell, Franklin
Hervey, James W.
Hawkins, Col. L
Hollyfield, William
Harris, M. B.
Harris, Thomas

Hay, S. R.
Hackett, Mrs.
Jones, Hon. W.
Johnston, N. R.
Johnston, John T.
Johnson, P.
Jones, Hardin
Jones, John W.
Jones, C. H.
King, D.
Lemeul, Martin
Lewis, Col.. S.
Lewelling, J. W.
Marshall, Dr. H
Morrison, T. J.
Murphy, Lawrence
Mydale, W.
McClary, W.
McFarland, W. J.
Montgomery, A. J.
McLarran, J. H.
Mason, M. B.
Mann, J. W.
Nolan, W. H.
Newell, Miss E. M.
Nichols, John
Nichols, A. J.
Orr, Buell
Oliver, Mrs.. A.

Park, Rev. Samuel	Scott, O. P.
Pharr, F. M	Thompson, Thomas
Potts,	Thompson, John
Patten, T.P..	Tomilson, Richard
Petty, John R.	Wally, John
Post, Sarah	Walker, V.
Provence, George W.	Water, George
Randolf, P.M.	Wise, John D.
Robertson, J.	Williams, Mrs. Nancy
Rogers, Miss E.	Williams, Miss Martha
Ringwald, M.	Williams, John L.
Saddleberry, Miss C.	Wilson, M. G.
Stevens, Benj.	Wilson, M. Louise
Stone, Oliver T.	Warren, Henry
Waters, George	Wyett, Mrs. Rhoda
Smith, William	Wyett, A. J.
Smith, William J.	Wynn, T. D.
Spell, Richard H.	Witherspoon, M. G.
Sturne, Lewis	Young, A. W.
Smith, O.	
Smith, Mr. Sarah Ann	

If the above letters are not called for before the first day of January next, they will be sent to the Dead Letter Office.

    Walter S. Spencer, P.M.

died

this morning at daylight, of flux, Gilbert Ragin, an old and much esteemed citizen, aged 43 years; his funeral takes place at the Baptist Church, 10 'clock tomorrow morning.

lost

by J. W. West of Sherman, Grayson County and J. Haing, two mares and one horse;

notice by R. Matthews, County Clerk of Hopkins County, that two mares were taken up by James M. Stell and taken before Josiah Smith.

****

From *The Standard,* October, 17, 1857

Bonham Hotel

It will be seen that Ben Christian of the Bonham Hotel, is still on hand and anxious to provide for the comfort of his old friends and traveling public. Ben is a considerate host, always pleasant and does his best at all times.

the River

The steamer *Effort* arrived at Fulton on Monday from Shreveport having occupied several days in pulling out the raft accumulated in the Red Bayou. The river has long been high enough for navigation to points above here and we presume the *New Era,* which left Pittsburgh on the 26th with goods for Rhine & Bros. will be at he landing before many days.

Titus County Court

Next Monday, the District Court of Titus County will commence.

we call attention to

the advertisement of a mule lost by Rev. A. Cummings;

the advertisement by Bagby & McDonald that they have a superb lot of stores of various patents. All who want had better take a look at them. A fine assortment of cooking, heating and parlor stoves, Charter Oak cooking stoves, a fine lot said to be the best stoves now in use.

married

at the residence of E. P. Wallis, by the Rev. Mr. Stone, Mr. W. R. Tompson to Miss Martha Wallis.

memorials for Gilbert Ragin

by G. H. Wooten, B. H. Epperson, J. W. P. McKenzie, Committee of the Masons Friendship Lodge;

By John Anderson, A. H. Corley, B. H. Norwood, Committee from the Colfax Lodge of the Order of Odd Fellows.

Notice by J. C. Hart that he has placed his notes and accounts in the hands of S. H. Morgan for collection. Take warning and pay up at once. S. H. Morgan is my agent and attorney in my absence from the State and is authorize to transact any and all of my business.

****

From *The Standard,* October 24, 1857

financial affairs in New York

There has been a run on the Park Bank today.[28] All demands were met. There is a panic in the bank stock market and such stock have suffered enormous depreciation. A proposition of the merchants to the bank to increase the loans three million dollars has been rejected.

we call attention to

the advertisement of stray horses by R. M. Davis, living three miles south of Rockwall, Kaufman county;

the advertisement of A. G. Malton of Tarrant, Hopkins County;

to the card of Mary Ragin. It will be seen that she intends to continue the business of her late husband and that the old customers of the house and the public generally can be accommodated as heretofore;

to the advertisement by William Collier that a Red River place is for sale.

the financial crisis

The financial revulsion in the cities is overwhelming to men who have been banking or doing any large business mainly based on credit. Banks, which our Texas Kite fliers have been clamoring for the past two years, are going through the course common to them all in all times of difficulty, whenever, they should be able to show a capacity for usefulness. Having inflated the stock and produce markets by their heavy issues upon facilities and by flooding the country with paper, they have induced excessive importing and the consequent exportation of gold and silver. We learn bankers, merchant, large manufacturers in turn give way and laborers are thrown out of employment; starvation comes and thousands of the poor have to be fed at houses of public charity. This being so, railroads and other stocks, but yesterday in good standing and considered safe dividend paying property, are way down and the man who was but yesterday rich, in his own estimation and in the estimation of others, finds he has little to nothing, depreciated stocks that it is almost disreputable to own being his all, and, if he has liabilities maturing, he is in agony to now how to meet them. The banks will not accommodate. Private money lenders have become scarce.

the river

is falling some. The *ERA* got up above Rowland on Thursday but turned back from the plantation of Mrs. Gaffney's.

Titus County

The District Court opened in Titus county on Monday evening, Hon. William S. Todd presiding. Not much important business had come up when we left (Thursday evening late) except the old case of Euker and Shoemaker, which occupied upwards of two days, we believe. The jury had not rendered their verdict when we left.

There were present at the court the following attorneys from abroad: Hervey Dillahunty, S. H. Morgan, Mosely and Wilkinson, T. J. Rogers, Martin Rogers, S. H. Pirkey and B. W. Musgrove.

Titus county is in flourishing condition. Its cotton crop, as we learn, is one of the best, if not the very best, that they have ever had. Corn in Titus is sufficient for the necessities of the county. It sells at $1 per bushel. Mt. Pleasant has improved a little in buildings. There is plenty of water at Jefferson for navigation and boats occasionally arriving and departing.

****

From *The Standard,* October 31, 1857

newspaper news

Maj. W. M. Houghton, Post Master at Monticello Post Office in Titus County and William Hayes at Buchanan Post Office in Titus County are agents of *The Standard*.

we call attention

to the advertisement of Shreveport Insurance company which is prepared to take risks on all produce shipped on boats in good standing with the Board of Underwriters of the City of New Orleans;

to the card of B. W. Musgrove, Attorney and Counselor at Law, office at Tarrant;

to the card of W. M. Freeman Jefferson, who is not only still engaged in the receiving and forwarding business furnishing plantation supplies, but is making extra preparations for increased business by erecting a large fire proof warehouse.

the panic

The financial panic which is now the dominant excitement has overridden all business interests and closed nearly all the banks from one end of the country to the other. The New York banks, which, it was supposed would successfully resist, closed their specie vaults in joint agreement.

incorrect

Several of our exchanges in other states are giving currency to the rumor of a terrific fight in which Wigfall, Evans, two friends, one on each side, were killed. The whole story is a hoax, having no basis in truth. None of our notable citizens have been killed anywhere in the state. People are quite as peaceful in Texas as anywhere in the west and there are fewer desperate personal combats that there are in several other states that we know of.

new school in the Indian Nation

F. D. Piner, P. M. Fletcher and Calvin S. Love, Building Committee of Burney Female Academy in the Chickisaw Nation, solicit bids on the building which is to be 50 feet long, by 20 wide and a wing 20 feet by 60 feet, all two stories high.

****

From *The Standard,* November 7, 1857

we call attention

to the advertisement of J. C. Hearn & Bro, stone cutters, Lamar County;

to the advertisement of W. H. Gill that he has for sale two plantations and Negroes etc.;

to the advertisement of J. J. Reagan, County Clerk, of town lots for sale in Mesquiteville, Jack County.

cotton mill

We invite the attention of the citizens of our county and to subscribers generally to an article on our front page, showing an estimate of the expenses of erecting a cotton mill of certain dimensions and capable of doing a certain amount of work. We wonder that some of our enterprising capitalists do not go into the business. The profits would be much greater than allowed in the estimate.

immigration

The Grand Army of newcomers has commenced its movement. A strong column of it passes through here and we see from the *Quitman Herald*, that Wood County and a part of Titus are gaining large accessions. It is a fine season, food is plentiful and Texas is the Poor Man's Paradise and, at the same time, has the largest bodies of rich land waiting the proper culture of the heavy slaveholder of any state in the Union and these lands are low now, but rising yearly.

financial pressures

Our exchanges are full nearly to the exclusion of all else with the accounts of the financial embarrassments, more especially in the North. Our latest dates are still of a gloomy character but hopes are entertained that the blackest hours of the storm have passed. The sub treasury system has proved in the hands of the government a source of great benefit to alleviate the disasters that so threaten the whole commercial interests of the country.

lost

Notice by L. A. Ellis of Rondo Post Office in Lafayette, Arkansas that he has lost a calf pocket book.

administration of estates

Jas. G. Hamilton and J. P. Hamilton have been named Administrators of estate of Mary Moore, deceased, of Hopkins County;

John P. Hamilton has been named Administrator of estate of Isaac C Burson, deceased, of Hopkins County

crime patrol needed

"Dear Mr. DeMorse:

Being a taxpayer, living in the corporate limits of our town, I want to ask for information on whom devolves the duty of appointing an efficient patrol. During the last winter, there was considerable excitement in the community and the vigilance of the patrol produced a most salutary effect for several months in restraining lawless bands of Negroes from aggregating in and around the town. Now that we are either without a patrol, or if an appointment has been made, it is totally inefficient, our town swarms nightly with the very worst forms of Negroes which the county affords. Thefts are committed nightly and some of them are of the most daring kind, yet there is little or no chance of detecting the culprits. Again, I ask. 'Whose is the duty to appoint and efficient patrol? Does it belong to the corporation? If so, , have they made such appointments? Does the duty belong to the

County Court?"

In reply to the above queries, we would advise [Taxpayer] to make inquiry of our worthy mayor. If the writer has been the victim of any light fingered gentry, we can sincerely sympathize with him, as we also have been favored with several nocturnal visits during the last six to eight weeks. These nightly visitors are in no way particular as to how they help themselves before leaving the premises. Not having the fear of God before their eyes and disregarding the distinction between *meum* and *tuum*[29], they are equally expert at clearing a clothesline, examining the contents of the smokehouse or stealthily entering your bedroom, rifling your pockets or decamping with your watch, especially if left hanging on the bed head. So deeply indeed are our sympathies with our correspondent that we would earnestly endorse the adoption of such measures, as must necessarily tend to promote and better the state of things in our community.

humor

Why is a woman sweeter when she just gets out of bed in the morn?

Because then, she is arose.

****

From *The Standard,* .November 14, 1857

financial crisis

The financial crisis which has fallen like an avalanche on all the commercial cities of our country, but more especially on those of the Northern and Eastern States, has overwhelmed thousands in its ruins. Politicians and political analysts are busily engaged in advancing theories to account for the catastrophe and those theories are almost as various as the writers who are attempting to enlighten the public on the subject. The present state of things has not been brought about by the operation of any single cause, but by the combination of many we believe is beyond conjecture. Speculation of the wildest kind – extravagance scarcely surpassed by the wealthiest aristocracy of Europe, the multiplication of banks and the constituent facilities with which money can be secured to pander to the appetites and desires of those who wished to forsake the legitimate course of business and become suddenly millionaires, have all doubtless had their share in producing the present deplorable condition of things. The taste for extravagance has not been confined to the wealthier classes; it has extended its influence through all the ramifications of society. This morbid taste had to be satisfied and to do this excessive importation on foreign articles of luxury had to be resorted to, far surpassing our expectations and thus the imbalance of trade has been brought to be largely against us. The farmer and the planter are indebted to the merchants in the interior and they in turn are largely indebted to the merchant of the cities. They in turn are similarly circumstanced in relation to the banks as well as to foreign merchant and whatever affects one class of the community, affects all.

additional land to railroad companies

We notice that several newspapers in the state are advocating a change in the law, granting $6,000 a mile to all railroads in the state, on complying with certain conditions. We sincerely hope that the Legislature will let the present laws stand as is. If a company cannot grade a few miles of road on the land bestowed and then, a loan of $6,000 a mile to aid them in procuring iron for the rails and purchasing the cars for the equipment of the road, we question the propriety of squandering more of the State funds to aid them. The large bonus of land granted by the State ought surely to be sufficient in itself to build and equip any railroad which may be built in the state, but, in addition to this, the loan of $6,000 per mile should certainly be ample to satisfy the wishes of the most craving speculation. We do not desire to see all the surplus funds in the Treasury of the State bestowed on one or two companies in the field of internal improvement. Other roads will soon be in the field and we wish the State to husband its resources so that the different companies aiming at developing the great resources of this state in different directions may come in for an equitable share of the loan of public funds.

Hopkins county

The business of the week has closed and three trials for murder and one for manslaughter have been disposed of, two resulting in acquittals on the grounds of self defense, *viz* Thomas for the killing of Payne, Hanse for the killing of Golden; and, in the third, Keener and son, for the killing of Porter at Mount Pleasant in Titus county, the accused were found guilty of manslaughter and sentenced to imprisonment for one year. It was supposed, prior to the trial, that the second case would go hard with the party accused, but the evidence of apparent necessity was so strong that the jury made up their verdict in five minutes. In the Keener case, the accused have moved for a new trial.

The District attorney being absent, the State was represented by W. H. Johnson and C. L. Mann for the defense and J. T. Mills and T. J. Rogers and B. W. Musgrove. In the Thomas case, the State was represented by W. H Johnson, Van Sicle and Mann; J. T. Mills and T. L. Green for the defense. In the case against Haney, Mills, Green and Musgrove representing the State and for the defense Johnson and M. D. Rogers.

A large number of people have been in attendance on the court including a formidable array of witnesses in the Keener case from Titus. The Court was opened for business on Tuesday morning, the Judge being detained at home Sunday evening by the illness of his family and arriving on Tuesday morning about the usual time for opening court. Three days have been taken up with the three trials of murder and the result is that a large criminal docket for minor offenses and the entire new civil docket is untouched and lies over to next term. The attorneys from abroad in attendance have been John T. Mills and C. K. Holman from Lamar; T. L. Green from Fannin; William H. Johnson, T. J. Rogers and B. W. Gray from Titus and Martin Rogers from Cass.

Tarrant gives signs of improvement. One new house of good size has been erected by W. M. Kelly, whose name is to be found in our columns. The Ewings are about ready to put up another; Wilson & Jackson a third,. Dr. P. L. Smith a fourth and Barry & Moore, a new Drug House. There are now four dry goods stores in the place and two drug stores. The citizens have contracted for an artesian well for which they will pay $2500, water being insured.

The neighbor town of Sulphur Springs is also improving rapidly, as I am told. The County of Hopkins increases in population yearly by immigration and is in all respects a flourishing county. It can vote near a thousand, raises fine wheat crops, fair corn crops, and cattle and sheep crops that never fail. The main staple of Hopkins is the exportation of cattle. Actually, from its wire grass prairie, it sends off heavy droves of these which are just now finding a considerable market at Jefferson, at Black's new beef packing establishment.

Mr. Black was, or is, lately a citizen of Hopkins and the joint owner, with his brother, of the finest lot of sheep in the county, the last clip of which was sold here at 39 cents. The first importation of which died suddenly and without apparent cause in considerable number but several hundreds brought in last fall have all survived and proved healthy. All of whom I have inquired of concur in the statement that there cannot be a better sheep raising region upon earth than Hopkins, that they are entirely free from disease and need no other attention than being penned up at night. Occasionally, a stray wolf commits depredations, but, as soon as observed, is halted with a strychnine and is put out of the way.

It is surprising to me, upon the unvarying reports I receive, that they do not put more capital into sheep husbandry and make a main business of it. As the grass becomes less luxuriant from the long continued pasturage of cattle, it becomes more suitable for sheep and the outcome of the investments is immense. For instance .I have noted some data as follows:

John W. Matthews had six years since two ewes; he has sold more than $200 of mutton, $150 of wool and now has 150 head worth six dollars. This is without attention and a mere contingent of his main farming operations. Dr. McGee (Black Jack Grove) bought six years ago for $60, twenty ewes, was offered 1400 for his stock last spring. The Blacks and William T. Blythe are the only persons in the country with anything like considerable flocks. Each has about1400 head. The Blacks average clip lat spring was 6 pounds.

Relative to the beef packing establishment in Jefferson to which I adverted, I am advised it started with 25 hands from Louisville Kentucky accustomed to this business, and that the expectation is to pack up 3000 beeves this winter.

Hard times and banks breaking do not much effect Hopkins. People must have food, meat as well as bread, and Hopkins always has the beef and the pork, and I hope ere long, will also have large droves of sheep for mutton as well as fine wool. Corn is worth in the county about one dollar a bushel and is not very plentiful for the large gangs of hogs have to be fed, this year the usual supply of mast failing here, as elsewhere in the State.

Saturday night: The Court hears tomorrow morning the application for a new trial for the Keeners and a hundred or more cases lie over to next term for want of time to try. It is said that another week is needed for this county and I think it would be well to so rearrange the terms of the counties as to make an additional allowance for this. Aside from the present press of business, the county is becoming prosperous and the business will always be hereafter be greater than it has been heretofore. The Bar now here generally concur in this opinion and desire the change.

There is a savage Norther blowing everything cold here.

we call attention

to the legal card of William M. Ewing of Tarrant, Hopkins County. Mr. Ewing is a very trustworthy gentleman with whom we have been long acquainted;

to the advertisement of Jackson Weems of Wimsborough, Wood County, for a lost pony.

special election

In the election of a Justice of the Peace to fill the office vacated by the resignation of C. B. Sutton in this place, which came off on Saturday last, T. J. Crooks (Democrat) was elected over T. J. Mosely (Know Nothing) by a 12 vote majority.

power of attorney

During my father's stay in Austin this winter, I will act as his authorized agent in all matters pertaining to his business; Office on south east corner of Courthouse.

John C. Burks

Red River Presbytery

stands adjourned to meet again at Paris Lamar County at 6 o' clock p.m. on Saturday preceding the second Sabbath of December next.

Congregations are most earnestly and affectionately begged to send up representatives and, with them, full church records of communicants, accessions, infant and adult baptisms, of dismissals, expulsions etc. that we may definitely arrive at the statistics of the church. There is no order of the Presbytery requiring them to send up funds with their representatives to defray the costs of the commissioners to the next General Assembly. Twenty five cents from each member would be sufficient but, lest there should be someone who may not contribute anything, let those, who are able, give a dollar or five dollars.

T. C. Skidmore, Clerk of the Presbytery

look out

I forewarn all persons of removing any timber, either standing or fallen, from my land, known as the W.B. Crowder survey, lying two miles east of Daingerfield -

Jane Crowder

Notice all persons are hereby cautioned against trading for a tract of land set apart to Parthena Chaney and Eli Edmondson as the heirs of Margaret Edmondson, deceased, lying in Red River County and a part of the James Levin's league survey; as such lands belong to me and all persons trespassing upon that portion of said land will be prosecuted to the full extent of the law.

A. G. Melton, Tarrant

From *The Standard,* November 21, 1857

Would this be none sense

There is a woman in the East, so high minded, that she disdains to admit that life has common sense

Greenville, Hunt County

It is Friday evening and the day is exceedingly disagreeable –both rainy and cold - and the ground covered with soft mud. The District Court, which opened on Tuesday, concluded the last of the business before it this morning and was only half employed during the days preceding. The old shed of a court house is not fit to do any business in, except in pleasant weather. The county has a courthouse of brick now going up in the center of the square. It is not quite so large as it should be, although sufficient for a few years to come. It will be 40 feet square. The contractor is L.S. Lissenbee, whose card is in our columns. The work will be well done both in masonry and carpentry. Mr. Lissenbee can be recommended as a contractor who would not have bad work done But little business of importance has been before the court. The mot important case decided was that between Davis vs Hart for damages for "cowhiding".[30] The jury returned a verdict of $750 for Davis. The case goes up to the Supreme county. For plaintiff by J. E. Wilson and T. L. Green, for defendant R. H. Lane and J. J. Dickson.

Attorneys present from other counties were Lane, Green and Roberts from Fannin, Dickson from Red River, E. G. Benners and Martin Rogers from Cass; T. Johnson and M. Bolin from Titus; B. W. Musgrove from Hopkins; Mr. Sparks of the *Quitman Herald* who has been here and was at the Hopkins Court.

More persons than usual attended upon the Court. Indeed, the county is receiving considerable accessions of population and the increased strength manifests itself upon the courtyard. Fifteen families have just arrived from Grayson county, Virginia and there are newcomers from Alabama, Tennessee, Illinois and Missouri and some expected from Kentucky. Corn is worth one dollar a bushel and wheat is selling for a dollar and 25 cents and there is not much of either to be had in the county. Hunt drives a great many "beef" cattle, yearly has increasing capacities and considerable bodies of rich lands, perhaps two-thirds of the county rich. The South Sulphur, the Middle Sulphur and the forks of the Sabine, with the minor tributaries, water her territory.

Greenville has not improved rapidly but will show some new buildings upon the square next spring. The lumber for two new store houses is now upon the ground and these, with the new court house, will show the central square to better advantage than heretofore.

Saturday night: It is still raining steadily very heavy and has since Thursday night. Everybody is housed up, except the occasional straggler. Across the square, it looks gloomy outside, but cheerful fires and the house comfortable and conversations and magazines serve to while away the time. The only sound of labor come from the blacksmith's shop. We are awaiting the cessation of rain to travel towards Bonham but, wet or dry, have to go tomorrow. The Bonham attorneys were fortunate enough to get off before the rain but Jefferson, Mt. Pleasant and Clarksville are represented as "they can't get away". We are just as well off, as you are at home, and confident that the mud here is not any dirtier than with you.

I remain as ever yours,

C. De Morse

we call attention
to the card of L. W. Lissenbee architect. Mr. L. is now carrying on the construction of the Bonham Female Academy and the Court House of Hunt county;

to the card of John E. Wilson , Attorney at Law, Greenville, Hunt County. Mr. W. Is a competent attorney of several years practice and for several years has been a resident of Greenville.

sorry

In our last we neglected to call the attention of the Cumberland Presbyterians and the religious public generally to the advertisement of the meeting of the Presbytery to be held shortly in Paris.

humor

Why is a lady pulling on her corset like a man who drinks to drown his grief?

Because in so lacing herself, she is also getting tight.

please settle accounts

All those indebted to the firm of Dickson and Smith or to Smith individually will find to their interest to come forward and make immediate settlement or they will find their accounts in the hands of an Officer of the Law.

****

From *The Standard,* November 28, 1857

newspaper business

F. McCown will act as one of our agents at North Sulphur Post Office in Fannin County. H. H. Hofar will act as an agent for *The Standard* at Bonham, Fannin County.

we are indebted

to J. H. Burks and Major John Marshall for documents from Austin;

to Lt. Governor Runnels, Hon. S. H. Pirkey and E. D. McKenney for papers from Austin.

we call attention

to the card of Col. R. H. Lane, Attorney at Law in Bonham. Col. Lane is a long time resident and has a large practice;

to the special notice by Dr. J. McDonna for those who owe him to settle accounts as he is preparing to leave Clarksville for Paris;

to the notice of S. J. Galbraith, commissioner of deeds for several states, resident at Bonham. In the transaction of all land matters, powers of attorney between the residents of this and other states. Mr. Galbraith's authority may be a matter of much convenience.

advice

Don't touch the lute when the drums are sounding. A wise man remains silent, when fools are speaking

Fannin County

My last was written at Greenville during the prevalence of a rain, which lasted until Sunday and rendered traveling too uncomfortable to be performed, except under the requirement of stern necessity. Having choice books on hand and some magazines, we passed the time pleasantly enough, in comfortable quarters, in the Greenville Inn, until Monday morning, when the Sun shone upon us once more, after five days seclusion, and we headed for Bonham.

The creeks were not high and the roads were not so bad as we had anticipated. We found new settlements north of Greenville in the Tidwell Creek neighborhood. Riding over country generally pleasant and of good quality for cultivation, we got at night to John Austin's within seven miles of Bonham, where we were hospitably entertained for the night. Mr. Austin has a choice place, rich and commanding a fine view. From it to near Bonham is a very rich region of black timbered land, thickly settled.

I learn here that there a good many newcomers settling in the

County, several about Honey Grove. Near Kentucky Town, 300 wagons are encamped, while their owners look about for places to settle upon. These movers are mostly from Northern Missouri and Illinois. I hear that Lamar County also catches a great deal of the immigration. A gentleman fellow from the Choctaw side tells me that the crossings at the ferries leading into Grayson County, the route by which the northern immigration comes, is continual.

The business before the District Court was started before we got there and was not large. But a part of one day sufficed to dispose of all the old civil docket that was ready for trial. The criminal docket is now under consideration. Attorney from the other counties have been Jesse P. Marshall from Grayson; John T. Mills, W. B. Wright, W. H. Millwee and William M. Williams from Lamar; Hervey Dillahunty from Red River and William H. Johnson from Titus. There is a large number of people in town from the country, notwithstanding a severe norther.

A heavy mercantile business had been done here during the summer. Bonham is improving. This is not so perceptible on the Square, but a walk of several hundred yards north will show the visitor several new buildings, most of them private residences and some of them of tasteful construction. The new academy building is getting on up to the second story windows. It is of brick, 40 by 60 feet in size and a good piece of work. It will need a handsome portico to relieve its entire plainness of appearance. A new brick hotel of some size is talked about and I hope will be built because a good edifice of that sort is much needed and would be well sustained.

Since writing the above, the Court has progressed with the criminal docket. The only important case before it was the State against R. O. Rhodes for an assault with intent to kill. The jury found Rhodes guilty and sentenced him to two years service in the Penitentiary.

Honey Grove, Saturday night, 8 o'clock. Arrived here since dark and learn that a larger number immigrants are settling here about than for the last several years before, and the report here is that an immense train is on the road behind. A large body of these are said to be from western Virginia; many from North Carolina,

Kentucky and Tennessee. Many places about here are at prices between 6 and 8 dollars per acre. The region hereabouts is destined to be heavily populated. It is not held out in large tracts, but can be purchased in small bodies, is generally rich land and pleasant to view.

This place which is already a lively little village, already has one church, one school house, four respectable dry goods stores, a drug store, two hotels, a grocery, a stone cutters establishment, a blacksmiths shop, a wagon shop, a saddler's shop and a shoemaker's. Those who remember the place in 1842, as I do, when looking for the noted Honey Grove, we found a small clump of trees with one dwelling, in the center, and it nearly surrounded by water, the center of the little grove being low land, then filled by a heavy rain in which we had been riding, will recognize a pleasant change now. The little village is adjacent to the grove, but on high rolling prairie, with a skirt of timber contiguous and plenty of it in view. It has a decent sober thrifty looking population. Loungers and gamblers form no part of its population, but the residents of the county around as well as the villagers, are a moral, orderly, industrious people, taking interest in all subjects of public advancement and morality and generally well to do in the world. A steam flouring mill, on a large scale, is about to be put up, the machinery being here now. I predict that few more prosperous country neighborhoods will be found in Northern Texas five years from now, than that immediately around Honey Grove.

A correspondent from Kentucky Town writes: "We have a great deal of rain and a heavy immigration. Corn is worth 75 cents a bushel, wheat $1.25; pork at 8 cents a pound."

married

on the 8th instant in Fannin. Mr. William S. Gilliam of Lamar County to Miss M. Z. Whatly

Bibles, Bibles. Bibles

Advertisement by John Anderson, Secretary of the Red River

Bible Association, that Bibles of all sizes and in every variety of binding, 30 cents to 10 dollars, may be found at Bagby & Corleys store on the public square in Clarksville.

horse race

Notice by J. H. Darnal, stake holder, for a mile long "colt race" over the Clarksville Course.

****

From *The Standard,* December 5, 1857

the mails etc.

We are this (Thursday evening) without a single word of news, later than our last issue. We have sometimes failures in one of our mails but neither the eastern, the western or the southern have made their appearance in a week. The commercial troubles, which have overwhelmed in ruin such vast numbers of our mercantile and manufacturing companies and which have so materially deteriorated all kinds of railroad and state stocks, have been followed to some extent by all classes of our citizens throughout the length and breadth of the land. We have therefore looked with anxiety for the arrival of our eastern and southern mail in the hopes of being able to impart to our readers some favorable news.

we are indebted

to the Hon. J. H. Burks for Austin papers, although not of late date.

we call attention

to the advertisement for stoves for sale by Bagby and McDonald at Bagby' Tin Shop, near Honey Grove, in Fannin county;

to the advertisement of a stray horse by William Fitzhugh, Collin County.

Chickasaw and Choctaw Herald

We call attention to the advertisement for the prospectus of the *Chickasaw and Choctaw Herald* to be published at Tishomingo, Choctaw nation.[31] The publisher is J. T. Daviess and the Proprietor is H. McKinney. It will be devoted to the Science, Literature, Agriculture, Education and the advancement of the arts and manufactories among the Chickasaw and other civilized tribes of the Red Race as well as the news of the day. It will be the object of the Editor and Proprietor to make their paper interesting and useful to both the Red and the White, by making it a true record of passing events, among the civilized tribes of Indian and at the same time a source of information to the Red Man by giving him such news and information as to him may be interesting as well to keeping him regularly informed as to the prices and values of products. In short, the *Herald* is intended to be what a paper under these circumstances should, but what no paper heretofore established among the Indians has been. It will be a record of the customs, habits, laws and usages among the Indian tribe which cannot fail to be of interest to all persons desirous of obtaining information on this subject. It will at the same time convey to the Red Man the advanced state of Art and Sciences among the White Man and stimulate the Indians to the acquisition of knowledge and pursuits of industry. It will contain regular statistics of the number of inhabitants, a report of production, slaves and the wealth of the nations respectively.

The *Herald* will be independent in politics and religion.

doctor's rate agreement

Notice by Dr. George Gordon, Chairman and Dr. John R. Lyons, Secretary of the agreement and rates of charges of the physicians of Clarksville to which they agree to be bound for the next 4 years:

Dr. G. H. Wooten; Dr. O. B. Wade; Dr. J. A. Barry; Dr. E. S. Look; Dr. John McDonna and Dr. Thomas F. Titus

rates of charges

mileage (day time) $1 per mile

mileage (nocturnal) $1.50 per mile

town visits $2.50

Prescription and medicines $2 and upward

obstetrics - $15.00

detention: $12.00 fo 24 hours

consultation $6.00

Sherman Seminary

Located in Sherman, Grayson county and under the charge of Prof. O. D. Howe, Principal, M. A. Howe, Preceptress and teacher of Music.

Miss E. A. Blackon, associate principal and teacher of painting. The trustees of the institution are B. P. Smith President; W. E. Saunders M.D., Secretary; T. W. Randolph, Treasurer, R. D. King, L Richards –Coffee, W. C. Young; –Shannnn; J. Marshall, Trustees

Collin County

Dear Major

The Hon. District Court of Collin County, Judge Vortress of the Seventeenth Judicial District presiding, adjourned on Saturday evening the 31[st,] after having dispatched a docket of 250 to 300 cases.

Judge V. arrived here on Saturday the 17th and organized Court. On the same evening, he was attacked with a fever and, on Tuesday, was scarcely able to walk to the Courthouse. He then adjourned until the following Friday before which time it was necessary to call in a physician. He recovered very speedily and on Monday morning got to the Courthouse where he resumed his duties with untiring energy and assiduity .

There were but few important cases tried at the late term. One of the most important, however, was the State against Charles Exmon who was sentenced to the penitentiary for a term of 14 months upon a charge of larceny. There is also an indictment against Exmon for horse stealing. There were a number of indictments for perjury in obtaining colonial certificates under the Act of '52. You remember said act granted to residents of Peters Colony 160 and 320 acre certificates for those who resided in said colony bona fide from the year 1848 to 1857 for three years. It is a lamentable fact as ascertained upon testimony by the Commissioners of said colony, who have mot recently investigated those claims, that a large number of persons have fraudulently obtained certificates and located them in said colony when they were absolutely non residents of the colony.

At the final adjournment, the McKinney Bar met at the court house. Alex Berry was called to the Chair and Mr. Armstrong appointed Secretary and a Committees elected to draft resolutions expressive of the high regard the bar entertained for Judge Vortress, won by his courtesy, urbanity and ability.

democratic convention

There will be a meeting at the Courthouse on Saturday the 12th at 2 o'clock to appoint delegates to the Democratic convention to meet in Austin on th 8th of January next. The Democracy of Red River are invited to attend

administration of estates

Notice by J. M. Bivins, County Clerk Red River County that Nathan Hoss, Administrator of the estate of William F. Hamilton deceased, has filed his accounting

strays taken up

notice by P. M. Duke, Clerk of Bowie County, that a stray taken up by Thomas Luum was estrayed before D. M. Chisolm, a Justice of the Peace of precinct number 3. It had been appraised by Peyton B. Smith and E. D. Dickerson.

lost head right certificate

notice by C. B. Wilks that he has lost or mislaid the head right certificate of Wm. H. Griswell for 640 acres in Red River County and, after due notice, will apply to the proper office for a duplicate.

****

From *The Standard*, December 12, 1857

Red River

Plenty of water. The *Era* and the *New Era* and the *Effort* were at the landing place last week and went above.

new post office

A new post office called "South Sulphur" has been established at the house of E. B. Keith in Hunt County on the line from Greenville to Paris. Many of those on that route that have heretofore complained of inconvenience for post offices, could be served by either by this office or the new post office at Tidwell Creek, on the line from Bonham to Greenville. The Post master at either place can forward names to us of persons desiring *The Standard*.

we call attention

to the card of the Paris Hotel, R. B. Francis, Proprietor. The house is the most commodious in Paris, the Landlord very attentive and the stable excellently well kept and provided for.

thanks

We are certainly under many obligations to our neighbor of the *Quitman Herald* with whom we met at Tarrant and Greenville. If we do not copy his compliment (from the *Herald* of the 11th which we have not seen until this week), as is some times done by contemporaries, it is not the less highly valued.

we are indebted to Messrs. Pirkey, Burks ,Taylor and R. H. Ward of the Legislature and Mr. Clerk Haynie for late documents.

Lamar

The District Court is in progress, having been in operation since Monday afternoon and will likely continue a part of next week. The civil docket is not much. The criminal docket has been on trial for the past three days and continues tomorrow. A great many people are in attendance at the Court.

The following lawyers from abroad are here: W. H. Johnson of Titus, Dillahunty, Morgan, Murray, Epperson, Dickson, Sutton and Burks of Red River, Lane, Roberts and Davis of Fannin and Barber of Bowie.

Paris continues building up rapidly, but there is an evident approximation of tight times, which may perhaps check its growth for a while. It is, at present, far in advance of any other city in Northern Texas, in population and number of buildings. Of the houses, those that have been put up in the last year or two, are, many of them, neat structures, mostly of wood, but two or three of the stores last built upon the square are of brick, each two stories, covered with metal and having neat fronts. One or two more, as I learn, are to be put up in the Spring.

The Court room has been plastered and furnished with comfortable sets and is much improved in appearance.

Some late immigrants are settling in the county, which offers the inducements of rich soil, good schools and plentifulness of meat and breadstuffs and, although largely composed of prairie, has also plenty of timber. There is a decided spirit of progress here, not a little heightened by being the domicile of the Memphis and El Paso Railroad. The company's surveyors, who have been running lines of late, in the neighborhood of Bonham , returned this week and have taken up winter headquarters intending to get through with office work and do not more surveying, until they can meet with the surveyor of the Central Road and determine the point of junction. I am not advised of what the prospects of our road are at present, beyond this, that I know that the company has received subscriptions of a large amount of land on the basis of which to negotiate a loan. When that negotiation will be attempted, I do not know. I presume not very soon. I suppose, however, if the point of junction with the Central Road at or near the Trinity could be ascertained, the company may venture upon its present cash subscription to contract for the grading of 20 or 25 miles more of the route. This, however ought not to be done at any other part of the route than from that point of junction eastward. It would not be of practical utility to let out more grading now, upon the eastern end of the route, as there is no prospect of junction there with either the Cairo or the Ouachita road for a long time to come. I suppose that the Texas Central or the Houston road will continue to advance northward, energetically as it has heretofore done and from the first extension of that line eastward, the next work should be done by our company.

Apple wagons from Missouri have been around the Square all week, retailing apples at 50 cents to one dollar per dozen. With a connection to the Cairo and El Paso roads to this point, those apples would be worth perhaps two dollars per barrel. Fortunately, there are few Missouri products that we need. Even apples, we shall have little occasion to get from abroad in five years. Hempen manufactures may be necessary for us from that section. I know of nothing else and those I am satisfied can be produced here but perhaps will not be.

The cotton crop of this county will not exceed a half crop and, if full, would not be much. There is plenty of corn worth 75 cents a bushel and of wheat at one dollar per bushel. There will be pork to sell at 7 or 8 cents a pound.

We are pleased to note that Upshur County is receiving a full share of the immigration that is coming into Texas this season. There are quite a number of respectable families who have recently stopped in this county, some of whom have purchased homes and permanently located among us. Our Town has also received an accession of numbers to its population which has imparted an air of business to the place that we have never before noticed.

A goodly portion of those who are stopping with us are well to do in the world and will doubtless induce others to follow them, from the "States".

confessions of a horse thief

The large number of horses stolen from our citizens in Texas has become the most alarming evil and led in some cases to the summary vengeance of the Lynch Law.

We lay before our readers a confession of a horse thief at a late term of the Court of Burleson County. We trust that it may lead to the breaking up of the horse thievery gang declared to be in existence in this state and well organized.

"When he [Hugh Allen] first came to Texas, he met with Tom Middleton at Buck Horn in Austin. The accused was drunk at that place. Tom Middleton employed him to work for him. They immediately left Buck Horn for the town of Bastrop and, at the direction of Middleton, the accused stole a horse; then they started for the town of LaGrange and, on their way, stole two horses, one a paint. Middleton, up until this point, never told the accused that he was engaged in the regular employment of horse stealing. They then stole two on the Colorado River and, then on their way back to the town of Chappell Hill, Washington County, they stole three, a little black, a bay, a sorrel. They then stole two, a bay and a brown at the White's, near Colonel Kirby's. Accused said that they often stole horses in the day, as well as in the night. They then went to Col. Wm. Sledge's plantation, where they stole an old black mule. Middleton then went up the country to Mr. Griffiths for the purposes of stealing a fine horse. He did not succeed, but stole two others on his return. The accused stated that he had been engaged in stealing horses with the following named persons, to wit: Nat Berry, Bill Berry, both killed at San Antonio; three of the Samuels, who live down the county; three Batton boys, who live on Lost Creek; Hillard Putnam and Vandy Putnam; he, does not know where they live as they are young men having no wives; old Jim Cox, Burleson County, William Hutton, Reuben Dean, Washington County; Thomas Taylor of Eastern Texas, John Ake, a large raw boned man with sandy hair who lives in Arkansas and visits Texas for the purpose of stealing horses.

The accused says he has been shot at since he was in jail and thinks that Middleton did it, as he sent word that he intended to kill him for telling on the party. The accused was raised in the state of Alabama and came to Texas in July 1856. The name of his mother is Little; he is illegitimate. The name of the man who raised him is Joe Allen and lives in Benton county, Alabama.

Accused stated that Tom Middleton had informed him that he [Middldton] had killed a Jew pedlar and took from him all his valuable property; this occurred in one of the lower counties.

The Jury then received the charge of the Judge and retired to consider their verdict.

They returned in ten minutes with the verdict of guilty, assessing the penalty as two years at hard labor in the penitentiary.

****

From *The Standard,* December 19, 1857

we call attention

to the advertisement of the Alto House, Decatur, Wise County by Alexius Halsell, Proprietor;

to the advertisement of sheep strayed from Dr. James D. Scales, Kentucky Town;

to the advertisement of Forest Mail Stage Line from Marshall and Jefferson to Mt. Pleasant. Mr. Nesmyth, the proprietor is an energetic gentleman, who keeps up his line well;

to the advertisement of D. C. Russell. He offers a large stock of goods at cost and carriage;

to the advertisement of a Negro girl for sale by L. C. Alexander of Sherman, Grayson County;

to the advertisement of Negroes to be leased by the Executors of Wortham;

to the advertisement of a Negro lost by J. G. Gibson;

to the steamboat card of G. L. Kouns & Bros. Both of the boats were here last week and are well calculated for the low water trade. Our citizens will see that they propose to become a permanent attachment. We believe they are worthy of confidence.

mail facilities

We have private advises which satisfy us that our mail facilities in this region will be much improved at the next general letting. Our friends about Sherman and Gainesville will be benefitted. In this aspect, we take some credit to ourselves, although not all.

Wise County

Wise is a fine county, inhabited by sensible people, well to do in the world, if we may judge by an indication sent to us in the mail on Thursday evening. To be more explicit, we have not been in Wise, but we have the highest possible evidence of the good sense of the people and the fertility of the county for none but sensible people, living in good country, would have done what the people of Decatur, the County Seat of Wise, at the last session of the District Court - did, that is they made up a list of 25 new subscribers to *The Standard* and sent it to us. That is what we call sensible and when we visit them next Spring, as we intend to do, we doubt not that the list will be greatly increased for we have up in that region many old subscribers, who went for a time beyond the reach of our mail facilities and are now just getting once more what is within the pale of Uncle Sam's postal lines and will again come on our lists and hold converse with again as of old.

Wise county, however, in sober fact, judged otherwise than by the intelligent action of its people, and looking only at its soil, is a county of rich land, beginning to populate freely, and offers great incentive to settlers who would want lands cheap, yet rich. This cannot be so for a great length of time, but it is now. Wise is due west of Denton and has been more lately settled.

After a long and tedious travel from Hopkins County, by land and water, I arrived at due time at the high town of Taylorsville, on Tuesday morning at sunrise. This is one of the most beautiful situations in Northern Texas, presenting to the view to the west, a country interspersed with timber and prairie, for 30 miles, through which passes the much talked about West Fork, winding its way down to the three forks of the Trinity. To the South, a beautiful country is presented for 30 miles. To the east, a sightly prairie, rich and well watered, is presented. In richness, none can surpass it. To the North, now and then, a towering mound springs up on the high table prairie which tends to variate the view from the fair situation of Taylorsville. There are two stores in the town, one tavern, some other improvements going up.

There seems to be a considerable disposition among the people of Wise county to see that justice was administered to all who came knocking at the door. Judge E. H. Ventress presided. He is a young man, but highly respected by the Bar and I have no doubt that he will be an honor to the station he occupies. He resides in Williamson County. He is now in the place of Nat M. Burford of the 16th Judicial District.

There were some very exciting cases disposed Tuesday and Wednesday. The case of Moses P. Bell vs. Joseph Robinson. This was a case for damages for certain words used by the said Robinson to the prejudice of the said Moses. The Plaintiff was ably represented by speeches for about four hours from Messrs, H. C. Russell, Judge Everets and W. T. G. Weaver. The defendant was represented by John J. Good of Dallas. The Judge then drew a bead on the jury and then gave them one of the ablest charges I ever heard from the lip of any man on th Bench in Texas. The jury then retired for about one hour and on half and returned with a verdict of $250 for the plaintiff.

The next morning the most exciting case came up, that of the State against Martin and Clara, Slaves, for murder. The case was one that caused much excitement in Wise. The case came on. The State announced itself ready, so did the attorney for the defendants and the witnesses were put under rule. The State most singularly failed to make out the slightest presumption. Defendant introduced no evidence, the Judge gave the jury the law, the Jury retired for a few minutes and returned with a verdict of not guilty.

The attorneys in attendance were Judge Gustavus Adolphus Everets, W. T. G. Weaver of Cooke, J. A. Carroll of Denton; Lewellen and Robinson of Collin; Gen. John J. Good of Dallas and John C. McCoy, the District Attorney, also of Dallas; A. Y. Fowler of Fort Worth, W. A. Ellet, resident of Taylorsville, formerly of Red River and H. C. Russell of Wise County.

steamers collide

We give on our front page the details of the loss of the steamer *Opelousas*, of the Berwick Bay and Galveston lines in a collision with her alternate, the *Galveston*. The statements of the passengers show great neglect and disregard for human life for which we hope it will be practical for the courts to inflict the proper punishment. There was no providential reason why the collision should have occurred. After the collision, if the life boats of the two steamers had been in order ready for use, as it was the duty of the two captains to have them , every passenger could have been saved.. Of what use is it to provide the expensive appliances, if when they are suddenly wanted, the plugs are out of the bottoms and the oars are missing. There is no avoiding the conviction that the chief officers of both vessels were criminally careless and unfit for their positions and we know of no way to ensure better conduct than to punish them severely. Our last advise from New Orleans was that they were on trial before the District Court. The vessels were new and good ; their appointments, we doubt were not perfect, despite expensive. Their owner, Vanderbilt,[32] has all the practical knowledge, sagacity and capital necessary to insure complete preparation. The lives of the traveling public are too often reckless sacrificed and we have looked earnestly and desirously for a long time for some infliction of punishment upon careless captains, conductors which would have the effect to protect the life of those who fro the time are completely at their mercy.

Since writing the above, we see a statement that Captain Ellis has been acquitted. We shall read report of the evidence with interest. Somebody certainly was at fault decidedly and that some one captain, mate or man ought to be punished severely.

meeting of the Democrats of Red River County

At the meeting of the Democrats of Red River County held in the courthouse in Clarksville to appoint delegates to attend the convention in Austin, the following proceedings were had:

On motion, Maj. J. W. Sims was called to the Chair and W. P. Cornelius as Secretary. On motion of L. D. Henderson, John C. Burks was called upon to explain the purpose of the meeting after which, on motion, a committee was appointed to draft resolutions to wit -H. R. Latimer, L. D. Henderson, I. D. Lawson, L. C. Bailey and William Lawrence and , on motion, J. C. Burks was added to the Committee.

After a short absence, the Committee presented the following resolutions which were adopted unanimously.

Resolved: we endorse the convention system as the best of ascertaining the true sentiments of the people;

Resolved: we endorse the present administration, James Buchanan on all leading questions as so far developed;

Resolved: that delegates not exceeding five be appointed to attend at Austin and to represent Red River County to select suitable men as candidates to fill the important state offices which are to be filled by an election on in August next;

Resolved: we believe rotation in office proper is a democratic principle when applied with discretion.

The following gentlemen were put into nomination and unanimously elected as delegates. to wit Col. J. C. Burks, S. H. Pirkey, J. M. Bivins. H. R. Latimer and J. A. Bagby

On the motion of W. P. Cornelius, it was ordered that the proceedings of this meeting be given to Maj. Charles De Morse for publication.

murder trials

(from *The Henderson Democrat*)

"This is the fifth and last week of court for our District. A considerable amount of cases were not disposed of; not more than half of the civil docket was reached. The case of the State vs. William Oliver and also against Archibald Murphey has continued all of last week and will the balance of this week. On last Monday, Oliver's case was taken up. The Judge gave his charge to the jury on Saturday night at 11 o'clock. He was one of the men charged with assassinating William R. Wiggins of Cherokee County. Mr. Wiggins was in point of ability, respectability and standing one of the first men of the county. As he returned from supper about dark, he was fired upon by two men who were concealed by the road and was instantly killed. A fouler, baser more damning deed had never before been perpetrated in the state. The circumstances to us with unerring certainty identified the person who killed him. Oliver was a arraigned as one of those men. The jury brought in a verdict of guilty and–reader, what to you think his punishment was?–that he should spend three years in the penitentiary. The jury remained out in his case for several days.

On Monday last, the case against Murphey as an accessory in the same murder. We are satisfied in our experience and observation, we have never witnesses the trial of any case of more intense interest. There were a great number of witnesses on both sides and friends of both the prisoner and the deceased in attendance. His Honor, Judge Frazer, has displayed a remarkable degree of patience during the trial and has worked both day and night, and has given the highest evidence of his knowledge of the law and the rules of evidence. His charge in the Oliver case could not be surpassed.

P.S. The jury in the Murphey case brought back a verdict of not guilty in two hours deliberation."

If our neighbor at the *Democrat* has described all the aspects of the case against Oliver correctly, their verdict ought to damn the jury's reputation and their names should be printed in bold letters. We are satisfied that a dereliction of juries as well as other persons invested with high trust should be denounced. Jury trials are getting to be farces in the United States, where money and local influence are in the defense.

new goods for sale

Mrs. M. A. Ragin has received in addition to her other inventory, rock molasses, superior brown sugar, mackerel, dried apples, raisins, rice, cheese, figs, candies, fresh salmon in cans, pickles, beans, onions, soda, cigars, snuff, powder, shot caps, together with a very general assortment of dry groceries; Mrs. Ragin gives her thanks to a liberal public for past patronage.

****

From The Standard, December 26, 1857

Merry Christmas

Merry Christmas, gentle readers or should we confine our salutation to subscribers and exclude from our abundant felicitation the members of that Godless tribe who reap what they do not sow and avail themselves of our good wishes, while they rob us of our labor. However, we being charitably inclined and practicing the precept of the Divine Being whose terrestrial birth blessed the day and who taught charity as one of the chief virtues, we will permit the fragrance of our salutation to exhale upon those barbarians yet for a little while.

steam boat collision

We have the account of the Col. Edwards burning on the Red River by which means human beings lost their lives and much property was destroyed. Of course, no one was to blame. It is nobody's duty to prevent such incidents by close attention with the consideration that many lives depend on that attention. Watches are kept, but they are matters of form; they do not watch for anything and, if fire wants to burn, let it burn. We learn that James Garret of Hopkins County was on board with a drove of cattle. He escaped but lost his cattle.

weather

On Wednesday night at 7 o'clock it was raining freely. At 7, the next morning, it seemed unusually bright and, looking for a cause, we discovered that it had been snowing. The trees were clothed in a white dress and looked graceful and beautiful with small limbs bending slightly under the weight. The snow on the ground was four inches deep at morning. Yesterday morning, there has been little diminution of it, although some of it had melted from the trees but the earth and the roof tops were still thickly covered. This morning, however, more of the earth is perceptible, although the house tops are still pure white. and the general presentation to the eye everywhere is similar.

Christmas Festivities

Last night, we participated by special invitation in a supper and dance got up by the young gentlemen of the town at the Donoho House. The supper was the best we have seen yet in the place and the dance afterward was well attended and much enjoyed.

died

At a meeting of the young men of Paris at the office of N. W. Townes for the purpose of expressing their sympathy with the friends of Dr. Edwin F Carpenter, late of this place and their sincere regret for his untimely end. On the motion of A. H. Latimer, Richard . Peterson was called to the Chair and N. W. Townes was appointed Secretary.

On the motion of Benj. R. Ferney, it was ordered that a committee of not less than five be appointed to draft resolutions expressive of the sense of the meeting regarding the loss of Dr. Carpenter, who died near Philadelphia while attending medical lectures. The Committee was comprised of Benj. R. Ferney, Drs. A. J. Reduing,

J. S. Pettus, T. N. Pettus and A. H. Latimer;

in Honey Grove on the 18th of December, Lucinda Elizabeth, daughter of Thomas and Nancy Shaw, late of Tennessee.

great opportunity

$10,000 worth of goods to be sold at cost by D. C. Russel.

we call attention

to the card of J. L. Tucker, Ambro typist who can be found at the Donoho house. He would be happy to have the ladies and gentlemen call and see his style of work as the sphereotype[33] is something new and altogether superior to anything ever introduced before. It only wants to be seen to to show its advantages.

Forest Mail Stage Line from Marshall to Jefferson, Daingerfield and Mt Pleasant.

Fares from Marshall to Jefferson $2; from Marshall to Daingerfield $5; from Marshall to Mt. Pleasant $7.

The above line will run in connection with the Shreveport stages and railroad and the Henderson and Tyler stages and connect at Mt. Peasant with the Clarksville and western stage lines; notice by R. W. Nesmith.

In connection with the stage line, the proprietor keeps an extensive livery where travelers can procure hacks, buggies, carriage and saddle horses at all times on the most reasonable terms.

At Mt. Pleasant, Mr M. Bowman, who is a host himself, keeps entertainment for man and beast.

strayed

from Charles De Morse, a sorrel filly;

from Jas Scales of Kentucky Town, 27 sheep, five of them black

professional card

W. R. Hill, Attorney at Law, in New Orleans; he has been a citizen of Texas, laboriously and extensively engaged in the practice of law for more than 20 years.

Alto House

The Alto House in Decatur, Wise County; Alexius Halsell, Proprietor. This house opened during the present year at the county seat of the new county of Wise; he invites the attention of travelers and residents.

for sale

Notice by L. C. Alexander of Negro girl, 13 years old, which "I will sell for cash or barter for a boy or exchange for cattle at low rates"; inquire of A. M. Alexander of Sherman or the subscriber living 12 miles north of Sherman on the Red River.

runaway

notice by J. G. Gibson, living 12 miles north of Clarksville of runaway Negro, Julia; 23 years old; quite tall and of rather copper color. "She left me on December 13 and said to one of my Negroes that she intended to go to Clarksville and harbor until she could get some man to take her on."

****

ENDNOTES

1. The thrust of this item from an Exchange paper was humor. A woman's blouse, which was "close to her bosom' was made of cotton. However, on another level, the item is forbidding. *The Boston Liberator* was an early abolitionist paper and it reminds us that the War between the States was only four years off.

2. Strange sounding today, but the phrase "ready made clothing" speaks of a time before the American Civil War, when ready-to-wear apparel, which could be purchased using predetermined sizes, was not available, except for some coats and undergarments, Most clothing was made by tailors or at home. The Civil War with its need to manufacture thousands of uniforms and the invention of the sewing machine took the "ready to wear clothing" industry to new heights.

3. A safe, unfailing, at least to the diligent, drinking water supply was a gift of Nature, bestowed upon the citizens of Clarksville and Red River County. They did not take their water from rivers or creeks. Nor did they dig wells to the aquifers below or have springs gush it up under their noses. Instead, the townspeople allowed rainfall to run off into cisterns they had dug in the soft rock beneath the Clarksville earth. It appeared very efficient and healthy. In an issue six years earlier May 17, 1851, De Morse bragged

Our greatest element of health is pure water, the water that descends after atmospheric purification and is received and retained in cisterns in the solid rock, many feet beneath the surface. It is such water as we have found no where else, so cool that ice is no luxury here. Not so cold as ice would make it, but near it, that ice is unnecessary and no body feels the want of it; so cold that milk from a vessel let down to the bottom of a cistern will make the teeth ache.

The supply was inexhaustible, nothing less than the prior winter's rainfall, which in Clarksville is usually copious. Effort was required to dig the cisterns, but that was all that was needed to insure plenty of fresh cold water immediately available in a summer drought, without hauling.

4. Roland, sometimes and more accurately spelled "Rowland", was Clarksville's landing or the docks the town had on the Red River. It permitted the region to hook into the river commerce. The landing was just ten miles north of Clarksville. It had some stores (including "Rowland Bryerly's)" warehouses and its own name, Roland. You will not find Roland, on the map today, or even in the memory of the oldest citizen. But, it was there, at Roland, where the Red River planters and Clarksville merchants received the seed, equipment, manufactured goods and other necessities and luxuries they had been ordered the autumn before. It was at Roland also where, in winter and spring time, as the "navigation" of the river permitted, the planters would send by steamboat or flatboat their cotton down the Red River to Shreveport, where the Red River joined the Mississippi. From Shreveport, the market in New Orleans was only two days away by steamer. After the cotton was sold in New Orleans, it would be stowed on sailing ships and sent to the cotton and textile mills of either New England or London, where thousands upon thousands of workers waited to turn the nature's fiber into fabrics of fashion.

5. It is difficult for us today to imagine a Texas without highways and airports, connecting and making manageable the enormity of the State's geography. However, totally forgotten is the time, a generation before even the rail road, when internal transportation depended on the rivers of Texas. Indeed, the rivers themselves are nearly invisible today and, when recognized, more resemble the abandoned "canals" scarring the Martian face, than the infrastructure of the 1850s. How many in Dallas - once called the City of the Three Forks of the Trinity- know the location of those river beds today? Dams, lakes, flood control, irrigation and development, all have done their part to the withering of Texas rivers: the Brazos, Colorado, Sabine, Trinity, Guadalupe, San Antonio, Nueces, Rio Grande and, of particular importance to the

people of Clarksville and the Red River Valley, the Red River, with its Sulphur Creek.

The Red River is 1,360 miles long, the second longest in Texas. It stretches from the Mississippi and the Gulf of Mexico on one end, north to Arkansas, west across the entire state of Texas and then into the mountains of New Mexico. Although the Red River was by far the best means available to the farmer to send his crop to market and to receive his supplies in return, it was still a very difficult, often unreliable, route. The river was not deep and it was obstructed in places, with accumulated fallen trees and growths of vegetation, called *rafts*. Usually, the river began to rise in January or February, peaked in mid-spring and then declined until, by early summer, boats became rare. Sometimes, late fall would bring some more rains and the river would again be briefly "boatable." It would follow logically that, if ample rains brought navigation, droughts would hinder it. Texas river traffic was highly dependent upon the weather.

6. Archaic for "strayed". When livestock were found, their value was estimated by local citizens and the amount reviewed and fixed by the local Justice of the Peace. If the owner showed up, the finders of the animals were rewarded with a percentage of the appraised values.

7. The telegraph, invented in 1845, made messages almost instantaneous and opened up all sorts of opportunities from trans Atlantic cables to a the weather forecasting business. By 1852, there were 14,000 miles of telegraph wire laid, mostly in the northeastern United States.

8. When the Republic of Texas become a State, it maintained both its debt and its unappropriated lands. As part of the Compromise of 1850, Texas ceded its land claims for what is now New Mexico in return for $10,000,000 to reduce that debt. Some disputes arose in the payment of the second half of it which resulted in an offer for more money by Acts of Congress, which was accepted by the

Texas Legislature in 1857, despite the citizens having rejected it a year or so earlier in a general election.

9. In the election of 1856, it was neither the neophyte Republican party that worried De Morse nor the expiring Whigs. The former would be a foe for future, the latter was one of the past. Instead, the enemy was a familiar one that appears every so often on the American political stage, excites the attention of the electorate for a couple years and then dies out amid public disgust. It was termed Nativism - anti-foreign sentiment. A couple of years earlier, a new, secret version of it, had appeared on the scene, called Know Nothingism. Cloaked in secrecy it was anti immigrant and anti Catholic., an expression of unhappiness among the native born citizens of English /Scotch Irish/Dutch descent with the influx of these foreigners. De Morse was not among them. While no one could accuse him of being fond of "Popery", he detested their persecutors and frequently attacked the movement in *The Standard.*

Know Nothingism did not survive, soundly beaten in the 1856 election. It nevertheless had an effect as one of several agents that shaped the election of that year and the birth of the Republican Party.

10. Immigration to Texas was heavy. Incoming settlers purchased or leased the farms of the pioneers, who themselves were moving westward with the frontier. Many of the first residents of the region held land grants from Mexico or the Republic. Veterans had leagues of lands given them by a grateful government. Others owned head rights of land, originally granted them as inducements to settle. Some lost the certificates evidencing their or their predecessors' ownership and had to go to a lawyer to learn how to give notice and secure title, such as this one. If there was no response to the notice, the claimant could apply for new ones."

11. Bloomers - a new style of dress for women - is among the

earliest displays of the Feminist Movement, more than a half century away from even the ballot, much less full equality. The Women's Rights Convention at Seneca Falls, New York of 1848 under the leadership of Elizabeth Cady Stanton or the 1850 National Women's Rights Convention, led by Lucy Stone, in Worcester, Massachusetts,.

The style of dress might have begun in Europe. In Belgium, a style had developed for unmarried women to wear mens' garb to announce their condition. It received some attention on this side of the Atlantic Ocean, and in 1850 De Morse reported that, on the East Coast of the United States, ladies were taking to shirt collars and short jackets like men.

Many of the U.S. newspaper editors, De Morse included, accepted it as the right of a woman to dress as she felt most comfortable. They were mindful of the demand for equality being voiced by the same women who tended to dress in Bloomers, but, despite that red flag, they conceded to women "the right of ruling in petticoatdom":

12. William Becknell was known as the "Father of the Santa Fe Trade." He had been born in Virginia, and fought in the War of 1812. After a series of adventures, Becknell moved to Red River County. In the Texas War for Independence, he mustered a company of mounted volunteers known as the Red River Blues in July 1836. He subsequently commanded Red River militia companies in 1838, 1841, and 1842. He amassed a sizable estate in land and livestock in Red River and Lamar counties and also also owned a bridge across the Sulphur River.

13. The Town of Clarksville was managed by a "Corporation"" that is, by its Commissioners The bridges over the Delaware Creek were under its control. So was the graveyard, the public square and the jail. At different times, De Morse was critical of the Corporation's management, asking questions as " "What is the corporation of Clarksville doing? Is it doing anything? A good many tax payers wait patiently for an answer. It looks to the

uninitiated that the "City Fathers" were perfectly satisfied with their greatest improvement of encompassing the Square with drains and never expecting to do any more."

If pressure from the press was not enough, De Morse used his knowledge of the law to bend stubborn Commissioners to the will of the People, for whom De Morse was their self appointed spokesman, warning them that "that a gentleman of our acquaintance entertains a deliberate intention to report everyone liable to fines to the District Attorney at the next session of the District Court. The law has been examined and the fines are severe and recoverable upon motion. Fair warning now to all of you who are responsible for the wretched state of the several bridges over the main road from town.*"*

14. The election of 1856 was the Republicans, their first presidential contest. They included former Whigs and Norther anti slavery Democrats. This new party denounced the expansion of slavery and advocated a program of internal improvements. They nominated John C. Fremont, an explorer of the Far West with no political record.

15. As we recently learned by Hurricane Ike, Texas, not even its mid section, is immune from hurricane. But was this a hurricane or a tornado? Probably, the latter. It happened in May and it was one of several reported in Texas and Arkansas during a couple week period "leveling every opposing obstacle. Trees, fences, houses have all been prostrated and the deadened lumber in the cultivated sections have done extensive damage. We have heard of the ravages of the storm from several other districts south and east of this."

16. This refers to Oliver Hazard' Perry quote after the Battle of Lake Erie during the War of 1812: "We have met the enemy and they are ours: two ship, twp brigs, a schooner and a sloop."

17. By the 1850s, the eastern states had had their fill of emigrants from Europe. Texas, however, still encouraged immigration. There was so much land that had to be settled. De Morse called for those outside of Texas to come and settle.

The State's wide enough,

There's room for us all,

Room, boys, room.

A good portion of the immigration entered Texas by crossing the Red River near Clarksville. De Morse needed only to look out his window or stand on his front porch to view the immigration first hand. "For the last two weeks, scarcely a day has passed that a dozen or more mover's wagons have not passed through our Town." Passing through Clarksville gave the immigrants several options: to settle in Red River and surrounding counties. Or they could push out west along the Red River to the frontier counties, like Cooke, Montague or Parker. Or, at Preston in Grayson county, they could take the National Road south, to the Trinity region, or even as far as Austin and points below. De Morse was an exuberant supporter of immigration, boasting that "the country is filling up fast and deserves to - if ever rich soil and sunny clime deserved settlers."

The bulk of the newcomers, not unexpectedly, were from the American south. They were farmers, usually of cotton. Many were prosperous and brought their slave workforce with them. However, today's Texan might be surprised at how many immigrants came directly from Europe to Texas. The immigrant ships usually deposited their passengers at Galveston's, Texas' ocean port.

Often the emigrants came as part of colonies. French communists, the Utopian Icarian Colony, "living completely in common with order and economy and calling each other brother" settled in Titus county and then in the Peters Colony, about twenty miles north of Fort Worth. Another group, also of French origin, but following the socialist philosophy of Charles Fourier, called their colony La Reunion, just a few miles from Dallas. A group of Germans, sponsored by the nobility of the several German States, settled their excess population in central Texas, creating New Braufels and Fredericksburg in the process.

18. Charles De Morse and Texas could not be blamed for dreaming of a railroad. Railroads were all the rage in the United States, since Peter Cooper introduced Tom Thumb in 1830. By 1852, there were 12,500 miles of track in the United States. The demand across the nation for building railroads was huge, but the supply was limited and the price expensive. It would be well after the Civil War that the railroad would have much impact on Texas

19. Dalby Springs in neighboring Bowie county was, a century and a half ago, something of a sports resort and health spa to sneak off to in the summer time. It had sulphur hot springs considered therapeutic by the populace. They became popular, summer meeting place, for some of the upper crust of Northern Texas.

20. The deceased was the son of James Clark, a Tennessean-born adventurer of Scotch ancestry, and his wife Isabella, who had founded the town of Clarksville. When James Clark passed away, Isabella remarried Dr. George Gordon of the Town. Frank H. Clark became his step son and the family would continue as one of the more influential voices in Town.

21. A *tableau vivant*, French for "living picture", was the representation of a picture or scene by people properly costumed and posed. In other words, the women would dress up and the men would stare at them without giving offense.

22. Inflation? When Benjamin Franklin coined the phrase, it was "a penny saved , a penny earned".

23. Buck and Breck were, of course ,James Buchanan, the successful Democratic candidate for President whose inability to

avert the Civil War has been assessed as the worst single failure by a United States President. His running mate was John Cabell Breckinridge, a 36 year old from Kentucky. He was to become a Presidential candidate himself in 1860 for the Southern Democrats. With the War, he became a Confederate General and finally Secretary of War for the South.

24. The bois d'arc tree is indigenous to Northeast Texas, Southeast Oklahoma and Southwest Arkansas. A member of the mulberry family and related to the fig, it grows to a maximum height of 50 to 60 feet, with a trunk 1 to 2 feet in diameter, and thrives near creek and river bottoms. The wood is hard, flexible, durable, and resistant to moisture and soil. Early settlers also made bois d'arc grave markers, floors, gates, foundation blocks but the tree's real claim to fame was its use on the prairies as a hedge row fence before the invention of barbed wire in the 1870s.

25. R. W. B. Oliver, was a fellow member of the Bar with De Morse, having his office in Gainsesville

26. America's history has many chapters, among them the period of Manifest Destiny when many thought the United States should expand its territory to all of North America and even Central and South America. Filibusters were soldiers of fortune who fitted out expeditions to wage war against countries with which the United States was at peace.

One of the more successful of these was William Walker who enjoyed immense popularity. After an unsuccessful invasion of Mexico, he saw his opportunity in Nicaragua which was undergoing political turmoil at the time. One of the feuding political parties hired Walker and three hundred men of his men to come to Nicaragua and fight. Successful, Walker declared himself Commander in Chief, and then President, of Nicaragua, declaring English an official language and reorganizing currency and fiscal policy to encourage immigration from the United States.

Walker's empire did not last long. His army, thinned by cholera was run out by a coalition of central American countries and Cornelius Vanderbilt, who had his own designs on Nicaragua, as a short cut to California.

27. *La perce quipoise* is when one performer stands on the ground, holding a vertical pole, either in a leather sling or balanced on his shoulder or even his head. A second performer shinnies up the pole and does an acrobatic routine on it

28. This was among the opening salvos of successive failures of banks and businesses that has come to be known in history as the Panic of 1857, a downturn in the economy of the United States not unlike, in causes and effects, as our own in 2008. Gold pouring into the economy from California, the move by millions westward, plenty of credit to be had the and expansion of American firms into a precarious worldwide market gave America a sense of confidence which burst and fears grew that the Government would be unable to pay obligations in specie. Thousands of businesses failed, unemployment soared and there was great discontent in urban areas. It spread to the rest of the world. It would take the Civil War to pull the United States out of this depression just as World War II, twelve years later, ended the Great Depression of 1929.

29. Latin for "mine" and "yours".

30. Is this cattle rustling?

31. In his May 12, 1855 issue of *The Standard,* De Morse explained to his readers that " [t]here is a tradition in the tribe that there were three brothers named Choctaw, Chickisaw and Muscogee, who came from the far west each giving his name to a Nation - the first to wit, the Chickisaw and the Choctaw are now blended, speaking the same language. The Muscogees are now known as the Creeks. From the Creeks, sprang the Seminoles [or

wanderers] a tribe whose acts of violence it took years to repress in Florida.

The three tribes were among the Five Civilized Tribes, a loose confederation of North American Indians in the Indian Territory, formed in 1859. They had been deported to Oklahoma, under the Indian Removal Act of 1830, from their traditional homelands east of the Mississippi. Each organized an autonomous state, established courts, enacted a legal code, built schools and churches, and even developed a writing system based on one earlier devised by the Cherokee.

The Chickasaws established their capital at Good Spring on lower Pennington Creek when they were separated from the Choctaws in 1856. The place was given a new name, Tishomingo City, in honor of a famous tribal chief. Several stores, a cotton gin, a water mill, and a newspaper, the *Chickasaw and Choctaw Herald,* were established in the place.

32. This was the famous "Commodore" Cornelius Vanderbilt of New York, a legend in steamboat and railroad circles. Quitting school at age 11, he, five years later, had his own business, ferrying freight and passengers between Staten Island and Manhattan. A contemporary and rival of Thomas Fulton, he had, by the 1840s, a hundred steamships plying the Hudson, supposedly the largest employer at the time . The discovery of gold in 1849 in California gave Vanderbilt another opportunity, offering a shortcut via Nicaragua. There he encountered William Walker (see endnote 26) . Vanderbilt also "dabbled" in railroads, owning most of them in the east at one time or another

33. Today, with digital camera, cell phones shooting pictures and the like, we are well past the early days of photography. Not so in Texas and the United States in the mid 1850s. The rage then were Daguerrotypes or Ambrotypes, a complex and demanding process, taking about an hour to complete, using copper plates, glass and chemicals to help create the image. Sphereotypes, patented in 1856, was an improvement on th process.

INDICES

PEOPLE

A

ABBOT, M. P. - 7/5/56

AGERS, Eli - 11/22/56

AIKIN, Rev. Mr. - 5/31/56

ALEXANDER, A. M. - 9/20/56; 11/15/56;12/26/57

ALEXANDER, C. C. - 5/10/56; - 5/17/56; 5/31/56; 3/7/57; 9/5/57

ALEXANDER, L. C. - 12/26/57

ALFORD, B. D. - 9/19/57

ALFORD, J. P. - 9/6/56

ALIC - 10/11/56

ALLEN, Miss C. A. - 8/23/56

ALLEN, Hugh - 12/12/57

ALLEN, James E. - 6/7/56

ALLEN, James M. - 6/14/56

ALLEN, Joe - 12/12/57

ALLEN, M. W. - 3/14/57

ANANIAS - 7/5/56

ANDERSON, Charles - 6/7/56

ANDERSON, Rev. John - 7/5/56; 8/30/56; 10/11/56; 9/5/57; 10/17/57; 11/28/57

ANDERSON, Mrs. M. M. - 9/5/57

ANDERSON, Nathan - 5/17/56

ANDERSON, Samuel Bailey - 1/17/57

ANNIS, Mr. J. T. L. - 11/22/56

ARLEDGE, A. L. - 7/5/56

ARMSTEAD, B. H. - 8/16/56

ARMSTRONG, Matthew - 9/5/57

ARMSTRONG, Attorney - 11/15/56; 11/29/56;12/5/57

ARNOLD, L. W. - 11/29/56; 9/12/57

ASKEW, R. L. - 5/10/56

AUSTIN, John O. - 3/29/56

AUSTIN, William K. - 10/10/57

AUSTIN, Mr. - 11/28/57

AVANTA, Cary 10/10/57

AVANTA, John - 10/10/57

AYMAR, A.F. - 9/19/57

AYRES, Mrs. Caroline - 1/17/57

B

BABB, E. W.- 10/25/56

BAGBY, Arthur P. - 5/10/56

BAGBY, B. C. - 5/24/56; 5/31/56

BAGBY, Edward - 7/5/56

BAGBY, George H.. - 3/1/56; 3/15/56; 7/5/56; 7/26/56; 8/2/56; 8/9/56

BAGBY, Mrs. Jane - 8/9/56

BAGBY, Capt. John A. - 5/10/56; 8/2/56; 12/6/56; - 12/19/57

BAGBY, Miss Martha - 8/2/56

BAGGETT, John M. - 10/10/57

BAILEY, L. C. - 12/19/57

BAIN, R. M. - 1/17/57

BAKER, Gwen - 10/10/57

BAKER, Joseph - 2/16/56; 5/17/56

BALL, George B. - 7/5/56

BAKER, Miss Mary - 10/10/57

BALLARD, W. W. - 10/10/57

BANKSTON, James - 10/10/57

BARBER, esq. - 12/12/57

BARBOUR, Hon. L. - 3/14/57

BARNHART, F. G - 9/26/57

BARRIE, C. N. - 6/21/56

BARRIEr, M. T - 6/21/56

BARRY, Dr. Jasper A. - 3/8/56; 11/22/56; 1/3/57; 1/17/57 ;9/5/57; 12/5/57

BATEMAN, Jonathan - 11/22/56

BATEMEN, M. - 7/5/56

BATES, John Miflin - 3/8/56

BATES, Rev William - 7/26/56

BATTES, Maj. Wm. C .

BATTLE, R. .J. - 2/14/57

BATTON Brothers - 12/12/57

BEAVER, Benjamin L. - 12/20/56

BECKNELL, Capt William. - 4/26/56

BELL, Attorney - 11/29/56

BELL, Mr. - 3/7/57

BELLAMY, J. R. - 7/26/56

BENNERS, Benners , E. G. - 5/10/56; 6/14/56; 11/21/57

BENNERS, Mr. - 5/10/56; 8/2/56

BENNINGFIELD, William - 11/22/56

BENSON, Mr. - 1/17/57

BERRY, Alex - 12/5/57

BERRY, Bill - 12/12/57

BERRY, J.D.- 7/12/56

BERRY, Nat - 12/12/57

BIBLE, L. T. - 10/10/57

BILGE, Dr. J. H. - 10/10/57

BILLINGLEY, Henry L. - 11/22/56

BIRMINGHAM, P. W.. - 3/1/56

BISHOP, Col. A. - 12/6/56; 3/14/57

BIVINS, John M.. - 3/1/56; 3/29/56; 8/9/56; 10/ 04/56; 11/29/56; 1/3/57; 12/5/57; 12/19/57

BLACK, Ann - 1/3/57

BLACK, R. H. - 10/3/57; 11/14/57

BLACK, Mr. - 9/5/57

BLACKON, Miss E. A. - 12/5/57

BLACKWELL, Joel - 5/10/56

BLAIR, John - 8/16/56

BLAIR, Captain - 6/21/56

BLANKENSHIP, Mr - 1/3/57

BLOOODWORTH, Jesse D. - 5/17/56; 7/5/56

BLYTHE, William T. - 5/10/56; 11/14/57

BOGART, Samuel - 5/17/56

BOLIN, Malcolm - 4/19/56; 8/16/56; 10/11/56; 9/12/57; 9/26/57;11/21/57

BONE, Celestia Virginia - 6/7/56

BONE, Elizabeth A - 6/7/56

BONE, John W. - 6/7/56

BONNER, W. H. - 5/10/56; 5/17/56

BONNERS, S. G. - 3/8/56

BOSWELL, William - 1/17/57

BOURLAND, James - 9/5/57

BOWMAN, M. - 12/26/57

BOYLE, Attorney - 11/29/56

BRADFORD, William - 7/5/56

BRADLEY, Rev. C. J. - 12/6/56

BRADSHAW, G. - 5./17/56

BRECKENRIDGE, John C. - 10/11/56; 11/15/56; 11/22/56; 11/29/56; 12/6/56

BREM, T. J. - 6/28/5

BRITT, Mrs. Mary T - 1/3/57

BROMLEY, D. - 5/17/56

BROWDER, David - 11/22/56

BROWN, Anthony - 5/24/56

BROWN, Cicero - 1/19/56; 5/24/56

BROWN, - 10/10/57

BROWN, John Henry - 1/19/56

BROWN, L. - 5/17/56

BROWN, P. - 10/3/57

BROWN, Phdandrum - 3/1/56

BROWN, William H. - 2/16/56

BROWN, Mr.- 3/22/56; 11/22/56

BROWNELL, S. E. - 9/5/57; 9/19/57

BRUSH, Miss - 5/3/56

BRUTON, David - 6/21/56; 9/13/56

BRYAN, Benjamin - 7/5/56 10/10/57

BRYAN, Mary Ann - 7/5/56

BRYAN, Mrs. Sarah M. - 7/5/56-

BRYAN, Wilson - 9/26/57

BRYERLY, Rowland - 11/29/56

BUCHANAN, James - 8/23/56; 10/11/56; 11/15/56; 11/22/56; 11/29/56; 12/6/56; 12/19/57

BUCK, Stephen - 1/17/57

BULKLEY, C. A. - 3/7/57

BURCHER, Mrs. Mary F - 7/5/56.

BURE, William - 6/21/56

BURFORD, Nat. M.- 2/16/56; 10/25/56; 11/1/56; 11/15/56; 11/29/56

BURKE, E. - 7/5/56

BURKS, John C. - 5/3/56; 6/28/5; 11/29/56; 12/6/56; 3/7/57; 9/19/57; - 9/26/57; 10/10/57;11/14/57; 12/12/57; 12/19/57

BURKS, Col. J. H. - 5/10/56; 11/28/57; 12/5/57; - 12/12/57

BURNETT, Austin - 7/26/56

BURSON, Isaac C. - 11/7/57

BUSH, Miss Mary - 5/10/56

BUTLER, A. - 7/5/56

BUTLER, Charles - 7/26/56

BUTLER, John - 11/22/56 -

BUTLER, Miss Martha - 10/10/57

BUTT, Colonel - 11/22/56

C

CALDWELL, James. - 3/1/56

CALHOUN, James - 7/5/56

CALVIN, W. - 8/16/56

CAMPBELL, D. - 10/10/57

CAMPBELL, James - 10/10/57

CANADAY, Mr. - 7/5/56

CARNCROSS, Miss - 5/24/56

CARNCROSS Family - 5/24/56

CARPENTER, Dr. Edwin F. - 12/26/57

CARPENTER, Mr. - 12/6/56

CARTER, A. P. - 1/17/57

CARTER, D. - 8/16/56

CARTER, J. O. - 3/7/57

CARTER, Robert - 7/5/56

CASE, Miss Mary T. - 8/16/56

CECK, Valentin - 1/17/57

CHAFFIN, Green - 7/5/56

CHAMBERS, General T. J. - 1/26/56

CHANDLER, E. - 10/10/57

CHANEY, Parthena - 11/14/57

CHAPMAN, Edward - 8/16/56

CHERRY, N. A. - 5/17/56

CHILDRESS, Levi G. - 5/10/56

CHISOLM, D. M. - 2/14/57; 12/5/57

CHRISTIAN, B.F. - 2/13/56

CHRISTIAN, Ben - 10/17/57

CHRISTIAN, W. H. - 9/19/57

CLARK, E. - 8/16/56

CLARK, E. T. - 10/10/57

CLARK, Frank H. - 9/27/56

CLARK, James - 1/19/56; 9/20/56; 9/27/56

CLARK, James H. - 6/14/56; 7/26/56; 10/25/56; 3/14/57; 10/10/57

CLARK, John T. - 7/5/56

CLARK, N. P. - 3/22/56; 4/12/56

CLARKE, J. R. - 12/6/56

CLEVELAND, Gen. Benjamin - 7/5/56

COCKRELL, Mr. - 11/1/56

CODY, Miss E - 8/23/56

COE, Mr. - 5/10/56

COFFEE, Langston - 9/19/57

COFFEE, Nancy Anne - 9/19/57

COFFEE, - 12/5/57

COLLARD, W. E. - 10/10/57

COLLIER, Edie - 10/25/56

COLLIER, Mrs. Isabella - 7/5/56

COLLIER, Shandrich - 10/25/56

COLLIER, William - 10/24/57

COLLIN, James - 7/5/56

COLLINS, J. W. - 10/10/57

CONDON, Jackson - 10/10/57

CONE, John - 10/10/57

CONNER, Wesley - 10/10/57

COOK, William A. - 7/5/56

COOPER, Col. - 9/20/56

CORLEY, A. H. - 10/17/57

CORNELIUS, William P - 5/10/56; 3/7/57; 12/19/57

CORNELL, Watson - 8/16/56

COULTER, T. M., - 9/27/56; 9/5/57

COVEY, John W. - 11/22/56

COWAN, Thomas L. - 5/3/56; 5/10/56

COX, Jim - 12/12/57

CRABTREE, William - 8/16/56

CRAWFORD, J. F. - 5/24/56

CRAWFORD, W. - 10/10/57

CRITTENDEN; Wm. - 6/21/56

CROCKER, W. B. - 5/24/56

CROOKS, Thomas J. - 12/6/56; 11/14/57

CROWDER, Crowder, James - 9/5/57

CROWDER, Jane - 11/14/57

CROWDER, Mary - 9/5/57

CROWDER, W.B. - 11/14/57

CRUCE, William - 7/5/56

CRUTCHER, William - 8/16/56

CUADRAS, Mr. Joaquin - 9/19/57

CULLUM, John H. - 4/12/56

CUMMINGS; F. E. - 5/17/56

CUMMINGS; H. - 10/10/57

CUMMINGS; Rev. A. - 10/10/57; 10/17/57

D

DAGLEY, T. A. - 5/17/56

DALBY, Joseph G. - 10/10/57

DALBY, W. R. - 10/10/57

DALBY, Warren K. - 9/12/57

DALE, John P.. - 3/1/56; 8/9/56

DALE, T. H. - 8/9/56

DANFORTH, D. - 1/12/56; 9/19/57

DANIEL, J. M. - 1/17/57

DANIEL, T. - 10/10/57

DARIEN, Elias H. - 10/04/56

DARNAL, J. H. - 11/28/57

DARNELL, Mr. - 3/8/56; 8/2/56

DAUGHERTY, M. L. - 1/19/56

DAVIDSON, Miss E. - 1/17/57

DAVIDSON, L.C. - 1/17/57

DAVIDSON, Mrs. - 11/22/56

DAVIESS, J. T. - 12/5/57

DAVIS, Rev. A. L. - 5/24/56

DAVIS, Greenberry - 8/30/56

DAVIS, Miss Narcissa - 8/16/56

DAVIS, R. M. - 10/24/57

DAVIS, Attorney - 12/12/57

DAVIS - 11/21/57

DAWSON, W. N. - 5/10/56

DAY, Miss Clarinda - 10/10/57

DAY, Miss Mary E. - 10/10/57

DE MORSE, Charles - 4/12/56; 7/19/56; 7/26/56; 9/20/56; 9/27/56; 10/11/56; 12/6/56; 12/26/57; 3/7/57; 11/7/57; 11/21/57; 12/5/57; 12/19/57

DEAN, J. A. - 11/22/56

DEAN, Dean, Reuben - 12/12/57

DEAN, Willis - 8/2/56

DEBERRY, Henry D. - 1/3/57

DEKING, Lorenzo D. - 5/10/56

DENNIS, Thomas - 5/17/56

DICKERSON, E. D. - 12/5/57

DICKERSON, T. J. - 5/17/56

DICKSON, Clement - 1/17/57

DICKSON, Miss F. - 10/10/57

DICKSON, J. J. -3/8/56; 11/21/57; 12/12/57

DICKSON, John B. - 5/3/56; 5/24/56

DICKSON, Miss Sally R. - 5/24/56

DILLAHUNTY, Hervey - 5/10/56; 11/15/56; 11/22/56; 10/10/57; 10/24/57; 11/28/57; 12/12/57

DISLEY, Capt. George H. - 8/16/56

DOAK, Miss Margaret A - 9/6/56

DOAK, Nelson - 5/10/56; 9/6/56

DODD, Mrs. Elizabeth - 11/22/56

DOLLAR, W. G. - 5/10/56

DONOHO, Mary W. - 7/26/56; 11/1/56; 2/21/57

DOUGHERTY, Charles - 5/17/56

DOYLE, James - 10/10/57

DRAKE, Thomas - 10/10/57

DUDLEY, W. N. - 7/5/56

DUGAN, Geo. C. - 2/16/56; 3/8/56

DUKE, Andrew J. - 8/16/56

DUKE, Duke, P. M. - 9/6/56; 10/10/57; 12/5/57

DUKE, Col. William J. - 10/10/57

DUNLAP, Rev Mr. - 1/3/57

DUNLASS, R. R. - 4/26/56

DUNN, Miss Harriet - 10/10/57

DURANT, Col - 11/15/56

DURDEN, Mr. - 10/11/56

DURFEE, Chas- 8/9/56

DUTIES, James C. - 3/8/56

DYER, H. P. - 5/24/56

DYER, James - 5/24/56

E

EASTON, John C. - 1/19/56; 1/26/56; 2/16/56; 4/5/56; 11/29/56; 10/10/57

ECHOLS, Benjamin R. - 10/10/57

EDMONDSON, Eli - 11/22/56; 11/14/57

EDMONDSON, Margaret - 11/14/57

EDMONDSON, Turner B. - 12/6/56

EDMONSON, K. - 10/10/57

EDMUNDSON, T. B. - 9/5/57

EDWARD - 9/20/56

ELKIN, P. - 10/10/57

ELLIOT, G. F. - 1/17/57

ELLIOT, L. C. - 9/13/56

ELLIS, L. A. - 11/7/57

ELLIS, S. H. - 2/14/57

ELLIS, Stephen. - 1/17/57

ELLIS, Captain - 12/19/57

EMANUEL - 9/20/56

EMBRY, H. J. - 10/10/57

ENGLISH, Judge - 3/8/56; 5/3/56; 5/10/56

EPPERERSON B. H. - 10/17/57

EPPERERSON, Benjamin H. - 1/3/57

EPPERERSON William - 10/10/57

EPPERERSON, - 12/12/57

ERWIN, N. C. - 9/26/57

ESTES, Edward A.- 10/25/56

EUKER - 10/24/57

EVANS, Miss B.A. - 7/5/56

EVANS, H. C. - 11/22/56; 10/10/57

EVANS, Henry - 10/10/57

EVANS, Jesse - 8/16/56

EVANS, L. D. - 5/17/56. 7/19/56; 8/9/56; 9/20/56

EVANS, Lucinda - 7/5/56

EVANS, Wm. - 5/10/56

EVERTS, Gustavs A. - 10/25/56; 11/29/56

EWING, Dr. J. ..A - 1/17/57

EWING, John M. - 8/23/56; 9/20/56

EWING, William M. - 5/10/56; 1/3/57; 9/5/57; 11/14/57

EWINGS, - 11/14/57

EXMON, Charles - 12/5/57

F

FARBER, C. A. - 10/10/57

FARIS Attorney - 10/25/56

FARLEY, Mr. - 7/5/56

FARRAR, James J.. - 3/1/56
FAULKNER, John - 1/12/56
FAVORS Miss Josephin - 12/6/56 e
FEATHERSTON[E] William B,- 9/20/56; 10/25/56; 9/5/57
FERNEY, Benj. R. - 12/26/57
FERRETT, John - 10/10/57
FILLMORE, Millard - 5/10/56; 8/23/56
FISHBACK, Elizabeth - 9/5/57
FISHBACK, Isaac H. -8/2/56; 9/5/57
FISHER, M - 10/10/57
FISHER, M. W. - 10/10/57
FITCH, W. D. - 3/14/57
FITZHUGH, William - 12/5/57
FLEMING, Adaline - 11/22/56
FLEMING, W.D. - 7/5/56
FLEMING, William - 1/17/57
FLEMING, Mr. - 2/21/57
FLEMINGTON, S. - 9/5/57
FLETCHER, P. M. - 10/31/57
FLETCHER, W. L. - 7/26/56
FLOYD, James B. - 7/5/56
FORD, M. F. - 7/5/56
FOREMAN, M. - 7/5/56
FORT, J. W. - 5/17/56
FOWLER, A. J. - 11/15/56
FOWLER, John H. - 5/17/56
FOWLER, Jonathan - 5/10/56
FRANCIS, R. B. - 6/7/56;

12/6/56; 9/12/57; 12/12/57
FRANKLIN, B. T. - 5/17/56
FRANKLIN, G. W. - 1/17/57
FRANKLIN, John, M.D. - 8/16/56; 11/22/56
FREEMAN, Henry - 11/22/56
FREEMAN, W. M.
FREMONT, John C. - 10/25/56
FREYER, Mr. - 5/24/56
FULLBRIGHT, David - 3/7/57
FULLBRIGHT, Judge - 5/3/56; 5/10/56
FULLER, Fuller, B. F. - 1/12/56; 9/5/57; 9/19/57
FULLER, Flora - 9/19/57
FULLER, Ida, - 9/19/57
FULLER, John W - 10/10/57
FULLER, Mr. - 11/22/56
FULSOM, Susan - 11/22/56
FULTON, Clarissa - 1/19/56
FULTON, Samuel M. - 1/19/56
FURLONG, Dr. Luther K. - 10/10/57

G
GAFFNEY, Mrs. - 10/24/57
GAGE, W. W. - 10/10/57
GAINES, Gen. Henry H. - 7/5/56; 10/10/57
GAINES, Thomas - 5/17/56
GAINES, Wm. C. - 11/1/56
GALBRAITH, S. J. - 5/24/56;

11/28/57

GALBREATH, Samuel C - 1/17/57

GAMBELL, Joseph - 8/16/56

GAMBILL, Wm. - 5/24/56

GAMMAGE, W. L. - 11/22/56

GARR, A. - 5/17/56

GARRET, James - 12/26/57

GARRETT, John - 5/10/56

GARRISON, Rev Thomas F. - 6/7/56

GATTIS, M. J. - 9/5/57; 9/19/57

GATTIS, M. R. - 9/5/57; 9/19/57

GEORGE; - 10/11/56

GIBBONS, J. C. - 5/17/56

GIBBONS, John - 7/5/56

GIBSON, E. F. - 9/5/57; 9/19/57

GIBSON, J. G. - 12/26/57

GIBSON, Robert - 5/17/56

GIBSON, Mrs.- 5/3/56

GIDDENS, W. W. - 7/5/56

GILL, W.A. - 7/5/56

GILL, W. H. - 11/7/57

GILLIAM, James - 8/30/56; 3/7/57

GILLIAM, William S. - 11/28/57

GLASS, A. M. - 11/22/56

GLASS, Alexander - 11/22/56

GLASS, Henry D. - 10/04/56

GLOVER, Martin - 5/31/56; 10/25/56

GOFF, Thomas - 1/17/57

GOFF, Wm. W. - 5/10/56

GOLDEN; - 11/14/57

GOLDMAN, A. - 2/14/57

GOOD, Gen. John J. - 3/1/56; 10/25/56; 11/15/56; 10/10/57

GOOD, Rev. Mr. - 1/17/57 -

GOODMAN, J. P. - 5/10/56

GORDON, Dr. George -1/19/56; 5/3/56; 5/10/56; 9/27/56; 11/22/56; 3/7/57; 12/5/57

GORE; Miles - 1/19/56

GOULD, Miss Virginia - 8/16/56

GRAG, Milton, - 2/16/56

GRAHAM, R. H. - 8/2/56

GRAHAM, Rev. Jas. - 12/6/56

GRANT, Carrol - 9/20/56

GRAY, Judge - 4/26/56

GRAY, B. W. - 5/10/56; 11/14/57

GREEN, J. W. - 5/17/56

GREEN, M. L. F. - 10/3/57

GREEN, T. C. F. - 10/3/57

GREEN, Turner L. - 1/19/56; 5/10/56; 5/31/56; 8/2/56; 8/16/56; 3/7/57; 10/3/57; 10/10/57; 11/14/57; 11/21/57

GREGG, Mrs. Virgina A - 8/16/56.

GRIDER, Attorney - 10/25/56

GRIFFITHS, Josiah - 10/10/57

GRIFFITHS, Nathan E. - 5/31/56

GRIFFITHS, Mr. - 12/12/57

GRIGGS, D.C. - 8/16/56
GRISWELL, Wm. H. - 12/5/57
GUEST, Martin Sr., - 1/3/57
GUEST, Martin Jr, - 1/3/57
GUEST, Wm. - 5/3/56; 5/10/56; 11/29/56
GUFFEE, John - 5/17/56

H

HACKETT, A.A. - 7/5/56
HACKETT, Mrs. - 10/10/57
HAING, J. - 10/10/57
HALE, John W. - 7/5/56
HALEY, William - 11/22/56
HALL, Dr. Alfred - 9/5/57; 9/19/57
HALL, Dr. B.F. - 11/29/56
HALL, Miss Mary E. - 11/22/56
HALSELL, Alexius - 12/26/57
HAMILTON, James G. - 5/10/56; 11/7/57
HAMILTON, James M. - 10/04/56,
HAMILTON, John P. - 11/7/57
HAMILTON, Robert S. - 10/04/56
HAMILTON, William F. - 12/5/57
HAMPTON, Mr. - 9/5/57; 9/12/57
HANCOCK, Joseph P. - 11/22/56
HANCOCK, Lewis C. - 1/3/57

HANSE, - 11/14/57
HANSON, Col. H. C. - 9/13/56
HANSON, Col. S. T. - 9/6/56
HARBINGER, Attorney- 10/25/56
HARDIN, Mrs. Sarah M. - 8/16/56
HARDY, Edie - 10/25/56
HARGRAVE, Glen - 8/16/56
HARGRAVE, Wm. - 5/10/56
HARGRAVES, H. H. - 5/10/56
HARMAN, L.G. - 1/12/56; 5/10/56; 5/31/56; 8/23/56; 9/20/56
HARMAN, Thomas - 1/3/57
HARMON, Rev. Dr. - 8/16/56
HARRIS, Mrs. Elizabeth G - 1/17/57
HARRIS, J. B. - 5/17/56
HARRIS, J. G. - 9/26/57
HARRIS, M. B. - 10/10/57
HARRISs, H C. - 1/17/57
HARRIS, Thomas - 10/10/57
HARRISON, L. L. - 10/11/56
HART, J. C. - 6/28/5; 9/27/56; 3/7/57; 10/17/57
HART, Hardin - 10/25/56; 10/10/57
HART, M. - 1/19/56
HART, Martin - 10/25/56; 11/22/56
HART, W. F. T. - 9/5/57
HART, Dr. - 5/10/56

HART, - 11/21/57

HARTELL, Franklin - 10/10/57

HATMAKER, Col. - 9/20/56

HAWKINS, Henry - 9/20/56

HAWKINS, Col. L - 10/10/57

HAY, S. R. - 10/10/57

HAYES, William - 1/17/57; 10/31/57

HAYNIE - 12/12/57

HAYS, Miss M. J. - 5/17/56

HEAD, John - 8/16/56; 1/17/57

HEARN, T. B.- 2/28/57

HELMAN, Mr. S. - 7/26/56

HELTON, E. J. - 5/17/56

HENDERSON, L. D. - 5/3/56; 5/10/56; 5/31/56; 3/7/57; 12/19/57

HENDRICKS, H. G - 5/17/56; 10/25/56; 11/22/56

HENDRICKSON, Attorney - 10/25/56

HENNINGS, F. - 8/16/56

HENRY, William F. - 8/16/56

HENRY, Mr. - 5/24/56

HENSLEE, J. N. B. - 1/12/56

HENSLEE, K. C. - 5/24/56

HENSLEY, Archibald V Darby - 8/16/56

HENSLEY, William - 8/16/56

HERDNON, Jacob W. - 8/16/56

HERVEY, James W. - 10/10/57

HIGBY, Attorney - 10/25/56

HIGRIGHT, Richard - 11/22/56

HILL, Aaron - 7/26/56

HILL, John P. - 5/10/56

HILL, Col. W.R. - 9/19/57; 12/26/57

HILL, Wm. - 5/17/56

HILL, Mr..- 3/22/56; 3/14/57

HOBBS, W. H. - 5/17/56

HOBSON, G. W. - 3/14/57

HOFAR, H. H. - 11/28/57

HOFFMAN, John - 11/15/56

HOGAN, H. C. - 5/17/56

HOLAFIELD, C. R. - 7/5/56

HOLLAND; E. J. - 1/19/56

HOLLIDAY, Mr. - 2/14/57

HOLLIS, Mr. - 9/26/57

HOLLUM, Ira - 11/22/56

HOLLYFIELD, William - 10/10/57

HOLMAN, C. K. - 11/14/57

HOLYFIELD, C. P. - 5/17/56

HOOKER, James - 5/17/56

HOOKS, William - 3/7/57

HOOTEN, James - 5/10/56

HOPKINS, Henry - 2/16/56

HOPKINS, J. E. - 5/10/56; 12/20/56

HOPKINS, Joslin - 2/16/56

HOPKINS, Miss Mary A. - 9/5/57

HOPKINS, Miss N. A. V. - 12/20/56

HOPKINS, Richard M. - 10/25/56; 9/5/57

HOSS, Nathan - 12/5/57

HOUGHTON, Maj. W. M. - 10/31/57

HOUSE, Eliza - 7/26/56

HOUSE, R. M. - 5/17/56

HOWE, M. A. - 12/5/57

HOWE, O. D. - 12/5/57

Howell, Alfred T. - 5/17/56; 5/24/56; 7/5/56

Howell S., - 1/19/56

HOWES, Mr. - 9/27/56

HOWETH, William - 7/26/56

HUFF, J. A. - 10/11/56

HUGHART, Edward - 8/30/56

HUGHES, Reece - 9/5/57

HUPPERS, George W. - 11/22/56

HUSKEY, L. C. - 11/22/56

HUSKEY Silas - 8/16/56

HUTCHINSON, R. C.- 3/22/56

HUTTON, William - 12/12/57

HYDE, Hyde, Jordan - 5/17/56

HYDE, John K. - 7/26/56

J

JACKSON, Andrew - 5/10/56

JACKSON, John M. - 1/3/57

JAMES, Mr. - 7/26/56

JAMISON, Davidson - 7/5/56

JANES, H. S. - 10/11/56

JANES, Jarret , - 11/29/56

JANES, Margaret - 11/29/56

JANES, W.C. , - 11/29/56

JARRETT, John - 5/10/56

JEFF, - 9/5/57; 9/12/57

JEFFERSON, Thomas - 12/6/56

JIM, - 10/11/56

JOBE, Jonathan - 10/10/57

JOHNSON, Alexander - 10/3/57

JOHNSON, C. B. - 5/17/56

JOHNSON, G. W. - 9/13/56; 9/27/56; 5/17/56

JOHNSON, Geo. - 6/14/56

JOHNSON, H. D. - 8/16/56

JOHNSON, Mrs. J. - 5/17/56

JOHNSON, Jean - 9/19/57; 9/26/57

JOHNSON, John T. - 10/10/57

JOHNSON, L. S. - 5/17/56

JOHNSON, Mrs. M. - 5/17/56

JOHNSON, Col. M. T. - 3/14/57

JOHNSON, Martha M. - 10/3/57

JOHNSON, N. R. - 10/10

JOHNSON, P. - 10/10/57

JOHNSON, P. J. - 5/17/56

JOHNSON, Robert - 5/24/56

JOHNSON, Sam - 9/12/57

JOHNSON, T. - 11/21/57

JOHNSON, Wesley - 5/10/56

JOHNSON, William George -

JOHNSON, William H. - 4/26/56; 5/10/56; 11/15/56; 6/14/56; 9/12/57; 10/10/57; 11/14/57; 11/28/57; 12/12/57; 10/3/57

JOHNSON, Mr. - 10/04/56

JONES, C. H. - 10/10/57

JONES, Colin E. - 11/22/56

JONES, H. - 8/16/56

JONES, Hardin - 10/10/57

JONES, J. P. - 7/5/56

JONES, John W. - 10/10/57

JONES, Parson - 3/7/57

JONES, R. M. - 9/20/56

JONES, R. S. - 5/24/56

JONES, Dr. R. T. - 5/17/56

JONES, W. - 5/17/56; 10/10/57

JONES, Wm. - 1/26/56; 3/1/56; 8/16/56

JONES, Mr. - 1/12/56

JUDGE; - 9/19/57

JUGE, Dr.J. .M - 5/17/56

JULIA; - 12/26/57

K

KEENANS, - 10/18/56

KEENER, J. M. - 1/17/57

KEENER - 11/14/57

KEITH, E. B. - 12/12/57

KELLY, Harry - 7/5/56

KELLY, W. M. - 9/5/57; 11/14/57

KENNEDY; J. - 1/12/56

KERBEY, Joseph - 11/22/56

KIMBELL, Mrs. John - 7/19/56

KING, D. - 10/10/57

KING, James - 8/16/56

KING, L. H. - 1/12/56

KING, R. D. - 12/5/57

KIRBY, Colonel - 12/12/57

KITCHING, William - 5/17/56

KNOX, F. - 8/16/56

KOSCIOSCO, G. D. - 11/22/56

KOTTWITZ, A. S. - 9/5/57

L

LADD, Romulus - 6/21/56

LAND, J. N. - 1/17/57

LANE, Robert H. - 3/8/56; 5/24/56; 5/31/56; 10/25/56; 11/15/56; 11/28/57; 9/12/57; 10/10/57; 11/21/57; 12/12/57

LANGFORD, Maj. A.R. - 8/16/56

LANKFORD, Benjamin - 1/19/56

LATIMER, A.H. - 5/10/56; 12/26/57

LATIMER, H. R. - 5/3/56; 5/10/56; 3/7/57; 12/19/57

LAUGHLIN, C. H. - 11/22/56

LAWRENCE, William - 8/2/56; 12/19/57

LAWSON, I. D. - 12/19/57

LEDBELLY, J. W. - 8/16/56

LEDBETTER, J. N. - 9/20/56

LEIGH, Charlie - 8/23/56

LEIGH, John W. - 10/25/56

LEMEUL, Martin - 10/10/57

LEMONS, Attorney - 11/15/56

LESTER, Mr. - 7/5/56

LEVIN, James - 11/14/57

LEWELLEN, Thomas - 10/25/56; 11/29/56; 10/10/57

LEWELLING, J. W. - 10/10/57

LEWIS, Col.. S. - 10/10/57

LEWIS, William N. - 1/17/57

LIGHTFOOT, H. C. - 11/29/56 -

LINDSEY, J. C. - 11/22/56

LIPE, Moses - 9/5/57

LIPSCOMB, Judge - 1/3/57

LISSENBEE, L. W. - 12/13/56; 11/21/57

LITTLE; Miss - 12/12/57

LONG, Henry - 5/17/56

LONG, Jacob - 5/31/56; 7/19/56

LONG, Thomas - 1/12/56; 8/16/56

LOOK; Dr. E. S. - 11/22/56; 12/5/57

LOOK, Mrs. S. - 7/5/56

LOOP, John - 2/14/57

LOVE, Calvin S. - 10/31/57

LOWE, D. W. - 10/3/57

LOWERY, Mr. - 3/14/57

LUALLEN, Isaac - 10/04/56

LYNCH, James - 5/17/56

LYONS, Dr. John R. - 11/22/56; 9/19/57; 12/5/57

M

MADDEN, R. W. - 5/24/56

MAGEE, John C.- 10/10/57

MALLOW, Michael - 10/25/56

MALTON, A. G. - 10/24/57

MANN, C. L. - 11/14/57 -

MANN, J. W. - 10/10/57

MARLER, W. W. - 9/26/57

MARSHALL, Dr. H - 10/10/57

MARSHALL Marshall, J. - 12/5/57

MARSHALL, Jesse P. - 11/28/57

MARSHALL, Major John - 11/28/57

MARSHALL, Attorney,- 10/25/56

MARTIN, Daniel - 6/14/56

MARTIN, Mr - 4/12/56

MASON, M. B. - 10/10/57

MATTHEWS, John W. - 5/10/56; 11/14/57,

MATTHEWS, R. - 10/10/57

MATTHEWS, R. E. - 5/10/56

MATTOX, Wiley A. - 5/17/56

MAUDLING, Presley - 9/6/56

MAYFIELD, A. P. B. - 10/11/56; 12/20/56

MAYO, Thomas J - 7/26/56

MCBRIDE, Sherwood - 5/17/56

McCALL, Marshall - 11/22/56

McCAMANT, A.S. - 5/17/56; 5/24/56

McCAMANT, James W. - 5/17/56

McCARLEY, George W. - 5/10/56; 8/9/56

McCARTY, Joseph - 5/17/56; 5/31/56

McCLARY, W. - 10/10/57

McCown, F. - 11/28/57

McCOY, J. C. - 2/16/56 ;4/5/56; 10/25/56; 11/15/56; 11/29/56

McCROREY, John - 11/22/56

McDONALD, Mrs. E. - 11/22/56

McDONNA, Dr. John - 11/22/56; 11/28/57; 12/5/57

McFARLAND, A. J. - 5/24/56

McFARLAND, Jacob - 2/14/57

McFARLAND, W. J. - 10/10/57

McGEE, Dr. - 11/14/57

McGILL, Sarah - 6/28/5

McGILL, Thos. - 6/28/5

McKASSAN, J. S. - 1/19/56

McKASSON, John L. - 5/24/56

McKENNEY, E. D. - 1/12/56; 1/19/56; 1/26/56; 5/10/56; 5/31/56; 10/10/57; 11/28/57

McKENZIE, J. W. P. - 1/26/56; 10/17/57

McKINNEY, H. - 12/5/57

McLANE, Dr.- 7/12/56; 10/10/57

McLARRAN, J. H. - 10/10/57

McLAUGHERY, J. F. - 5/17/56

McREE, J. D. H. - 5/10/56

McWILLIAMS, Capt. - 10/18/56

MEHRMANN,[Merriman], Mr. - 10/11/56

MELTON, A.G. - 5/10/56; 11/14/57

MENARD, Michel B - 9/27/56

MIDDLETON, Tom - 12/12/57

MILLER, J. D. - 5/10/56

MILLER, N. O. - 11/29/56

MILLS, Sumpter. R. G. - 3/8/56 ;5/10/56; 5/31/56; 6/7/56; 7/19/56, 8/2/56; 9/20/56; 11/22/56; 11/29/56; 12/6/56; 10/10/57

MILLS, John T. - 3/1/56; 3/8/56; 5/17/56; 9/20/56; 10/25/56; 11/15/56; 11/22/56; 11/29/56; 3/7/57; 9/5/57; 9/12/57; 9/19/57; 10/10/57; 11/14/57; 11/28/57

MILLS, William G. - 5/17/56

MILLSTEAD, John - 7/5/56

MILWEE, William H. - 3/8/56; 5/17/56; 7/19/56; 9/12/57; 11/28/57

MONTGOMERY, A. J. - 10/10/57

MONTGOMERY, Mr. - 5/10/56

MOODY, L. - 5/17/56

MOORE, A. - 7/5/56

MOORE, H. T. - 7/5/56
MOORE, Lewis W. - 5/17/56
MOORE, Mary - 11/7/57
MOORE, Martin L. - 7/5/56
MOORE, N. J. - 5/3/56
MOORE, S. J 2/28/57
MOORE, Samuel - 12/20/56; 5/17/56
MOORE, William - 10/11/56; 2/14/57
MOORE, Captain - 2/28/57
MOORE, Dr. - 1/3/57
MORGAN, Simpson H. - 1/12/56; 4/5/56; 5/17/56; 5/31/56; 7/19/56; 10/25/56; 3/7/57; 9/19/57; 10/17/57; 10/24/57; 12/12/57
MORRILL, Amos - 1/12/56; 3/8/56
MORRIS, Henry - 9/5/57
MORRISON, T. J. - 10/10/57
MOSBY, Fortunaus S. - 11/22/56
MOSE - 10/11/56
MOSELY, James - 5/17/56
MOSELY Samuel F. - 9/19/57
MOSELY , T. J. - 10/24/57; 11/14/57
MOSS, Daniel P. - 9/12/57
MOSS, Wm. - 1/12/56
MOSSINGTON, Charles - 9/5/57
MOSSINGTON, Sarah - 9/5/57
MURPHY, Hugh - 11/22/56

MURPHY, J. C.- 2/28/57
MURPHY, J. M.
MURPHY, Lawrence - 10/10/57
MURRAY, J. A. N. - 3/8/56;12/12/57
MURRAY, Joanna - 7/5/56
MUSGROVE, Bushrod W. - 3/8/56; 5/10/56; 6/7/56; 11/15/56 10/10/57; 10/24/57; 10/31/57; 11/14/57; 11/21/57
MYDALE, W. - 10/10/57

N

NATHAN, Henry - 9/20/56; /5/57
NAYLOR, W. L. - 7/5/56
NEATHERY, Robert - 5/10/56
NEIGHBORS, Major - 5/3/56
NELSON, , Dr. A. J. - 5/17/56
NELSON, John W. - 7/5/56
NESMITH, R. W. - 3/8/56; 12/6/56; 12/26/57
NEWELL, Newell, Miss E. M. - 10/10/57
NEWELL, Isaac - 5/17/56
NICHOLS, Nichols, A. J. - 10/10/57
NICHOLS, John - 10/10/57
NICHOLSON, J. D. - 5/17/56
NICHOLSON, A. J. - 5/24/56
NICHOLSON, Attorney - 11/29/56
NOLAN, W. H. - 10/10/57

NORTON, George B. - 8/16/56
NORWOOD, B. H. - 10/17/57

O

OCHILTREE, Hon. W. H. - 2/16/56
ODOM, Jesse - 5/10/56
OLDHAM, Mrs. Anne S. - 11/1/56
OLDHAM, W. S. - 11/1/56
OLIPHANT, W. D. and J. B. - 11/22/56
OLIVER, Mrs.. A. - 10/10/57
OLIVER, Edward - 7/5/56
OLIVER, R. W. B. - 7/26/56; 2/28/57 ;10/10/57
ONEAL, D. - 7/5/56
ORR, Buell - 10/10/57
ORTON, B. - 5/24/56
OWENS, James - 11/22/56

P

PACE, A. E. - 5/24/56; 9/5/57
PADRICK, John - 11/22/56
PAFF, William - 5/10/56
PAGE, H. - 10/11/56
PARISH, J. C. - 1/19/56
PARK, Rev. Samuel - 10/10/57
PARK, William - 8/16/56
PARKS, James - 3/1/56; 5/10/56
PARRISH, J. C. - 9/5/57
PARTAIN, M. H. - 2/21/57

PATTEN, T.P.. - 10/10/57
PATTON, N. B. - 2/14/57; 3/14/57
PAXTON, Hanson - 9/20/56
PEACOCK, Wilson - 1/12/56; 5/10/56; 11/15/56
PENNINGTON, Samuel - 7/5/56
PENNYPACKER, George M. - 11/29/56
PENNYPACKER, Julia E. - 11/29/56
PERKINSON, B. H. - 9/26/57
PETER, Dr. Lemuel - 8/2/56
PETERSON, Richard - 12/26/57
PETTUS, J. S. - 12/26/57
PETTUS, T. N. , - 12/26/57
PETTY, John R. - 10/10/57
PHARR, F. M - 10/10/57
PHELPS, Alpha - 7/5/56
PHILLIPS, Preston G. - 1/3/57
PIERCE - 12/6/56
PINER, F. D. - 10/31/57
PIRKEY, Sherwood H.- 1/19/56; - 9/20/56; 2/14/57; 9/12/57; 10/24/57; 11/28/57; 12/12/57; 12/19/57
PISTOR, Charles - 9/19/57
PITTS, Bartley - 5/17/56
POE, Aexander - 11/22/56
PORE, W. H. - 5/10/56
PORTER, Ben - 10/18/56
PORTER - 11/14/57

PORTEY, Matthew - 8/16/56
POSEY, E.M. - 5/10/56
POST, Sarah - 10/10/57
POTTS, - 10/10/57
POWERS, William - 3/8/56
PRICE, D. O. - 7/5/56
PRICE, Robert - 5/17/56
PRICE, Mrs. - 9/12/57
PRINCE, John H. - 12/6/56
PRITCHETT, David B. - 10/3/57
PROCTOR, T. - 5/10/56
PROVENCE, George W. - 10/10/57
PULLIAM, William M - 10/25/56
PUTNAM, Hillard - 12/12/57
PUTNAM; Vandy - 12/12/57

R

RAGIN, Gilbert - 9/5/57; 10/10/57; 10/17/57
RAGIN, Mary - 10/24/57
RAGIN, Reason - 9/5/57
RAGSDALE; Martha - 1/12/56
RAGSDALE, Smith, - 1/12/56; 1/26/56; 5/10/56
RAGSDALE, Thomas - 5/17/56; 9/5/57
RAINEY, S. D. - 5/17/56
RANDOLF, P.M. - 10/10/57
RANDOLF, T. W. - 12/5/57
RARRAR, Edwin - 10/10/57

RATCLIFF, Benjamin - 7/5/56
REAGAN, J. J. - 11/7/57
REAGAN, Judge - 4/26/56; 5/31/56
RECORD, Gen. James O. - 4/12/56
RECORD, John - 4/12/56
REDUING, Dr. A. J. - 12/26/57
REED, Joseph - 7/5/56
REEVES, George - 3/7/57
REVELS, James C. - 11/22/56
REYNOLDS, Mrs. Sarah - 8/16/56
REYNOLDS, William G. - 3/14/57
RHINE, Henry - 5/10/56
RHODES, R. O. - 11/28/57
RICE, A. M..D. - 12/20/56
ROUTH, J. Virgil - 11/22/56
RICHARDS, L. - 12/5/57
RICHARDSON, Miss Mary E. - 10/25/56
RICHIE, B. L. - 5/17/56
RICHIE, John - 5/17/56
RIDDLE, E. - 12/20/56
RIDDLE, Elam - 4/19/56
RIDDLE, John L. - 9/26/57
RIDDLE, T. G. - 12/20/56
RIDDLE, Wm. S. - 9/26/57
RINGWALD, M. - 10/10/57
RITCHEY, James - 8/2/56
ROBBINS, John - 1/3/57

ROBERTS, L. M. - 7/5/56

ROBERTS, Samuel A. - 10/25/56; 11/15/56; 9/5/57; 11/21/57; 12/12/57; 9/12/57

ROBERTSON, J. - 10/10/57

ROBINSON, Mr. - 3/22/56

RODER, Nancy Lee - 9/19/57

ROGERS, Miss E. - 10/10/57

ROGERS, Martin C. - 5/10/56; 10/24/57; 11/14/57; 11/21/57

RODGERS, R. B. - 3/7/57

ROGERS, T. J. - 5/10/56; 10/24/57; 11/14/57

ROLAND, B. - 7/5/56

ROLAND, C. R. - 5/31/56

ROUTH, W.A. - 5/24/56

ROUTH, A. J. - 5/24/56

RUNNELS, Lt. Governor H. R. - 1/19/56; 2/14/57; 11/28/57

RUSK, Hon. J. - 5/17/56

RUSK, T. J. - 3/15/56; 3/14/57

RUSSEL, Isham - 8/16/56

RUSSELL, Alexander J - 1/3/57.

RUSSELL, David C. - 9/6/56; 1/3/57; 9/12/57; 12/26/57

RUSSELL, H. - 5/10/56; 12/19/57

RUSSELL, Miss Sarah A. - 6/7/56

S

SADDLEBERRY, Miss C. - 10/10/57

SALTER, Mr. - 5/24/56

SAMUELS Brothers - 12/12/57

SANDERS, H. - 5/10/56

SAUNDERS, M.D., William. E. - 3/14/57; 12/5/57

SCALES, Jas - 12/26/57

SCALLON, John - 8/16/56

SCHACKLEFORD, Mr. - 10/04/56

SCOTT, L. Lawrence - 9/26/57

SCOTT, O. P. - 10/10/57

SCOTT, R. H. MD - 11/22/56

SCRUGGS, J. A - 7/26/56

SCRUGGS, Rev. - 4/12/56

SEALES, Miss - 1/17/57

SELLERS, Sam - 5/10/56

SEXTON, John - 1/3/57

SHANAHAN, J. B. - 11/1/56; 2/14/57

SHANNNON; - 12/5/57

SHARP, A. - 7/5/56

SHARP, Abram - 7/5/56

SHAW, Lucinda Elizabeth, - 12/26/57

SHAW, Nancy - 12/26/57

SHAW, Susan - 7/5/56

SHAW, Thomas - 12/26/57

SHECK; J. S. - 9/26/57

SHELTON, Miss Mary - 11/22/56

SHERRIL, R. C. - 12/6/56;

9/5/57

SHERRY, Barney - 11/22/56

SHERRY, P. - 1/17/57

SHIRLEY, Captain Lewis - 8/2/56

SHOEMAKER, - 10/24/57

SHOOKS, Mr. - 1/17/57

SHUMAKER, J - 8/16/56

SIMPSON, Jas. B. - 5/10/56

SIMS, Brahas - 1/19/56

SIMS, F.M.- 3/22/56

SIMS, Jr., J. W. - 5/10/56

SIMS, Major James W. - 5/3/56; 5/10/56; 3/7/57; 12/19/57

SIMS, Josh - 11/22/56

SIMS, William B. - 1/12/56; 5/10/56

SIMS, William S. - 1/17/57

SIMS, Mr. - 3/8/56

SISLER, esq - 11/29/56

SKELTON, D. K. - 8/16/56

SKIDMORE, James - 5/17/56

SKIDMORE, S. D.- 10/25/56

SKIDMORE, T. C. - 11/14/57

SLEDGE, Col. Wm. - 12/12/57

SMATHERS, Elisha F. - 1/3/57

SMITH, B.P. - 3/14/57; 12/5/57

SMITH, D. C. - 1/17/57

SMITH, D. F. - 7/5/56

SMITH, Mrs. D. F. - 5/17/56

SMITH, Henry - 1/19/56

SMITH, J. G. - 5/17/56

SMITH, Josiah - 6/7/56 ;10/10/57

SMITH, N. R. - 4/26/56

SMITH O. - 10/10/57

SMITH Dr. P. L. - 11/14/57

SMITH, Peyton B. - 3/8/56; 12/5/57

SMITH, Col. Robert W - 7/5/56

SMITH, Samuel. - 3/1/56

SMITH, Mrs. Sarah Ann - 10/10/57

SMITH, William - 10/10/57

SMITH, William J. - 10/10/57

SMITH, General - 3/22/56

SMITH, Dr. 2/28/57

SMITH Judge - 2/28/57

SMITH - 11/21/57

SMITHER, Col. John H. - 2/14/57

SNEED, B. J. - 4/5/56

SORRELL, Rev., - 7/5/56

SPARKS, Hardy - 11/22/56

SPARKS, Mr. - 11/21/57

SPELL, Richard H. - 10/10/57

SPENCER, Walter S. - 10/10/57

ST. CLAIRE, Daniel - 5/17/56

STEELE, Miss Ellen - 8/16/56

STELL, James M. - 10/10/57

STEPHENS, Josh - 9/26/57

STEPHENSON, W. - 6/21/56

STEVENS, Benj. - 10/10/57

STEVENS, F. M. & Co - 7/5/56

STEVENS, H. - 8/9/56

STEVENS, Squire - 9/19/57

STEVENSON, Sen. Logan - 5/17/56

STONE,, Blewitt - 10/3/57

STEWART, Hugh M. - 6/7/56

STONE, Rev A. M. - 9/5/57; 10/17/57

STONE, Oliver T. - 10/25/56; 11/15/56; 11/29/56; 10/10/57

STOUT, W. B. - 3/8/56; 5/10/56

STRICKLAND, Daniel - 11/29/56

STROTHER, Miss Sarah E. - 8/23/56; 9/20/56

STROTHER, William - 8/23/56; 9/20/56

STURNE, Lewis - 10/10/57

SUMMERS, John A. - 2/16/56; 5/10/56; 5/31/56; 9/20/56; 11/15/56 ;12/20/56; 10/10/57

SUTPHIN, James G. . - 3/1/56

SUTTON, Courtes B.- 6/21/56 10/ 04/56; 11/29/56; 12/6/56; 3/7/57; 3/14/57; 10/10/57; 11/14/57; 12/12/57

SUTTON, Norbonne - 3/8/56; 10/10/57

T

TALBOT, Isabella - 7/26/56

TALBOT, John A. - 2/14/57

TANNER, Lewis - 10/11/56

TAYLOR, John C . - 1/17/57

TAYLOR, Thomas - 12/12/57

TAYLOR, William - 7/5/56

TAYLOR, - 12/12/57

TERRY, E. W - 9/26/57

TERRY, John - 7/5/56

THAYER, W. T. - 3/7/57

THAYER, William H. - 5/17/56

THEBO, C. H. - 8/16/56

THOMAS, James W. -3/8/56 5/17/56; 7/5/56; 8/16/56; 11/22/56; 1/3/57; 1/17/57

THOMAS, John D. - 5/17/56

THOMAS, S. H - 1/17/57

THOMAS, W. - 8/16/56

THOMAS, - 11/14/57

THOMPSON, B. F. - 3/14/57

THOMPSON, John - 10/10/57

THOMPSON, Josiah - 9/13/56

THOMPSON, Kezziah - 9/13/56

THOMPSON, Miss Rett - 11/22/56

THOMPSON, Thomas - 10/10/57

THOMPSON, W. - 3/14/57

THOMPSON, William S. - 1/17/57

THRESHER, - 5/10/56

THROCKMARTIN, Dr - 10/25/56

THROCKMORTON, Attorney - 11/29/56

TINNIN, William - 5/17/56;

1/17/57

TITUS, R. B. - 8/16/56

TITUS, T. F. - 9/5/57

TITUS, Dr. Thomas F. - 12/5/57

TOAKE, Mr. - 9/27/56

TODD, William S. - 3/8/56; 3/22/56 ;4/12/56; 5/10/56; 5/31/56; 8/2/56; 8/23/56; 11/15/56; 11/22/56; 11/29/56; 12/6/56; 1/3/57; 2/28/57; 3/7/57; 9/5/57; 9/19/57; 10/24/57

TOM - 9/20/56

TOMILSON, Richard - 10/10/57

TOMILSON, Attorney -

TOMPSON, W. R. - 10/17/57

TOWNES, Nathaniel W. - 3/8/56; 5/17/56; 10/25/56; 11/15/56; 10/10/57; 12/26/57

TRUEBLOOD, A. H. - 5/24/56; 9/5/57

TUCKER, J. L. - 12/26/57

TUDER, K. L. - 12/20/56

TURNER, August J. - 8/16/56

TURNER, John - 7/5/56

TYLER, William - 2/16/56; 3/8/56

V

VADEN, L. - 5/10/56

VAN ZANDT, W. - 7/5/56

VAN ZANDT, William - 8/16/56

VAN DERLIN, D.C. -3/22/56

VAN SICLE - 11/14/57

VANCE, Miss Mary - 8/16/56

VANDERBILT, Cornelius - 12/19/57

VANSICKLE, Ron. A - 11/15/56

VASS, Eli - 5/10/56

VISAR, Peter - 5/10/56

VON SICKLE, Ben - 5/10/56

VORTRESS, Judge - 12/5/57

W

WADDELL, C. K. - 9/20/56

WADE; Dr. O. B. - 7/5/56; 12/5/57

WADSWORTH, K. M. - 7/26/56

WAGLEY, Joseph - 8/2/56

WALCOT, B. S. - 5/17/56

WALKER, James - 7/5/56

WALKER, John - 7/5/56

WALKER, V. - 10/10/57

WALKER, Wesley C. - 8/30/56

WALKER, William G. - 8/16/56

WALKER, Mr. - 12/20/56

WALLIS, E. P. - 10/17/57

WALLIS, Miss Martha - 10/17/57

WALLY, John - 10/10/57

WARD, Asa - 11/22/56

WARD, James J. - 5/10/56; 3/14/57

WARD, R.A. - 11/22/56

WARD, Robert H. - 5/31/56; 12/12/57

WARDLOW, Mary - 7/5/56

WARE, John - 8/9/56

WARE, Dr. - 5/10/56

WARREN, Henry - 10/10/57

WARREN, Jacob - 7/5/56

WASDEN, John - 11/29/56

WASHBURN, Mr. - 11/22/56; 9/19/57

WASHINGTON, George - 12/6/56

WASSON, A. C. - 11/22/56

WATER, George - 10/10/57

WATSON, Coleman - 3/14/57

WEATHERFORD, Money - 5/17/56

WEAVER, Attorney - 11/29/56

WEBB, J. D. - 5/17/56

WEBB, Milton - 5/17/56

WEBB, Rev. Mr. - 12/20/56

WEEMS, Jackson - 11/14/57

WEISNER, L. D. - 11/22/56

WELCH, James - 9/26/57

WELCH, M. C - 1/17/57

WELDIN, W. T. - 5/17/56

WELLES, B.S. - 7/5/56

WELLES, Isaiah W. - 3/1/56 ; 4/26/56; 7/19/56

WELLS, Annie V. - 8/2/56

WELLS, James S. - 8/2/56

WELLS, Lewis S. - 8/2/56

WELSCH, O. G,- 10/25/56

WEST, Major Edward - 5/10/56; 12/6/56; 3/7/57

WEST, John W. - 1/12/56; 5/10/56; 10/10/57

WHATLY, Miss M. Z. - 11/28/57

WHEAT; Mrs. Harriet E - 6/14/56.

WHEELER, Ambrose - 8/16/56

WHITACKER, Mrs. Nancy - 8/16/56

WHITAKER, Mrs. M.E. - 11/22/56

WHITAKER,, Robert F. - 7/5/56

WHITE, E. H. - 5/17/56

WHITE, - 12/12/57

WHITFIELD, Lewis - 1/19/56

WIGFALL, - 10/31/57

WIGGINS, Dr. - 8/16/56

WIGHT, R. - 9/5/57

WILBER, E. - 5/17/56

WILKINS, William - 5/10/56

WILKINSON, J. P. - 1/19/56; 11/22/56

WILKINSON, Attorney - 11/15/56; 10/24/57

WILKS, C. B. - 12/5/57

WILLIAM, James - 3/15/56

WILLIAM, Mr. - 9/19/57

WILLIAMS, Williams, J. D. - 1/12/56

WILLIAMS, Williams, John L. -

10/10/57

WILLIAMS, Miss Martha - 10/10/57

WILLIAMS, Mrs. Nancy - 10/10/57

WILLIAMS, Sam - 12/6/56

WILLIAMS, Wm. M. - 3/8/56; 5/17/56; 10/25/56; 9/12/57; 10/10/57; 11/28/57

WILLIS, L. - 9/26/57

WILLISON, Mary Ann - 6/7/56

WILLISON, Thomas - 6/7/56; 10/10/57

WILSON, John E. - 5/17/56; 5/31/56; 7/5/56; 8/23/56; 11/21/57

WILSON, John J. - 8/16/56

WILSON, M. G. - 10/10/57

WILSON, M. Louise - 10/10/57

WILSON, Miss S. - 1/17/57

WILSON, Thomas R. - 3/7/57

WIMBERLY, G. S. - 7/5/56

Winn, John - 8/16/56

WISE, John D. - 10/10/57

WITE, W. T. - 9/26/57

WITHEE., John W. - 10/11/56

WITHERSPOON, M.G. - 10/10/57

WOFFORD, John - 7/5/56

WOLEY, S. J. - 5/17/56

WOMBLE, John - 10/3/57

WOOD, John - 5/10/56

WOOD; William M. - 10/10/57

WOODBRIDGE, J. C. - 5/17/56

WOOLAM, Rev. J. C. - 11/22/56

WOOLEY, Mr. - 3/1/56

WOOTEN, G. H.1/12/56; 5/3/56; 5/10/56; 11/22/56; 10/17/57; 12/5/57

WOOTEN, Judge J. B. - 3/7/57

WORDLOW, Miss M. - 8/16/56

WORTHAM, Augusta C. ; - 11/29/56

WORTHAM, Hon. H. - 5/17/56

WORTHAM, James D. - 11/29/56

WORTHAM, Julia E. - 11/29/56

WORTHAM, Mary J. K. - 11/29/56

WORTHAM, Timothy - 11/29/56

WORTHAM, Wm. A - 5/10/56

WREN, Johnson - 5/10/56; 5/31/56

WRIGHT, Geo. W. - 3/1/56; 5/17/56; 7/19/56

WRIGHT, M. - 7/5/56

WRIGHT, Travis G.. - 3/1/56; 5/17/56; 11/29/56

WRIGHT, William B. - 5/17/56; 11/22/56; 11/29/56; 10/10/57; 11/28/57; 9/12/57

WRIGHT, Mr. - 5/24/56; 7/19/56

WYETT, A.J. - 10/10/57

WYETT, Mrs. Rhoda - 10/10/57

WYETT, Mr. - 5/3/56

WYNN, John C. - 8/16/56
WYNN, T.D. - 10/10/57
WYNN, Col. William - 1/3/57
WYSE, John B. - 8/16/56

Y

YATES, Dr. Lafayette - 5/17/56; 9/5/57

Young, A.W. - 10/10/57. -

YOUNG Young, Charles W. - 6/21/56

YOUNG Young Miss D. C. - 5/17/56

YOUNG, H. F. - 8/16/56; 3/14/57

YOUNG, Harriet M. - 8/2/56

YOUNG, Rev J. D. - 1/17/57

YOUNG, James - 8/16/56

YOUNG, Milton A - 8/2/56

YOUNG, Thomas - 5/10/56

YOUNG, W. C. - 12/5/57

YOUNG, W. H. - 1/17/57

YOUNG, W. T. - 8/16/56

YOURNES, John - 10/3/57

YUHANCE, Mr. - 2/14/57

INDEX OF PLACES

Alabama - 1/19/56; 4/19/56; 5/10/56; 5/17/56 ; 9/19/57;11/21/57; 12/12/57

Alton - 11/29/56; 9/12/57

Anderson County - 7/5/56

Arkansas - 1/12/56; 4/19/56; 5/3/56; 5/10/56; 5/17/56; 9/20/56; 9/27/56; 11/15/56; 12/6/56; 12/20/56;1/3/57; 10/3/57; 12/12/57; notes 5 and 15

Atlantic Ocean - note 11

Austin - 1/19/56; 3/22/56; 8/16/56; 10/11/56; 1/3/57; 10/3/57; 10/10/57; 11/14/57; 11/28/57; 12/5/57; 12/12/57; note 17

Bandera Pass - 3/22/56

Bastrop - 12/12/57

Belgium note 11

Belton - 12/20/56

Benton county, Alabama - 12/12/57

Birdville - 11/29/56

Black Jack Grove - 6/14/56; 11/14/57

Blanco river - 5/3/56

Blundells Creek 1/12/56

Bois d'Arc creek - 11/22/56

Bonham - 5/3/56, 5/10/56; 5/24/56;5/31/56; 6/7/56; 6/14/56; 6/21/56; 7/5/56; 7/19/56;8/2/56; 9/20/56; 11/22/56; 11/29/56; 12/6/56; 3/7/57; 9/5/57; 9/19/57; 10/3/57; 10/10/57; 11/21/57; 11/28/57; 12/12/57

Boston, Bowie County - 3/29/56 ;5/3/56; 6/14/56; 7/19/56; 8/2/56; 8/9/56;9/6/56; 9/20/56 ; 9/19/57;10/10/57;

Boston, Mass.. - 1/3/57

Bowie County - 3/22/56; 3/29/56; 5/3/56; 5/31/56; 6/14/56; ;7/19/56; 8/2/56; 8/9/56; 8/16/56; 9/6/56; 9/13/56; 9/20/56; 9/27/56;; 10/25/56; 11/29/56; 2/14/57; 2/21/57; 3/14/57; 9/5/57; 9/12/57; 9/19/57; 10/3/57; 10/10/57; 12/5/57; 12/12/57; note 19

Brazos - note 5

Buchanan, Titus County - 10/31/57

Burkham's Creek - 1/3/57

Cairo - 7/5/56

California - 2, 4/12/56; notes 28 and 32

Camden - 4/19/56

Campbell County, Ky - 4/5/56

Campte - 10/18/56,

Canada - 1/19/56

Cass - 1/12/56; 4/12/56; 5/10/56; 5/31/56; 8/2/56; 8/23/56; 9/20/56; 10/18/56; 11/15/56; 12/6/56; 9/19/57,11/14/57; 11/21/57

Castroville - 5/3/56

Cedar Brake - 3/22/56

Cedar Hills - 5/17/56

Cedar Springs - 11/15/56

Chappell Hill, Washington County - 12/12/57

Cherokee County - 12/19/57

Chicago - 7/5/56

Choctaw Creek 1/12/56

Choctaw Nation - 11/28/57; 12/5/57

Cibola, - 3/22/56

City of the Three Forks of the Trinity- - note 5

Clarksville - 1, 3; 1/12/56; 3/8/56; 3/29/56; 4/5/56; 5/10/56; 5/17/56; 6/14/56; 7/5/56; 7/12/56; 7/26/56; 8/16/56; 9/20/56; - 9/27/56; 10/04/56; 10/25/56; 11/1/56; 11/22/56; 12/6/56; 1/3/57; - 1/17/57; 2/21/57; 3/7/57; 9/5/57; - 9/12/57; - 9/19/57; 10/10/57; 11/7/57; 11/21/57; 11/28/57; 12/5/57; 12/19/57; 12/26/57; notes 3, 4, 5, 13,17 and 20

Clear Creek - 3/14/57

Cloud Spring, 3/14/57

Collin County - 1/19/56; 3/1/56; 3/29/56; 5/17/56;

248

5/31/56; 7/26/56 ; 8/2/56; 8/16/56; 11/1/56; 11/15/56; 11/29/56; - 12/6/56; 1/3/57; 3/14/57; 10/10/57; 12/19/57

Colorado County - 9/27/56; 10/11/56

Colorado River - 12/12/57; note 5

Columbus, Colorado County - 9/27/56; 10/11/56

Comanche Peak, Johnson County - 9/26/57

Connecticut - 1/19/56

Cooke County - 1/19/56; 3/1/56; 3/29/56; 4/12/56; 5/31/56; 7/12/56; 7/26/56; 8/16/56; 10/11/56; 11/29/56; 3/14/57; 9/5/57; 10/10/57; 12/19/57; note17

Corpus Christi - 4/12/56

Corsicana - 4/12/56

Coryell county - 10/25/56; 11/29/56

Cuba - 2/28/57

Cut Off, the - 4/19/56

Daingerfield - 7/5/56; 11/14/57; 12/26/57

Dalby Springs - 8/16/56; 8/23/56; 9/12/57; 10/3/57; note 19

Dallas County. - 3/1/56; 3/29/56; 7/26/56; 8/16/56; 10/25/56; 11/1/56; 11/15/56; 11/29/56; 10/10/57; 12/19/57

Dallas town - 3/1/56; 5/17/56; 5/31/56; 10/25/56; 11/1/56;

11/15/56; 11/29/56; 10/10/57; notes 5 and 17

Decatur, - 12/19/57; 12/26/57

DeKalb - 5/17/56; 6/14/56; 7/19/56; 9/13/56; 9/20/56; 9/27/56; 9/19/57

Delaware creek - 1/12/56; 1/26/56; 5/3/56; note 13

Denton town - 11/29/56

Denton County - 3/1/56; 3/29/56; 8/16/56; 10/25/56; 11/29/56; 10/10/57; 9/12/57; 12/19/57

Dinwiddie County, Virginia - 1/3/57

Douglassville - 7/19/56

East Fork - 1/3/57

Eclectic Grove - 9/5/57

Elliot and Hays landing - 3/29/56

Ellis;County - 10/25/56; 10/10/57

Elm Flats - 11/29/56

Elm Fork of the Trinity - 11/29/56; 3/14/57

Exeter, New Hampshire - 1/3/57

Fannin County - 1/19/56; 1/26/56; 2/16/56; 3/8/56; 3/22/56; 3/29/56; 4/12/56; 5/24/56; 5/31/56; 7/5/56; 7/26/56; 8/16/56; 8/30/56; 9/20/56; 9/27/56; 10/25/56; 11/15/56; 11/22/56; 11/29/56; - 9/5/57; 9/12/57; 10/3/57; 11/14/57; - 11/21/57; 11/28/57;

12/5/57; 12/12/57

Fisher's Prairie - 4/19/56

Florida - note 31

Fort Towson - 9/20/56

Fort Worth - 11/29/56; 12/19/57; note17

Fredericksburg - note17

Fulton - 3/29/56; 9/27/56; 10/18/56; 2/21/57; 10/17/57

Gaines Landing - 4/19/56; 7/12/56 ; 7/26/56; 9/20/56; 9/5/57

Gainesville - 7/12/56; 7/26/56; 10/11/56; 2/28/57; 3/14/57; 10/10/57; 12/19/57; note 25

Galveston - note17

Galveston - 7/19/56; 9/27/56

Georgia - 1/19/56

Germany - 2; 1/19/56

Good Spring note 31

Grand Ecore - 6/14/56

Grayson county, Virginia - 11/21/57

Grayson County, Texas - 1/12/56; 3/1/56; 3/29/56; 5/31/56; 6/7/56; 7/26/56; 8/2/56; 8/16/56; 9/20/56; 9/20/56; 10/25/56; 11/15/56; 11/22/56; 12/6/56; 3/7/57; 3/14/57; 9/12/57; 10/10/57; 11/28/57 ; 12/5/57; 12/19/57; note 17

Great Britain, - 2; 9/19/57

Greenville - 5/17/56; 5/24/56, 7/5/56; 8/23/56; 11/15/56; 1/3/57; 3/7/57; 10/10/57; 11/21/57; 11/28/57; 12/12/57

Guadalupe - note 5

Gulf of Mexico - 7/19/56; note 5

Harrison County - 1/12/56; 7/26/56; 1/3/57

Hart's Bluff - 9/20/56

Hart's Creek - 3/14/57

Hays County - 7/19/56

Hempstead County Arkansas - 5/10/56

Henderson County - 9/13/56.

Hickory Creek - 11/29/56; 9/12/57

Hill County - 10/25/56, 11/29/56

Honey Grove - 9/27/56; 9/19/57; 11/28/57; 12/5/57; 12/26/57

Hopkins County - 1/12/56; 3/1/56; 3/8/56; 3/29/56; 4/26/56; 5/10/56; 5/31/56; 6/7/56; 6/14/56; 7/5/56; 8/23/56; 9/13/56; 9/20/56; 11/15/56; 11/29/56; 12/20/56; 1/3/57; 3/7/57; 9/5/57; 10/3/57; 10/10/57; 10/24/57; 11/7/57; 11/14/57; 11/21/57; 12/19/57; 12/26/57

Houston - 9/27/56; 10/25/56; 12/6/56

Howels Store - 3/14/57

Hudson River - note 32

Hunt County - 3/29/56; 5/17/56; 5/31/56; 7/5/56; 7/26/56; 8/16/56; 8/23/56; 10/11/56; 10/25/56; 11/15/56; 11/22/56; 12/6/56; 1/3/57; 10/10/57; 11/21/57 11/14/57; - 11/21/57 11/21/57; 11/28/57; 12/12/57

Illinois - 1/19/56

Indian Territory - note 31

Ireland - 2

Jack County. - 11/7/57

Jasper County 2/28/57

Jefferson - 3/8/56; 3/29/56; 4/19/56; 5/10/56; 7/5/56; 9/20/56; 10/18/56; 12/6/56; 12/20/56; 2/28/57; 3/7/57; 9/5/57; 10/3/57; 10/10/57; 10/24/57; 10/31/57; 11/21/57; 12/19/57; 12/26/57 Johnson County - 9/26/57; 10/10/57

Jonesboro - 1/17/57

Kaufman County -3/1/56; 5/31/56; 7/19/56; 10/24/57;

Kenton County, Ky - 4/5/56

Kentucky Town - 11/29/56; 9/12/57; 11/28/57; 12/19/57; 2/26/57

Kentucky - 1/19/56; 5/17/56; 6/7/56; 11/15/56; 12/20/56; 2/28/57; 9/5/57; 11/14/57; 11/21/57; 11/28/57; note 23

Kiamitia - 3/8/56; 9/20/56; 9/27/56; 1/17/57; 2/21/57; 2/28/57; 9/26/57; 10/10/57

Lafayette County - 1/3/57,

LaGrange - 12/12/57

Lamar County; - 1/12/56; 1/19/56; 2/16/56; 3/1/56; 3/8/56; 3/29/56; 5/10/56 5/17/56; 5/31/56; 6/7/56; 8/16/56; 9/27/56; 10/25/56; 11/15/56; 11/22/56; 11/29/56; 12/6/56; 12/20/56; 1/3/57; - 1/17/57; 3/7/57; 9/12/57; 9/19/57; 10/10/57; 11/7/57; 11/14/57; 11/28/57; 12/12/57; note 12

Leon - 11/15/56

Linden - 4/12/56; 7/19/56

Little Rock - 1/12/56

Lockhart - 11/1/56

London - - note 4,

Lost Creek - 12/12/57

Louisiana - 1/26/56; 5/17/56; 12/6/56; 1/3/57

Louisville - 7/5/56; 9/5/57; 11/14/57

Manhattan.- note 32

Marshall - 1/3/57; - 12/19/57

Massachusetts - 4/19/56

McKinney, - 1/19/56; 4/5/56; 4/26/56; 7/26/56; 8/2/56; 10/25/56; 11/1/56; 11/29/56; 9/19/57; 10/10/57; 12/5/57

Memphis - 7/5/56

Mesquiteville - 11/7/57

Mexico - 10/11/56; notes 10 and 26

Middle Sulphur - 11/21/57

Mill Creek - 9/13/56; 9/20/56; 9/27/56; 12/6/56; 9/5/57

Mississippi River- 1/19/56; 4/19/56; 5/17/56; 7/26/56; 9/5/57; notes 4, 5 and 31

Missouri - 1/19/56; 12/20/56; 11/21/57; 11/28/57; 12/12/57

Montague - note 17

Monticello, Titus County - 10/31/57

Montreal - 9/27/56

Mount Pleasant - 1/12/56; 4/19/56; 6/21/56; 7/5/56; 7/12/56; 8/23/56; 10/18/56; 10/10/57; 10/24/57; 11/14/57; 11/21/57; 12/19/57; 12/26/57

Mountain City - 7/19/56

Mt Vernon - 8/30/56

New Braufels - note 17

New England 2; note 4

New Jersey - 2/16/56

New Mexico - note 5 - note 8

New Orleans - 1/19/56; 3/8/56; 3/15/56; 4/26/56; 5/3/56; 5/17/56; 6/7/56; 6/14/56 ; 7/5/56; 7/19/56; 8/16/56; 9/6/56; 9/20/56; 10/18/56; 11/1/56 ; 2/21/57; 3/7/57; /14/57; 9/5/57; 9/19/57; 10/3/57; 10/31/57; 12/19/57; 12/26/57; note 4

New York - 2; 1/12/56; 1/19/56; 5/10/56; 7/19/56; 9/20/56; 10/24/57; 10/31/57; note 32

Newark - 2/16/56

Nicaragua - 9/5/57; notes 26, 32

North Carolina - 1/19/56; 11/28/57

North Sulphur Post Office - 11/28/57

Northampton, Massachusetts - 3/14/57

Nueces, - note 5

Nueces Valley - 4/12/56

Ohio - 10/25/56

Oklahoma - note 31

Olmus river - 5/3/56

Paris - 1/12/56; 1/19/56; 5/3/56; 5/10/56; 5/17/56 ; 5/24/56; 5/31/56; 6/7/56; 8/2/56; 8/16/56; 9/20/56; 9/27/56; 11/29/56; 12/6/56; 12/20/56; 12/20/56; 1/3/57; 3/7/57; 9/5/57; 9/19/57; 10/10/57; - 11/14/57; 11/28/57; 12/12/57; 12/26/57

Parker County - 8/16/56; 10/25/56; 11/29/56; 12/6/56; 10/10/57; note 17

Pennington Creek - note 31

Pennsylvania - 1/19/56; 10/11/56

Philadelphia - 1/12/56; 7/19/56; 12/26/57

Pilot Point, - 11/29/56

Pine Bluff - 9/26/57,

Pine Creek - 2/21/57

Pittsburg, Upshur County -

9/6/56; 9/19/57; 10/17/57

Plano - 5/17/56

Preston - 3/7/57; note17

Prussia - 1/19/56

Red Bayou - 10/17/57

Red River - 1; 1/19/56; 1/26/56; 2/23/56; 3/8/56; 3/15/56; 3/29/56; 4/19/56; 5/3/56; 5/10/56; 6/7/56; 8/16/56; 9/6/56; 9/13/56; 9/20/56; 9/27/56; 11/15/56; 11/29/56; 1/17/57; 2/14/57; 2/21/57; 2/28/57; 3/7/57; 3/14/57; 9/5/57; 10/17/57; 10/24/57;12/12/57; 12/26/57; notes 4, 5 and17

Red River County - 3; 2/16/56; 4/26/56; 5/10/56; 5/31/56; 6/7/56; 8/2/56; 8/30/56; 9/20/56; 10/4/56; 10/11/56; 10/25/56; 11/22/56; 11/29/56; 12/6/56; 1/3/57; 2/14/57; 2/28/57; 3/7/57; 9/5/57; 9/19/57; 9/26/57; 10/3/57; 10/10/57; 11/14/57; 11/21/57; 11/28/57; 12/5/57; 12/12/57; 12/19/57; notes 3, 12and 17

Red River Valley - note 5

Rio Grande - note 5

Rockwall - 7/19/56; 10/24/57,

Rondo Post Office, Lafayette, Arkansas - 11/7/57

Rowland, [Roland]- - 1/19/56; 3/29/56; 5/3/56; 9/20/56; 9/27/56; 11/29/56; 1/17/57; 2/14/57; 2/28/57; 9/26/57; 10/24/57; - note 4,

Rowlett survey - 5/17/56

Rowletts Creek - 5/17/56

Sabine river - 10/11/56; 11/21/57; note 5

San Antonio - 3/22/56; 4/12/56; 6/14/56; 9/5/57; 12/12/57

San Patracio - 4/12/56

San Antonio - note 5

Santa Fe - 4/26/56

Savannah, Red River County - 9/5/57

Seneca Falls, New York note - 11

Sevier County, Arkansas - 10/25/56

Sherman - 5/17/56; 6/7/56, 8/2/56; 9/20/56; 9/19/57; 10/10/57; 11/1/56; 11/15/56; 12/5/57; 12/19/57; 12/26/57

Shreveport - 1/12/56; 1/26/56; 4/19/56; 7/5/56; - 9/6/56 ; 9/20/56; 11/1/56; 2/28/57; 10/17/57; 12/26/57; note 4,

Smith County. - 11/15/56; 11/22/56

South Carolina - 1/19/56

South Sulphur - 11/14/57; 11/21/57; 12/12/57

Spanish Bluffs - 9/20/56

Spencer - 9/5/57,

St. Louis - 7/5/56; 9/13/56; 9/27/56

Staten Island - note 32

Sulphur Creek. - notes 5 and 12.

Sulphur Fork - 3/22/56; 3/29/56; 7/19/56; 8/16/56; 9/6/56; 9/20/56

Sulphur Spring, Hopkins County - 9/5/57; 9/26/57

Sulphur Springs, Hunt County - 10/3/57

Tarrant, - 1/12/56; 3/29/56; 5/10/56; 7/5/56; 8/16/56; 11/29/56; 2/14/57; 9/5/57; 10/3/57; 10/10/57; 10/24/57;10/31/57; 11/14/57; 12/12/57

Taylorsville, 3/14/57; 12/19/57

Tennessee - 1/19/56; 5/17/56; 10/25/56; 12/20/56; 3/7/57; 11/21/57; 11/28/57; 12/26/57; note 20

Tidwell Creek - 11/28/57; 12/12/57

Tishomingo, Choctaw nation. - 12/5/57; note 31

Titus County - 1/12/56; 2/16/56; 3/29/56; 4/19/56; 5/10/56; 5/31/56; 6/7/56; 6/21/56; 7/12/56; 8/16/56; 8/30/56; 9/20/56; 10/11/56; 10/18/56; 11/15/56; 12/20/56; 1/3/57; 9/12/57; 9/19/57; 9/26/57; 10/10/57; 10/17/57; 10/24/57; 11/7/57; 11/14/57; 11/21/57; 11/28/57; 12/12/57; note17

Trinity River - 7/19/56 ;11/22/56; 11/29/56; 12/12/57; notes 5 and17

Tyler - 1/12/56; 11/22/56;

2/14/57; 10/10/57

Upshur County - 8/23/56 ; 9/6/56; 9/13/56; 9/19/57; 12/12/57

Van Zandt County - 1/12/56

Vicksburg - 4/19/56

Vicksburg road - 4/19/56

Virginia - 1; 1/19/56; 5/10/56; 10/25/56; 2/28/57; 11/28/57; note12.

Waco - 2/14/57; 3/14/57

Wadsworth Bluff, 3/14/57

Warren - 9/5/57

Washington, Arkansas - 1/12/56; 4/19/56; 7/26/56, 9/5/57

Washington County - 12/12/57

Washington DC - 7/19/56

Washita. - 3/7/57

West Fork - 12/19/57

White Oak Creek - 3/29/56

White Oak Shoals - 6/7/56

Williamson County - 12/19/57

Wimsborough, Wood County, - 11/14/57

Wise - 8/16/56; 10/25/56; 11/29/56; 12/6/56; 3/14/57; 10/10/57; 12/19/57; 12/26/57

Wood County - 11/7/57

Worchester, Massachusetts, note 11

Zillaboy Creek - 11/29/56

GENERAL INDEX

Academy for Males - 5/10/56

Alamo Rangers - 9/5/57

Albany Times, the - 10/18/56

Alexander and Jackson - 8/2/56

Allen Power Thresher and Separator - 3/7/57

Allwood Academy - 5/3/56

Alto House, the - 12/19/57; 12/26/57

American Almanac - 1/3/57

American Party - 3

Austin State Gazette, the - 5/3/56

Aymar Brothers - 9/19/57

Bagby & Corleys - 9/5/57; 11/28/57

Bagby & McDonald - 10/17/57; 12/5/57

Bagby' Tin Shop - 12/5/57

Baptist Church - 1; 5/3/56; 12/6/56; 10/10/57

Barry & Moore - 4/5/56; 8/16/56; 1/3/57; 9/5/57; 11/14/57

Baptist1

Battle of Lake Erie ' -note 16

Beman & Co. - 7/26/56; 9/5/57

Berry Rodgers & Rust - 7/12/56 ,

Berry & Wallis - 7/12/56

Berwick Bay and Galveston Lines - 12/19/57

Black Republicans - 5/10/56; 10/25/56

Bonham Enquirer, the - 9/19/57; 11/15/56

Bonham Female Academy - 11/21/57

Bonham Hotel - 1/26/56; 2/13/56; 10/17/57 -

Bonham Male Academy - 11/22/56; 9/5/57

Bonham Masonic Female Institute - 2/23/56; 8/2/56; 9/20/56;11/22/56; 12/6/56; 12/13/56; 9/5/57

Boston Liberator - note 1

Bryarly & Co - 3/8/56

Buck Horn in Austin -

255

12/12/57

Bullion & Connally - 9/5/57

Burford and Good. - 3/1/56

Burney Female Academy - 10/31/57

C.P. Thompson's - 5/3/56

Cairo Rail Road - 12/12/57

Campaign Democrat, the - 9/20/56

Catholics - 2; note 9

Cherokee Nation - 3/22/56; note31

Chickasaw and Choctaw Herald, the - 12/5/57; note31

Chickasaw - 12/5/57; note31

Chickisaw Nation, - 10/31/57

Choctaw Nation - 1/19/56; 9/20/56 ; note31

Civil War - notes 2, 18, 23 and 28

Clarksville Advocate, the - 10/10/57

Clarksville Classical Mathematical and Mercantile Academy - 10/11/56

Clarksville Female Academy -8/9/56; 10/11/56; 9/5/57; 9/19/57

Clarksville Female Institute - 5/3/56; 7/12/56; 8/2/56; 8/30/56

Clarksville Female Seminary - 5/3/56

Clarksville Hotel - 1; 1/19/56; 3/8/56; 5/10/56; 6/28/56; 7/5/56; 3/7/57

Clarksville Male Academy - 8/30/56; 10/11/56

Clarksville Male and Female Institute - 9/5/57

Clarksville Messenger, the - 3/8/56

Clarksville Municipal Corporation - 5/3/56; 10/25/56

Clarksville Race Course - 11/28/57

Col. Edwards, the Steamer- 12/26/57

Cole and Williams - 7/19/56

Colfax Lodge of the Order of Odd Fellows - 10/17/57

Colt's pistol - 10/18/56

Columbia the Land of the Free - 12/6/56

Comanches - 3/22/56

Compromise of 1850 - note 8

Congressional Globe. 3/14/57

Cottage Inn - 7/26/56

Creeks - note 31

Creek War - 5/10/56

Crutchfield House - 11/1/56

256

Cumberland Presbyterian Church - 4/26/56

Daily Union, the - 8/9/56

Darnall and Dickson - 8/2/56; 9/5/57

Darnall & Hunt - 5/3/56; 9/27/56; 9/5/57

Davis Bro. & Bayless, - 6/7/56; 9/5/57

Declaration of Independence - 7/26/56; 2/14/57

Delta , the - 9/20/56

Democratic party - 3; 3/29/56; 4/26/56; 5/3/56; 5/10/56; 5/17/56; 5/24/56; 5/31/56; 7/5/56; 8/2/56; 10/18/56 ;11/15/56; 11/22/56; 11/29/56; 12/6/56; 2/14/57; 3/7/57; 3/14/57; 11/14/57; 12/5/57; 12/19/57; note 14

Dickson & Smith - 11/21/57

Dillahunty and Wright - 6/7/56; 10/10/57

Donoho Hotel - 5/3/56; 7/26/56; 8/2/56; 12/6/56; 1/3/57; 2/21/57; 12/26/57

Douglassville Male and Female Seminary - 12/6/56,

Dred Scott decision - 2

Eagle Hotel - 4/5/56

Effort, the Steamer - 1/19/56 ;6/7/56

Effort, the Steamer - 10/17/57; 12/12/57

Eight Judicial District - 1/12/56; 2/16/56; 3/29/56; 4/5/56; 10/10/57

El Paso Rail Road - 12/12/57

Emery Wheat Thresher - 11/1/56

Enquirer, the - 12/6/56

Epperson's Ferry - 3/29/56

Era, the steamer - 10/24/57; 12/12/57

Erie the steamer - 2/14/57; 2/28/57; 9/5/57

Fanny Fern, the steamer - 3/8/56; 11/29/56; 12/20/56

Fathered & Bingham - 10/3/57

Father of the Santa Fe Trade," - note12

Five Civilized Tribes - note31

Forest Mail Stage Line - 12/19/57; - 12/26/57

Fort Belknap - 11/22/56

Fort Chadbourne - 11/22/56

G. L. Kouns & Bros. - 12/19/57

Galveston, the Steamer - 12/19/57

Galveston News, the - 1/3/57

Georgetown Independent, the - 12/20/56

Great Depression of 1929 - note 28

Greenville Inn - 11/28/57

H. Rhine and Bros. - 4/26/56; 9/20/56; 10/25/56; 11/1/56; 11/29/56; 12/13/56

Hail Columbia - 7/26/56

Heald, Massle & Co. - 4/26/56

Henderson Democrat - 12/19/57

Henderson stage line - 12/26/57

Hope, the steamer -1/19/56; 3/8/56 3/14/57

Houston Rail Road - 12/12/57

Houston and Red River Rail Road, - 1/3/57

Icarian Colony, " - note17

Ike, Hurricane - note 15

Indian Nation - 10/31/57

Indians - 3/22/56; 5/3/56; 11/22/56

Indian Removal Act of 1830 - note31

Industrial Revolution - 2

Inman & Bros. 8/16/56

Institution of the Blind - 5/10/56

J. C. Hearn & Bro. - 11/7/57

J. A. Beard & May - 3/22/56

J.P. Dale and Bros. - 1/12/56

Jefferson Hotel - 5/3/56

Jefferson Herald, the - 8/23/56; 9/27/56

John Simonds, the Steamer - 7/12/56

Johnson Williams & Townes - 10/10/57

Johnson and Bro, - 5/17/56

Jonadab Temple - 6/21/56

Julia, the Steamer - 3/22/56; 3/29/56

Kickapoos - 11/22/56

Know Nothings - Know Nothings - 2, 3; 3/29/56; 5/10/56; 8/2/56; 10/18/56; 11/14/57; note 9

Lamar Enquirer, the - 3/7/57

La Reunion, - note17

LaSalle County (Illinois) Sentinel, the - 7/26/56

Lewis Wells & Bros. - 8/16/56

Lipan Apaches - 5/3/56

Lone Star - 1/19/56

Lynch law - 12/12/57

Manifest Destiny - note 26

Marion - 1/19/56,

Marshall - 12/26/57

Masonic Hall United - 4/5/56

Masons Friendship Lodge - 10/17/57

McKenzie Institute - 1/12/56; ½6/56; 7/12/56; 8/2/56; 8/16/56

Memphis, El Paso and Pacific Railroad Company - 5/17/56; 8/16/56; 12/6/56; 1/3/57; 2/14/57; 12/12/57

Methodist church - 1; 9/27/56; 10/ 04/56; 10/11/56

Mexican War - 9/27/56

Milam Masonic Lodge - 5/31/56

Milam Masonic Institute - 6/14/56; 8/9/56

Milam Male and Female Academy - 10/25/56; 9/5/57

Mills & Mills - 1/12/56; 1/19/56; 10/10/57

Moore's Landing - 2/23/56; 3/29/56

Morrill vs De Morse - 3/8/56

Mt Pleasant Hotel - 4/19/56

Muscogees - note 31

National Road - note17

National Women's Rights Convention - note 11

New Orleans Crescent, the - 3/22/56

New Era, the Steamer - 10/17/57; 12/12/57

New Orleans Picayune - 7/12/56

Ninth Judicial District - 4/26/56; 10/10/57

Odd Fellows - 3/8/56; 6/7/56; 2/14/57; 3/7/57

Odd Fellows -

Opelousas, the Steamer - 12/19/57

Ouachita Rail Road - 12/12/57

Palestine American, the - 11/15/56

Panic of 1857 - 2, note 28

Paris Female Academy - 1/3/57; 12/6/56

Paris Female Seminary - 7/19/56; 12/6/56

Paris Hotel - 6/7/56; 11/29/56; 9/12/57; 12/12/57

Paris Male Academy. - 3/1/56

Parish's Steam Mill - 11/22/56

Park Bank - 10/24/57

Peters Colony - 12/5/57; note 17

Prairie Eagle, the - 11/15/56

Presbyterian Church - 1; 7/5/56 ;1/3/57

Princeton college - 5/31/56

Quitman Herald, the - 11/7/57; 11/21/57; 12/12/57

R. M. Jones, the Steamer - 6/7/56; 10/18/56

Rangers - 3/22/56

Red River Bible Association - 11/28/57

Red River Blues note - note 12

Red River Presbytery - 11/14/57

Republican party [see also Black Republicans] - 3, notes 9 and 14

Red Store - 9/20/56

Reub White - 1/3/57; 1/17/57; 2/14/57; 2/21/57

Rhine Bro. & Co; - 1/3/57; 10/3/57; 10/17/57

Richmond Examiner, the - 4/12/56

Runaway, the Steamer - 1/19/56; 3/8/56; 3/29/56

Russel & Rice - 5/10/56

S. L. McFarland and Co. - 5/10/56

S. Boynton and Co. - 7/12/56

San Antonio Texan, the - 5/3/56

Schackleford and Johnson - 10/ 04/56

Seminoles - note31

Seventeenth Judicial District - 12/5/57

Shawnees - 9/27/56

Sherman Seminary - 12/5/57

Shreveport Insurance company - 10/31/57

Sims & Bloodworth - 1/12/56

Sixteenth Judicial District - 1/19/56; 1/26/56; 2/16/56; 3/29/56; 4/5/56; 10/10/57; 12/19/57.

Sixth Judicial District - 1/26/56

Snell and Milwee - 8/23/56

Sommes and Hill - 3/14/57

St. Charles, the Steamer - 6/14/56

Standard, (the Clarksville Standard) - 1, 3; 1/12/56; 4/12/56; 6/21/56; 11/15/56; 11/29/56; 12/6/56 ; 3/7/57; 9/26/57; 10/31/57; 11/28/57; 12/12/57; 12/19/57; notes 9 and 31

Star Mills - 10/3/57

Star Spangled Banner - 1/12/56; 12/6/56

State Gazette - 1/3/57

Stiewig's Steam mill - 3/29/56

Sulphur Springs Hotel - 9/12/57

Sutton & Sutton - 1/17/57; 10/10/57

Syracuse Chronicle, the - 3/8/56

Templars - 1/12/56; 7/5/56; 2/14/57; 2/21/57; 3/7/57

Terraqueous Transportation Company - ½6/56

Texas Almanac, - 1/3/57

Texas Central Rail Road - 12/12/57

Texas Debt Bill - 2/16/56

Texas House of Representatives - 2/16/56

Texas Legislature - 3/22/56

Texas War for Independence - note 12

Tom Thumb - note 18

Tranquit Temple of Honor - 8/30/56

Transylvania Law School - 9/27/56

Transylvania Female Academy - 8/23/56

Truman and Hopkins plantation - 5/17/56

Tyler stage line - 12/26/57

Underground Railroad - 2

Union, The (magazine) - 3/8/56;

Union, The Steamer- 2/14/57

Union Hotel - 5/10/56

U. S. Congress - 2

U. S. Supreme Court - 2

Victoria - 1/19/56; 3/29/56; 5/3/56; 6/7/56

War of 1812 - notes 12 and 16

Washburn's Southern Circus - 9/19/57; 9/26/57

Washington Telegraph, the - 9/27/56

Weaver & Weaver, - 10/10/57

Webb and Saufley - 6/7/56; - 8/16/56

Weekly Messenge, the - 3/8/56

Wells & Bro. - 11/29/56

Whigs - 3;5/10/56; 11/29/56 - 11/29/56; notes 9 and 14

White Cliffs, the - 10/18/56

White Rock Presbytery - 4/26/56

William M. Ewing & Bro, - - 1/3/57; 9/5/57

Wilson and Jackson - 7/12/56; 9/5/57; 11/14/57

Women's Rights Convention - note 11

Wooten & Lyon s - 7/12/56; 10/10/57

World War II - note 28

Other Heritage Books by Richard B. Marrin:

Abstracts from the New London Gazette:
Covering Southeastern Connecticut, 1763-1769

Abstracts from the New London Gazette:
Covering Southeastern Connecticut, 1770-1773

Abstracts from The Connecticut Gazette
(Formerly The New London Gazette*):*
Covering Southeastern Connecticut, 1774-1776

A Glance Back in Time: Life in Colonial New Jersey (1704-1770)
as Depicted in News Accounts of the Day

Going to Court in Texas: Riding the Circuit, 1842-1861

New Jersey During the Revolution, as Related in the News Items of the Day

The Paradise of Texas, Volume 1: Clarksville and Red River County, 1846-1860

Passage Point: An Amateur's Dig into New Jersey's Colonial Past

Runaways of Colonial New Jersey: Indentured Servants,
Slaves, Deserters, and Prisoners, 1720-1781

Other Heritage Books by Richard B. Marrin and Lorna Geer Sheppard:

Abstracts from The Northern Standard *and the Red River District [Texas]:*
Volume 1: August 20, 1842-August 19, 1848

Abstracts from The Northern Standard *and the Red River District [Texas]*
Volume 2: August 26, 1848-December 20, 1851

Abstracts from The Clarksville Standard
(Formerly The Northern Standard*)*
Volume 4: 1854-1855

Abstracts from The Clarksville Standard
(Formerly The Northern Standard*)*
Volume 5: 1856-1857

Other Fireside Fiction by Richard B. Marrin:

The Retaking of America

www.ingramcontent.com/pod-product-compliance
Lightning Source LLC
Chambersburg PA
CBHW070728160426
43192CB00009B/1362